Castro

# Castro

**THIRD EDITION**

Sebastian Balfour

PEARSON
Longman

Harlow, England • London • New York • Boston • San Francisco • Toronto
Sydney • Tokyo • Singapore • Hong Kong • Seoul • Taipei • New Delhi
Cape Town • Madrid • Mexico City • Amsterdam • Munich • Paris • Milan

PEARSON EDUCATION LIMITED

Edinburgh Gate
Harlow CM20 2JE
United Kingdom
Tel:+44 (0)1279 623623
Fax:+44 (0)1279 431059
Website: www.pearsoned.co.uk

First edition published in Great Britain in 1990
Second edition 1995
**Third edition 2009**

© Sebastian Balfour 1990, 2009

The right of Sebastian Balfour to be identified as author
of this work has been asserted by him in accordance
with the Copyright, Designs and Patents Act 1988.

ISBN: 978-1-4058-7318-5

*British Library Cataloguing in Publication Data*
A CIP catalogue record for this book can be obtained from the British Library

*Library of Congress Cataloging-in-Publication Data*
Balfour, Sebastian.
    Castro / Sebastian Balfour. – 3rd ed.
      p.  cm.
    Includes bibliographical references and index.
    ISBN 978-1-4058-7318-5
    1. Castro, Fidel, 1926–  2. Cuba–Politics and Government–1959–1990.  3. Cuba–Politics
and government–1990–  4. Heads of state–Cuba–Biography.  I. Title.
F1788.22.C3B35 2008
972.9106′4092—dc22
[B]

2008030473

10  9  8  7  6  5  4  3  2  1
12  11  10  09  08

Set by 35 in 9.5/12pt Celeste
Printed in Malaysia (CTP-VVP)

*The Publisher's policy is to use paper manufactured from sustainable forests.*

# Contents

# List of Plates

# Preface to the Third Edition

After 19 months of convalescence from a serious intestinal problem, during which he temporarily delegated his role as head of state to his brother Raúl, Fidel Castro announced on 18 February 2008 that he would no longer stand as President and Commander in Chief of the Armed Forces. The declaration brought to a close his almost 50 years at the helm of the Cuban Revolution.

This new edition is therefore a retrospective analysis of his extraordinary political career. It has been substantially revised to take into account the last 12 years of his role as the head of state as well as the new documents, articles and books on the Cuban revolution that have emerged during that time. The revisions include an epilogue, a new Chapter 10, and an extensive modification of all other chapters from the Prologue to the Bibliographical Essay at the end.

I am indebted once again to Jean Stubbs for her incisive comments on the draft of the last chapter and the epilogue and to Pedro Pérez Sarduy for his useful overview of the evolving political situation in Cuba today; also to my wife Gráinne Palmer for her helpful suggestions as a non-specialist about some of the chapters. None of them bears responsibility for any errors in the text, or for the balance of interpretation.

June 2008

# Publisher's acknowledgements

The publishers would like to thank the following for permission to reproduce copyright material:

Plate 1: © Bettmann/Corbis; Plate 2: © Alejandro Ernesto/EFE/Corbis; Plate 3: © Bettmann/Corbis; Plate 4: Corbis; Plate 5: © Hulton-Deutsch Collection/ Corbis; Plate 6: © Sygman/Corbis; Plate 7: © Reuters/Corbis; Plate 8: © Claudia Daut/Reuters/Corbis; Plate 9: © Claudia Daut/Reuters/Corbis; Plate 10: © Jose Goitia/Corbis; Plate 11: © Cuba Debate/epa/Corbis; Plate 12: © epa/Corbis.

# Prologue

The story of Fidel Castro can have few parallels in contemporary history. Most of the outstanding Third World leaders of the twentieth century like him emerged out of the anti-colonial struggles of the post-war period but none played such a prominent and restless part on the international stage and none survived as head of state for as long as he did. While he was in power, Castro survived nine US Presidents. It is difficult to think of many other political figures in the latter half of the last century who were so controversial and whose careers touched on so many issues of global significance: US hegemony, Soviet–American relations, Third World nationalism, revolution and social justice, Third World debt, war and peace in Central America and Africa.

Castro's rise to power seems to defy plausibility. With virtually no resources at first, he overthrew a US-backed military dictatorship and under the nose of the most powerful state in the world steered his small, Americanised island into Communist waters. For almost 50 years, the US government has tried and failed to destroy his regime by subversion and coercion, by invasion by proxy and economic embargo. The two greatest powers in the world went to the brink of nuclear war over the right of Cuba to have nuclear missiles. Decades later and contrary to expectations, the Cuban Revolution survived the collapse of Communism.

The most striking feature of Cuba under Castro was the disparity between its size and economic clout and the role that it played in world affairs. To find a comparable example, as one historian has pointed out, one has to look back to the Portuguese and Dutch empires of the seventeenth century or to eighteenth-century Britain.[1] Castro and Cuba have been immensely influential across the globe, especially in the Third World. Driven by the vision of one man, Cuba has become one of the best-educated

and healthiest societies in the world with one of the lightest carbon foot-
prints on the globe. Yet its people have also suffered the effects of exile and
emigration on such a mass scale that tens of thousands of Cuban families
remain divided across the Straits of Florida. Cuba is run by a populist, one-
party socialist state that limits individual and collective freedoms in the
name of security and ideological correctness and imprisons its most active
political dissidents. It also seeks to mobilise its citizens as a nation in arms in
perpetual war with its hostile enemy to the north, the most powerful nation
in the world.

Yet by any standard of probability the Cuban Revolution should have
failed. Years before, Castro survived numerous death threats as a student
leader and at least one assassination attempt. Almost all the radical leaders
of his generation were gunned down by the police or by rivals. Taken out of
context, moreover, his whole revolutionary enterprise appears reckless. His
attempt to launch a nationwide rebellion in 1953 by trying to seize a military barracks in eastern Cuba with a little over a hundred badly armed men
seems somewhat overambitious. He was lucky in the extreme to survive the
bloody reprisals of the army after most of his lieutenants were murdered in
cold blood or tortured to death when they were captured. Three years later,
in the hope of overthrowing the military dictatorship of Fulgencio Batista,
Castro landed in nearly disastrous circumstances from a yacht in a swamp
in a remote south-eastern corner of Cuba with an even smaller force. He
should not have escaped the rapid military encirclement of his group. Even
subsequently, it should have been easy for the Cuban army to seek out his
band and eliminate it. That the guerrilla campaign that followed eventually
led to the defeat of a US-backed army and air force seems a highly improb-
able outcome. And finally, that a small sugar island 90 miles from Florida
and permeated by American culture should declare itself the first and only
Communist state in the Western hemisphere appears bizarre in the extreme.

Yet the astonishing and unique process of the Cuban Revolution is less
incongruous in the light of Cuban history. Few of Castro's actions were
without historical precedent. The attempted seizure of military barracks, the
coastal landing in eastern Cuba and the guerrilla campaign in the mountains of the East were all part of a long tradition in Cuba. The second and
successful War of Independence against the Spanish, for example, had been
launched in 1895 when its leaders had landed on hidden coves in the easternmost corner of Cuba. The subsequent guerrilla war had led to the defeat
of the army of the Spanish empire. Indeed, the degree to which the 1959
Revolution and Castro's career as a revolutionary leader echo the past is
remarkable. Some of the parallels were the result of coincidence; many were

due to similarity of conditions; others were sought by Castro himself. The popularity of Castro can be attributed to a great extent to the fact that he came to symbolise for many Cubans a long-cherished hope of national liberation from neocolonial dependence. When a dove alighted on his shoulder as he made his victory speech in Havana in 1959 (there is no reason to suppose that it had been trained to do so) the illusion was complete; it must have seemed to many there that Castro was predestined to realise the long-frustrated aspirations of 140 years of struggle.

And indeed one gets the sense from some orthodox accounts of the Revolution that all happened as it was supposed to. Unable to understand the historical forces at work in the Revolution, even the CIA fell victim to wacky theories and supernatural plots. Among the more exotic of their many abortive attempts to eliminate Castro was a plan to get his beard to fall out by having a CIA agent dust his shoes with the drug thalium, on the grounds, presumably, that his success lay in his charisma and his charisma lay in his beard. Even more far-fetched was a scheme originally suggested by Ian Fleming, the creator of James Bond, at a dinner party with the Kennedys to stage-manage the Second Coming of Christ in Cuba. According to Senate Select Committee hearings in 1975, the plan was to spread rumours around the island that the Saviour was about to return to earth to denounce Castro as an anti-Christ; on the appointed day, a bearded CIA frogman would emerge on a beach in Cuba claiming to be Christ while an American submarine would surface just over the horizon shooting star shells into the sky.[2]

If the Cuban Revolution is inconceivable without Castro, it is equally true that it succeeded as a result of a specific set of historical variables. Historians have stressed the peculiar economic and social structure of Cuba, distorted by its uneven and dependent development.[3] The Revolution also owed its survival to the size and strategic position of Cuba, situated almost within sight of the coast of Florida and therefore a prize asset during the expansionist administration of Khrushchev. The subsequent economic and military aid of the Soviet Union was essential in keeping the regime afloat and in allowing it to play a role in world affairs out of all proportion to its size. After the collapse of Soviet and East European socialism, Cuba suffered a calamitous decline in both its economic health and its international status. On the other hand, the shift in global economic power and the emergence of left-wing regimes in Latin America in the new millennium rescued Cuba from its isolation and propped up its failing economy.

Yet no structural or conjunctural factors can obscure the exceptional individual role played by Castro in the history of Cuba since 1956. Some of the orthodox panegyrics on Castro imply that the Revolution was due largely to his leadership. Castro was the first to decry such simplistic versions of history.[4] It is true he displayed qualities that accounted in some measure for his successes. Among these were his dogged persistence in the face of intolerable odds, his luck (if that can be described as a quality), courage, integrity, political intuition, ability as a facilitator of ideas without being a particularly original thinker himself, and political flexibility in pursuit of strategic goals. Yet Castro's early personal triumph derived largely from the peculiar historical conditions that existed in Cuba in the 1950s.

Any account of his career cannot fail also to be an interpretation of the Revolution itself. The central theme of this book, consequently, is the interaction between Castro's special qualities as a political leader and the historical conditions that he and his supporters encountered and worked on.

## Notes

1    A. Hennessy, 'The Cuban Revolution: a wider view'. Paper to the Conference 'Cuba 30 Years On: the Dynamics of Change and the International Dimension', University of Warwick, 12–14 May 1989.

2    W. Hinckle and W. W. Turner, *The Fish is Red: The Story of the Secret War against Castro* (Harper & Row, New York, 1981), pp. 18 and 109–10. Also P. Bourne, *Castro* (Macmillan, London, 1987), p. 212.

3    For the debate about the exceptionalism of the Cuban Revolution, see L. Whitehead, 'On Cuban Political Exceptionalism' (Oxford, Nuffield College Politics Working Paper 2003-W1, 2003). For further discussion of the literature on Castro and the Cuban Revolution, see the bibliographical essay at the end of this book.

4    For example, F. Castro, *Nothing can Stop the Course of History* (Pathfinder, New York, 1986), p. 23.

# CHAPTER 1

# Pictures of the Past, Visions of the Future

*'Revolutionary governments are driven by pictures of the past as much as by visions of the future'*

Hugh Thomas, *Cuba: the Pursuit of Freedom*

When Fidel Castro entered the world of university politics in 1945 as a 19-year-old law student, two great historical events dominated the political rhetoric of his peers: the independence struggles of 1868 to 1898 and the revolutionary movement of 1927 to 1933 that had led to the overthrow of the dictator Machado. For student radicals, both events were interwoven into a picture of Cuban history as an incomplete and thwarted revolutionary process.

The largest island in the Caribbean, commanding the approaches northwest to the Gulf of Mexico and south to the Caribbean Sea, Cuba had been an important strategic centre of the Spanish empire in the New World. Almost 20 years before its conquest in 1511, Columbus had been struck by its beauty and also by its commercial potential. Topographically, Cuba is very varied. Three mountain ranges dominate the island, one in the centre and the others at its western and eastern ends, the tallest and most extensive being the Sierra Maestra in the east. Between the mountain ranges stretch wide and fertile plains on which are situated the main towns and where all but 5 per cent of the population lives. The island's shoreline is also diverse, from the low marshlands of part of the south-western coast to the mountains that rise sharply from the south-eastern shore. The coast is dotted with innumerable small natural harbours and a few miles offshore on each side of the island lie hundreds of tiny uninhabited islands and keys.

Under Spanish rule, Cuba had been dominated by the military, the clergy and the colonial administrators. Beneath this top echelon had been an elite of Cuban-born Spaniards or Creoles and much further down the social scale, the mulattos of mixed black and white race. The indigenous Indian population had been wiped out by conquest, disease and maltreatment, and so black slaves or ex-slaves occupied the bottom rung of this rigid hierarchy, providing the bulk of the labour force for the wealth that flowed to the metropolis from the sugar, tobacco and coffee plantations. Cuba thus became, in its racial mix, a typically Caribbean island, though with a stronger presence of whites than elsewhere in the area. Of its present 11.3 million inhabitants, 51 per cent are mulattos, 37 per cent are of European descent, 11 per cent are black and 1 per cent are Chinese.[1]

The Republic of Cuba had been born in 1902 after 400 years of colonisation by Spain. The battle for independence, waxing and waning for 30 years, had been a destructive and bloody affair, particularly in the final war of 1895–8; the toll it had taken of the male population was such that there were few men in their sixties when Castro's revolution took place in 1958.[2] It had also been a revolutionary struggle against slavery. The rank and file of the Cuban armies that threw themselves at the Spanish troops were black ex-slaves. A bitter war of attrition had been fought against the planters; many a former slave returned to burn down the canefields of his old master. In the first War of Independence, the mulatto general who led one of the armies, Antonio Maceo, had refused to enter into peace negotiations with the Spaniards unless they included the question of the abolition of slavery.

The struggle for independence had also been a fight against imperialism; on several occasions Castro described Cuba as 'the nineteenth century's Vietnam'.[3] Some of its leaders feared that once Cuba had broken away from Spain it would be swallowed up by the United States, which was at the time in a particularly expansionist mood. There had been talk earlier of the United States buying Cuba from Spain and some slave owners, looking towards the Confederate states in the South, had briefly flirted with the idea of its annexation by the United States because the Spanish government was tightening up its laws concerning slavery. In 1898, worried by the threat to North American assets of the continuing war in Cuba and determined to oust the old empire from the Caribbean, the United States declared war on Spain and after two months of hostilities forced it to give up its last colony. The new independent Cuba was thus born in the shadow of the eagle. Under the so-called Platt Amendment of 1901, the United States reserved to itself the right to intervene in the affairs of Cuba in order to prevent any other foreign power from exercising undue influence and to maintain 'stable government'. Despite this seemingly well-meaning paternalism, the four interventions by the US government between 1898 and 1920 were intended to ensure above all that Cuba maintained policies which favoured the increasing American investments on the island.

Indeed, it was US capital that re-colonised Cuba. Long before independence, giant American companies had moved in to exploit Cuba's natural resources. US investments on the island accelerated in the first quarter of the century and by 1926 were valued at $1,360 million, based in the sugar industry, and in railways, mining, tobacco, banking, commerce, real estate and other sectors. US capital controlled the telephone service and the gas and electricity industries among others.[4] But it was sugar that set the tune in Cuba. Under a long-standing agreement, the United States committed itself to buying up to half of Cuba's sugar crop each year, thereby guaranteeing profits for the Cuban planters, foreign currency and jobs. The Cuban sugar quota set by the US Congress, however, was a mixed blessing because it meant that the United States could punish Cuba by reducing the price and amount of the quota if it stepped out of line. Thus the remaining Cuban sugar crop could be sold on the world market but only to the extent that it did not affect US sugar growers; otherwise, the sugar lobby on Capitol Hill would force down the quota. A Louisiana senator is reported in the Cuban press in 1955 to have made the following warning to the Cubans: 'I represent in the American Senate a vast sugar-producing area of the United States. And I have to demand here whatever benefits that area. . . . Cuba has exceeded its production [of sugar]. . . . It is we who permit your country to produce.'[5]

The United States also controlled Cuba's internal market. The Platt Amendment was replaced in 1934 by a more modern instrument of neo-colonial domination, the Reciprocal Trade Agreement, whereby in exchange for the sugar quota, US exports to Cuba were given preferential tariffs. The effect was to dampen any efforts at creating import substitution industries in Cuba and to discourage cheaper imports from elsewhere. The Agreement therefore served to lock Cuba's economy even more tightly into that of the United States. In 1957, another American senator called on Congress to lower the sugar quota because Cuba had just announced its intention to build two flour mills, thereby threatening the export of US flour to the island. A Cuban employers' review reacted sharply, stating in the conditional tense what was already a reality: 'Cuba would have to resign itself to having its economy "frozen" on the one hand by the limited US sugar quota and by world competition, and on the other by having to keep its internal market unchanged for the benefit of foreign exporters.'[6]

Any policy of modernising Cuba's economy, any effort to regenerate Cuban society thus came to mean two related things in particular: to shake off its dependence on the United States, and to break out of the yoke of its sugar monoculture. Before the first marines landed in Cuba to supervise the new Republic, the writer and poet José Martí, icon of Cuban independence, had warned against US expansionism. In a famous passage from his last and incomplete letter, written the day before he died in a cavalry charge against Spanish troops in 1895, Martí referred to the US as the 'monster': 'I have lived in the monster and I know its entrails: my sling is that of David.'[7] Martí believed that the danger of US interference or aggression extended to the whole of the American continent south of the Rio Grande, to what he termed in his writings 'America'. 'The contempt of the formidable neighbour – who does not know it [America] – is the greatest danger facing our America, and it is vital, for visiting day is close by, that the neighbour gets to know it and gets to know it soon, so that it is not treated with contempt.'[8] Martí feared above all that the United States would replace Spain as a colonial power in Latin America. More effectively than the old colonial power, however, the United States came to dominate the Cuban economy and that of many Latin American countries, shaping their societies and gearing their production to the demands of its own economy without permanently occupying their territories (except for Guantánamo Bay). As late as the early 1930s, the dollar was the only paper currency in circulation in Cuba. The struggle for independence was seen by successive generations of radical young Cubans as unfinished business.

The 'Apostle' Martí was an obligatory reference in the speeches of all political figures in the Cuban Republic, from generals to gangsters. But his official image was as a spiritual, millenarian patriot, free from any trace of anti-imperialism or rebelliousness. Such was the range of Martí's thought, expressed in poems, prose, newspaper articles and letters, that it was possible to select different ideological messages to suit the circumstances. It was the student rebels of the 1920s who rediscovered the radical Martí, and this alternative picture of the national hero was channelled through successive generations of students and left-wing leaders to the new university class of the 1940s.[9] Castro became one of the most dedicated disciples of Martí. The new aspiring liberator of Cuba saw him as a guide to action and a source of legitimacy. Castro never lost an opportunity to link himself publicly with the revolutionary traditions embodied by Martí, and in the darkest moments of his endeavour he was able to find some inspiration from the example of Martí's political labours. Imprisoned after his abortive attempt to storm the barracks of Moncada in 1953 and contemplating the seemingly impossible task of creating a revolutionary movement in Cuba, Castro wrote to a friend:

*the similarity of situations reminds me of Martí's efforts to bring together all Cubans worthy of the fight for independence; each one had their history, their glories, their feats, each one believed they had more rights than or at least equal rights with the others; only the work of love, understanding and infinite patience of one man with less glory attached to him than others was able to achieve the miracle. . . . For this reason, perhaps, the pages of Cuban history I most admire are not to do with the heroic deeds on the battlefield but that gigantic, heroic and silent task of uniting Cubans for the struggle.*[10]

In fact, striking parallels can be found between the lives of Martí and Castro. Both were sons of Spanish immigrants. Both were imprisoned for their political activities on the same island, the Isle of Pines off the west coast of Cuba. Like Castro before his landing on the island in 1956, Martí had raised money for his own expedition among Cuban exiles in Florida and on the Eastern seaboard of the United States. Martí had disembarked on a remote beach in eastern Cuba in difficult circumstances, though not as hazardous as those encountered by Castro about 288 kilometres further west some 61 years later. Indeed, the dictator Batista was so sure that Castro would take the same route as Martí that he ordered air surveillance missions on the southern coast of Oriente; in the event, the new would-be liberator landed on its western coast.[11] Castro's attempted seizure of the Moncada barracks in 1953 coincided with the much-publicised centenary of Martí's birth, allowing Castro to claim that he and his men, the 'generation of the centenary', were the true heirs of the 'Apostle'. Martí's party, the Cuban Revolutionary Party (PRC), like Castro's movement later, embraced radicals of different and in some measure contradictory political tendencies. Among the members of the PRC were socialist and anarcho-syndicalist workers, many of them immigrant tobacco workers living in Florida. A final, less important parallel was the use both Martí and Castro made of US journalists to publicise their cause while engaged in guerrilla warfare, Martí's champion being George Eugene Bryson of the *New York Herald* and Castro's Herbert L. Matthews of the *New York Times*.

Martí represented a brand of romantic, republican nationalism that belonged to a very different period from that in which the young generation of the 1940s began their political careers. Nevertheless, there was a continuity of ideas between the two periods. Martí's words against the danger of US expansion struck a chord among radical nationalists like Castro who witnessed the contempt with which some Americans treated Cuba. In 1949, for example, Castro led a protest action against a group of drunken American sailors who had urinated on the statue of the national hero in Havana. Martí's call for Spanish America to declare its 'second independence', this time against the colossus of the North, also invoked an old tradition of Pan-Americanism without the United States derived from the epoch of the 'Liberator' of South America of the early nineteenth century, Simón Bolívar, to whom Castro was also deeply drawn.[12] This same vision can be found in Castro's restless efforts in the 1960s to create a continent-wide revolutionary movement or more recently to form a united front with other Latin American countries around the issues of debt and modernisation. Like Castro later, Martí believed that Cuba's struggle for independence was pivotal to the new balance of power in the American continent and beyond. 'We are holding a world in balance: it is not just two islands [Cuba and Puerto Rico] that we are going to free', he wrote in 1894. 'An error over Cuba', he said, referring to the danger of US invasion, 'is an error in America, an error among modern humanity.' Echoing Martí's words almost a century later, Castro remarked to foreign journalists in 1983 that 'North Americans don't understand . . . that our country is not just Cuba; our country is also humanity'.[13]

Martí's passionate belief in social justice, in the need for universal education, in the virtues of the countryside and land cultivation, found an echo in the young Castro. His conviction in the power of ideas and moral principles cannot fail to have influenced Castro, who gave special importance in his speeches and broadcasts in the 1950s to explaining his purpose and who rarely omitted in his speeches since the Revolution to make an appeal to rationality and ethics. Castro's language may be more prosaic but his faith in the capacity of ideas to move people to action was as great as Martí's when the latter wrote:

*Trenches of ideas are worth more than trenches of stone. There is no prow that can cut through a cloud of ideas.*[14]

Underlying this confidence in the power of will was a historicism or belief in the intrinsically progressive nature of history derived in Martí's case from the philosopher Krause.

Both Martí and Castro also possessed an organicist, almost ahistorical picture of a true Cuba, free from the aberration of dictatorship, whose essence was waiting to be discovered. Despite his espousal of Marxist-Leninist orthodoxy, Castro shared with Martí a vision of nationhood rather than class as the driving force of progress. In a passage highly reminiscent of Castro's words many years later, Martí wrote, with reference to the Latin American republics of the nineteenth century:

*The republics have purged in tyrannies their incapacity to understand the real elements of the country, derive from these the form of the government and govern with them. To govern in a new country is to create. . . . To know is to resolve. To know the country and govern it in accordance with this knowledge is the only way of delivering it from tyranny.*[15]

This notion of *cubanidad*, an essential Cuban way of being from which the country had been alienated, was transmitted from one generation of radicals to another and re-interpreted in the light of their own political ideas. It thus took the form of a radical nationalism or *cubanía rebelde*. Those who had gained power in the new Republic, whether as politicians or businessmen, were considered to have squandered the inheritance of the independence struggle. Without exception, the Cuban governments since 1902 had been characterised by graft and corruption on a scale that seemed to grow with each new President. The almost undisguised practice of using public office for self-enrichment became a way of life. In part, it was a custom derived from colonial days when Spanish officials – civil servants, judges, policemen, and the like – were paid low salaries in the expectation that they would make up the difference through graft. It was also indirectly an expression of the dependent and subordinate status of the Cuban elites. Hostage to the big neighbour across the Straits of Florida, whose entrepreneurs dominated so much of the island's economy, Cuba's rich men and rulers failed to project any set of universal values or mythology of nationhood of their own. Instead, their values were shaped by the culture of the United States; indeed, they tended to send their children to be educated in American universities, and many had second homes there. They were good at defending corporate interests but failed to unite around the collective defence of their class interests.

Moreover Cuba lacked any powerful institution that might serve to bind together the different social classes. The old landed oligarchy had been swept aside by war and technological change. Economic interests were expressed through narrow corporate channels rather than political parties. The Church had been discredited to some extent by its close association with the Spanish elite on the island. Unlike in most other Spanish American countries, where Catholicism destroyed the indigenous religions and served to integrate the poor into society, the Church failed to take root among the blacks of Cuba, among whom the African religious cult of *santería* was widespread. Without any unifying purpose to their hegemony, Cuba's rulers squabbled among themselves about the distribution of power and economic surplus, turning to their US godfather to settle disputes through armed intervention and a degrading form of paternalism, interim administration by American proconsuls. The belligerent US Senator Cabot Lodge wrote to Theodore Roosevelt in 1906:

*Disgust with the Cubans is very general . . . the general feeling is that they ought to be taken by the scruff of the neck and shaken until they behave themselves. . . . I should think that this . . . would make the anti-imperialists think that some peoples were less capable of self-government than others.*[16]

The political parties of the Republic had brought parliamentary democracy into disrepute by fraudulent electoral practices. So deep was political cynicism among Cubans that the feeling was widespread that they were incapable as a race of governing themselves. The patronising, racist image of Cuban incompetence shared by many Americans became absorbed into Cuban culture. The sentiment was expressed in the 1940s by the *choteo criollo*, a form of self-disparaging, cynical humour directed against the establishment.[17] The crisis of legitimacy in Cuba was exacerbated by the fragility of its governments faced with the fluctuations of sugar prices on the world market.

The twin blights of the Cuban Republic, its economic and cultural subordination to the United States and the corruption of its political life, were challenged by two successive student movements in the early and late 1920s. These became for the new rebels among Castro's generation an almost mythical reference point. Both occurred at times of severe economic dislocation caused by a crash in sugar prices on the world market and were accompanied by considerable labour unrest. The first movement coalesced around demands for the reform of the corrupt university system in Cuba but moved on rapidly to embrace a more wide-reaching critique of society. Cuba's leaders were accused of having betrayed the independence struggles by delivering the island over to American interests or passively acquiescing in US hegemony, and by indulging in self-enrichment at the expense of the people. The student movement of 1923 was part of a continent-wide revolt in Latin America by middle-class youth against imperialism and military dictatorship and for radical reform and nationalist regeneration. Deeply influenced by a combination of left-wing European ideas – anarchism, anarcho-syndicalism and Marxism – and indigenous movements such as the Mexican Revolution, the students were nevertheless moved also by the resentment of a new middle-class generation whose access to positions of influence was blocked by nepotism and political corruption. This same generational conflict would play an important part in later movements of youthful rebellion in both the early 1930s and the early 1950s.

The most outstanding leader of the 1923 generation of students was Julio Antonio Mella, who founded the Cuban Communist Party in 1925 with the old anarchist and close collaborator of Martí Carlos Baliño. Mella's murder in 1929 by the dictator Machado's assassins while he was in exile in Mexico won him a place in the already lengthy roll-call of martyrs for Cuba's redemption. It also saved him from the disrepute suffered later by the Party he had co-founded, which collaborated with the authoritarian governments of the 1940s in obedience to the zigzag policies of the Third International. In the figure of Mella in particular, Marxism remained one strand of the tradition of nationalist emancipation that the 1950s' generation would adopt.

Castro's generation, however, was more directly and profoundly influenced by the Revolution of 1933, which overthrew the dictator Gerardo Machado. That eventful year laid the basis for Castro's own revolution some 15 years later. An ex-general and wealthy businessman, Machado had succeeded the corrupt President Zayas in 1925 on a reformist campaign promising the repeal of the Platt Amendment and an ambitious programme of public works. It soon became clear, however, that Machado was out not only to enrich himself but also to concentrate even greater power in his own hands. In 1927 (the year after Fidel Castro was born) he got the Congress, packed with suborned supporters, to approve a constitutional amendment prolonging his term of office from four to six years and giving him an additional two years' term without re-election. Machado further strengthened his grip over Cuban politics by creating an extensive patronage network and by violently repressing the emergent opposition among students and in the labour unions. Machado's state terrorism was answered by the rise of urban terrorist groups. Bombs were thrown, armed opponents of the government exchanged gunfire in the streets with the police, and prominent labour and student leaders were tortured or gunned down by Machado's policemen.

Like their predecessors, the student rebels were impelled in part by personal frustration. The National University had been traditionally an important route to power and influence in society. But the widespread nepotism of Machado's government blocked the path of many an aspiring politician, aggravating the problems caused by the absence of career opportunities for graduates of the highly traditional university system in Cuba. The student rebels' manifestos were filled with anger at the corruption and authoritarianism of the Machado regime. Except for the demand for the restoration of democracy, however, the opposition to Machado among students and other groups was divided over objectives. These divisions, although shaped by the ideological preoccupations of the 1930s, were carried over in different forms into the next decade when Castro began his university career.

The majority faction of the student movement at that time was calling for an end to Cuba's dependency on the US and for a programme of social reforms. The left wing of the student movement, on the other hand, was led by Marxists and had a clearly anti-imperialist and anti-capitalist orientation. Another youthful organisation of the Left (later called Joven Cuba), led by the charismatic Antonio Guiteras, advocated a radical programme of reforms and a rather vague socialism. Unlike the Communists, who called for a united front among the anti-Machado forces, Guiteras believed that insurrectionary actions by small organised groups could lead the way to revolution. Among his first actions was the seizure of a small military barracks in the eastern province of Oriente; some 20 years later Castro was to attempt a similar action on a larger barracks in the capital of Oriente. For each group, the much-repeated slogan of the day, 'Revolution', meant a different thing, from the patriotic regeneration of Cuba to the seizure of power by the working class. Organised opposition to Machado was not confined to youth. Some middle-class professionals and bourgeois nationalists, recognising the need for political change (and anxious for more protectionist measures to safeguard Cuban industry), formed an underground terrorist organisation, the ABC, in an attempt to bring about Machado's fall by provoking US mediation.

Political unrest in Cuba in the early 1930s was aggravated by the post-1929 world slump, which forced down the price of sugar and tobacco on the world market. Labour dissent against wage restraint and unemployment began among the sugar workers in 1933 and spread throughout the island. Armed groups of workers in provincial towns staged small insurrections. Disturbed by the state of virtual civil war prevailing in Cuba, the new US President Franklin D. Roosevelt sent a special envoy to negotiate a transfer of power from Machado to a candidate more acceptable to the Opposition. The dictator, increasingly isolated among his own supporters, fled to the US one night in August 1933 and the presidential palace was sacked by the demonstrators.

However, the new provisional government, put together with the help of Roosevelt's envoy and filled with respectable conservatives, hardly matched the revolutionary atmosphere in the cities of Cuba. Machado's henchmen were being hunted down and lynched. The strikes continued. Sugar mills were seized by workers. Radical demands were spreading to new sections of society. Indeed, a new rebellion began in a totally unexpected quarter. Impelled by the fear of cuts and emboldened by the revolutionary turmoil, the army's NCOs staged a coup attempt that rapidly won the support of the students. Led by a sergeant stenographer of mixed mulatto and Indian origin, Fulgencio Batista, the revolt was couched in vague, redemptionist terms that would appeal to a wide constituency of discontent. Batista proclaimed:

*The revolution has not taken place merely for one man to disappear from the political scene but for a change of regime, for the disappearance of the colonial system that 31 years after the 20th May 1902 has continued to drown the country.*[18]

Attempts by conservative officers to mount a counter-coup failed and armed power rapidly came to lie in the hands of Batista, who elevated himself to the rank of colonel and chief of staff. Meanwhile, the students proclaimed a new five-man government headed by a professor, Ramon Grau San Martín, in which Guiteras became Minister of the Interior. Unable to secure recognition by the United States and to quell the unrest in Cuba (Guiteras unsuccessfully calling on workers to return to work in order to help the new cabinet), the government of Grau fell after 100 days.

The ex-sergeant Batista now held the future of Cuba in his hands, balancing for a short while the demands of students and workers against the interests of the anti-Machado but conservative sections of the bourgeoisie; indeed, Batista became the Bonaparte of the 1933 Revolution. From then on until 1959 he was to control political life in Cuba. Batista's rise to power had two broad explanations. Because of the institutional weakness of the different Cuban elites, the army was a relatively autonomous body and certainly the only organisation capable of imposing a political solution. Secondly, the officer class had been discredited to some extent by association with Machado while the NCOs, many of them from poor, rural, mulatto backgrounds, had been infected by the revolutionary atmosphere of the early 1930s. Batista turned on those who continued to agitate for the radical reforms promised by the Grau government: strikes were put down with violence, and Guiteras was cornered in a house in Havana with a few supporters and shot dead after a long gun battle. Yet through the governments he effectively controlled in the second half of the 1930s, Batista carried out a populist programme of reforms – limited land distribution, welfare schemes, paid holidays for workers and the like – which took up some of the demands of the revolutionary movement of 1933.

For Castro's generation of rebels, however, the 1933 Revolution represented yet another failure, albeit the most heroic, to realise what they saw as the historical aspirations of the Cuban nation stretching back to the independence struggles of 1868. This sense of frustration was felt on a deeply personal level. Individual self-esteem and 'national dignity' became intertwined. The evidence of North American domination was all around. Cuban middle-class culture was permeated by its values and there was much in the behaviour of Americans, from their ambassadors to their sailors, to suggest the inferiority of the Cuban race. The servility and corruption of generations of political leaders, including many who had fought in the Wars of Independence, were seen as a betrayal. On the other hand, the revolutionary legacy of the past was a violent one. Because the political system in Cuba had so signally failed to fulfil its promises, attempts to bring about real change had been carried out through insurrection, armed action and street riot. The student rebels, in particular, saw themselves as the true heirs of this nationalist tradition. They inherited from the past a conviction that it was their duty to carry on the unfulfilled struggle for independence and development on behalf of the true Cubans: the poor, the dispossessed, 'los humildes'. They also inherited a sense of their own power. It was the student movement that had led the fight to overthrow Machado and that had established the short-lived 'revolutionary' government of 1933. Despite the counter-revolution of Batista, students had forced the new government to recognise the inviolability of the university campus; the police were no longer allowed to enter its precincts.

When Castro enrolled in Havana University as a law student in 1945, the residue of the events of 1933–4 still dominated political life in Cuba. The action groups that had fought Machado still retained their guns even if they had lost their ideals. Some of the social and economic reforms that had been passed in the aftermath of the Revolution were enshrined in a new Constitution. Yet those who had profited by the upheaval had failed to honour its promises. While students were a privileged elite, from which traditionally the Cuban political class had drawn some of its leaders, their access to positions of influence through democratic channels and by virtue of merit continued to be blocked by the widespread use of patronage. The frustration felt by the new layer of students of the 1940s was deepened by the visible degeneration of the 1933 rebels into gang warfare and senseless vendettas. The new generation of rebels came to see it as their mission to pick up the banner of national regeneration that had first been raised in 1868 and had been dropped by the wayside. The indigenous historical models that were available to them were neither peaceful nor particularly democratic. Any profound political or social change had come about through violence. The system of parliamentary democracy had proved not only unstable but incapable of delivering reform. It had also been a source of bottomless corruption. The heroes of Cuban history were dead heroes, almost by definition – young martyrs. Almost all the great men who survived the last War of

Independence had become villains, seduced by power and wealth. The violence that brought about change arose from several sources: the insurrectionary strikes of workers, the struggles of peasants and land labourers, the old and continuing tradition of rural banditry, and student power.

The historical legacy thus passed on to the new generation of politically inspired youth was made up of several radical strands that were woven together into a more or less coherent picture of the past and an almost millenarian vision of the future: the fight of the ex-slaves for complete emancipation; the international struggle against imperialism; the utopian socialism and anarcho-syndicalism of Martí's working-class base; the liberal republicanism of Martí himself; the Communist movement of the 1920s; the student rebellion of the 1930s; the liberal nationalism of the middle class; and the almost unbroken struggle of Cuban workers in the town and the countryside for better wages and conditions. These different strands embodied contradictory aspirations, but they were bound together for the time being by the conviction that social and economic change was an indispensable component of national liberation. This radical heritage profoundly influenced the strategy of the young Castro in his rise to power.

## Notes

1  *Country Profile, Cuba* (World Resources Institute, 2006); CIA World Factbook (2007).

2  H. Thomas, *Cuba: the Pursuit of Freedom* (Harper & Row, New York, 1971), p. 1094.

3  Most recently in I. Ramonet, *Fidel Castro. Biografía a dos voces* (Random House Mondadori, Mexico and Barcelona, 2006), p. 35.

4  M. Azicri, *Cuba: Politics, Economics and Society* (Pinter, London, 1988), pp. 21–2.

5  *Bohemia*, 6 and 20 March 1955, quoted in M. Winocur, *Las clases olvidadas en la revolución cubana* (Grijalbo, Barcelona, 1979), p. 45.

6  From *Cuba Económica y Financiera*, May 1957, quoted in Winocur, *Las clases olvidadas*, pp. 40–1.

7  Letter to Manuel Mercado in J.J. Martí, *Martí y la primera revolución cubana* (Biblioteca Fundamental del Hombre, 1971), p. 133.

8  From Martí, *Martí y la primera revolución*, 'Nuestra América', p. 17.

9  A. Kapcia, 'Cuban populism and the birth of the myth of Martí', in C. Abel and N. Torrents, *José Martí: Revolutionary Democrat* (Athlone Press, London, 1986), pp. 32–64.

10  L. Conte Agüero, *Cartas del Presidio* (Lex, Havana, 1959), p. 60.

**11**  T. Szulc, *Fidel: a Critical Portrait* (Hutchinson, London, 1987), p. 298.

**12**  C. Franqui, *Family Portrait with Fidel* (Jonathan Cape, London, 1983), p. 9.

**13**  J.J. Martí, *Obras Completas* (Havana, 1894), vol. 3, pp. 142–3; F. Castro, *Conversaciones con periodistas norteamericanos y franceses* (Politica, n.p., 1983).

**14**  Martí, 'Nuestra América', p. 11.

**15**  Ibid., pp. 13–14.

**16**  Quoted in Thomas, *Cuba*, p. 481.

**17**  M. Solaun, 'El fracaso de la democracia en Cuba', *Aportes*, July 1969, pp. 72–3.

**18**  F. Batista, 'Proclama al pueblo de Cuba', *Pensamiento Crítico*, April 1970, p. 217.

# CHAPTER 2

# The Rebel

There was little in Castro's family background to suggest he would become a rebel. His father was a self-made man who had emigrated from Spain towards the end of the nineteenth century after participating in the last independence war in Cuba as a conscript in the Spanish army. Moving to the Mayarí region in Oriente, the easternmost province of Cuba, he had started his working life as a labourer laying the tracks for the railway of the local employers, the American United Fruit Company. Shortly afterwards, he had become a pedlar, selling lemonade to the plantation workers and then a variety of goods to local families. Like many Spanish immigrants, he was a hard worker and a determined saver, and with his savings he had leased land from the United Fruit Company and begun to plant sugar cane to sell to the American-owned mills. By dint of hard work and careful accounting, he had become a wealthy planter.

For all their affluence, Castro's family did not share the culture of the landowning class. His mother had been a maid and cook in the Castro household during his father's first marriage. Indeed, Castro's parents may only have been married after the birth of his two elder siblings and himself in 1926. By all accounts Castro senior retained his rough and hard-working ways and brought up his children with a firm hand and in a work culture. There had been no landed oligarchy in the area. The Mayarí region in which the family estate lay had begun to be exploited only in the late nineteenth century by American companies. Fidel Castro thus grew up among children of different social backgrounds, including the families of black immigrant labourers from Haiti. In his own rare accounts of his childhood, Castro liked to suggest that this early experience of socialisation among children of poor families was a formative influence on his political development.[1] It may have provided him with a certain social ease, yet he could not have helped feeling different, if only because his father owned most of the land and employed most of the workers in the immediate locality. Although he was not brought up with the traditional values of the landowning elite, Fidel did not belong either to the sophisticated urban culture of many of his future student companions. He was not a man of the people but nor was he a typical product of the upper or middle classes. How far this cultural indefinition played a part in Castro's formation is impossible to judge, but it may have influenced his own sense of being singular, even exceptional.

Castro displayed rebelliousness towards authority from an early age, frequently getting his own way through a combination of persistence and audacity. When he was 6 or thereabouts, the young Fidel was sent to Santiago with his elder sister to lodge at a teacher's house and receive private lessons. Two years later he began to attend a nearby school. Unhappy at the domestic austerity of his new home, where he felt permanently hungry in his first year, he and his sister and elder brother, who had joined them recently, decided one day to rebel against the rules of the house in order to force his family to make him a boarder. This first successful act of rebellion was followed by other equally audacious exploits. The youthful Castro seems to have developed an early sense of his capacity to prevail over higher authority, to get round people and mobilise support, as he himself claimed in interviews many years after. He was, in his own words, a born rebel rather than a born revolutionary.[2]

Later, he was educated in the strict almost military culture of Jesuit schools, first in the capital of Oriente, Santiago, and then in Havana. There, according to his own description, he imbibed values of self-discipline, enterprise, tenacity and 'personal dignity' that were the hallmark of Jesuit education.[3] The almost Spartan habits that he claims to have acquired during his schooling had not deserted him over 70 years later. At school, Castro stood out as a gifted athlete and a popular leader. In frequent excursions to the foothills of the Sierra Maestra near Santiago, he would go climbing and swimming and during his holidays would spend days exploring and hunting with a gun in the mountainous region around his father's estate, a practice that would stand him in good stead years later in his guerrilla war much deeper in the same Sierra Maestra.

Castro enrolled in the law faculty of Havana University in October 1945. He was then a tall, handsome 19-year-old brimming with vague ambitions and bold self-confidence. Photographs of the period reveal typically Spanish features; also a surprisingly boyish face and a rather formal, aloof bearing. He was soon embroiled in student politics; it was difficult to avoid them. Since the 1920s, Havana University had been one of the centres of political life. Cuba's political elite traditionally had drawn many of its members from graduates of the university, in particular from the law faculty. In a society where class interests and political parties were imperfectly integrated, the highly politicised student movement was an important source of support or opposition. Recent events, moreover, had given the student movement a new prominence. To understand the political stage on which Castro made his first bow, we need to look briefly at the development of post-1934 politics in Cuba.

Since he shot to power during the 1933 Revolution, the ex-sergeant stenographer Fulgencio Batista had dominated political life on the island. Batista never entirely forgot his origins as a man of the people, a 'humble mulatto' who had risen to the rank of non-commissioned officer in an army led by a white, upper-class elite. Although he had turned on the anti-Machado movement in 1934, establishing a new government more acceptable to the United States and the Cuban elites, he began to advocate a programme of social and political reforms that was hardly to the liking of his new allies. Through puppet cabinets, Batista carried out a series of measures designed to bring the sugar and tobacco industries under closer control of the state and to cushion the small growers and mill owners from the effects of fluctuating world prices. He also pushed through a number of reforms, such as limited land redistribution, social benefits for workers and a reorganisation of the tax system. The reformist drift of his policies was enshrined in the Constitution of 1940, a social democratic charter whose fulfilment became a major demand of the anti-Batista movement that Castro was to lead in the 1950s.

Conscious of the growing opposition of the business and professional elites in Cuba, Batista sought to extend his populist base, making much of his humble origins. He struck a deal with the Communists, legalising their party and allowing them to assume control of the newly reorganised labour confederation, the Confederación de Trabajadores de Cuba (CTC). The Communists, following the new popular front policy of the Comintern in 1935, welcomed Batista as a 'democratic and progressive ruler' and were rewarded with two cabinet posts in his post-1940 government.[4] Shortly after, they renamed the party the Partido Socialista Popular (PSP), signalling their increasing drift away from internationalism and towards social democratic nationalism. Because the conservatives were divided, the main focus of opposition to Batista was the followers of the wealthy physician and university professor Ramón San Grau, the president of the short-lived revolutionary government of 1933–4. In exile for a brief period in the United States, Grau had organised his middle-class supporters into a new party, the

Partido Revolucionario Cubano Auténtico, or Auténticos for short, indicating that they considered themselves the true heirs of Martí. In the elections of 1940, Batista, backed by considerable sums of money from newly won-over sections of the Cuban elites and with the support of the Communists, secured a majority of votes against the Auténtico coalition, which stood for the radical reformism of the 1933–4 government. Having for six years controlled political life from the wings, the ex-sergeant now became President of Cuba.

Apart from the army, now led by officers closely associated with his own fortunes, the new President had no organised base, nor did he ostensibly represent any one elite or social class in Cuba. In order to balance the different forces in Cuban society, with himself as the fulcrum, Batista followed an elaborate system of regulation and distribution that resembled in many respects a modern corporate state. The most powerful sectors of the economy – American and Cuban sugar growers and mill owners, cattle barons, tobacco farmers, industrialists and organised labour led by the Communists – bargained through the ministries for the protection of their monopolistic privileges, sharing out among themselves the income generated by sugar exports, or the losses when world prices fell. Batista also set out to buy political support by using the proceeds of the national lottery; union leaders, journalists, churchmen and the like received illegal pay-offs. State funds were also used to subsidise ailing companies and to stem unemployment.[5] Batista's mix of corporatism and populist nationalism was part of a widespread trend throughout Latin America in the wake of the Depression of the 1930s. In Argentina in the early 1940s, for example, Juan Domingo Perón set out on a similar path in an attempt to integrate capital and labour around a project of nationalist regeneration.

The Second World War years were a bonanza for the Cuban economy, the demand for sugar and minerals from the Allies drawing in considerable profits. Having amassed a fortune in real estate, Batista stood down in 1944, as he was required to do by the Constitution. His chosen successor was the prime minister, through whom he would have continued to exercise power had he won. In fact, the opposition coalition, led by the Auténticos, secured a slender majority against Batista's allies (who included the Communists). Grau San Martín was duly proclaimed President, bearing with him the hopes of many Cubans for social reform and honest government. Far from carrying out the promises of the 1933–4 movement, however, the Grau government inaugurated a new period of sleaze exceeding that of Batista's presidency.

The Auténticos were an electoral party whose leaders were drawn almost exclusively from the professional middle class. Without any organised base and confronted with potential opposition from the army and the Communist-controlled labour unions, they used their control of the state coffers to maintain a patronage system whose main clients were the armed action groups left over from the anti-Machado struggle. One of the first actions of the Grau government was to hand out public appointments, such as city chief of police and state director of sports, to leaders of the different factions to reward them for their backing during the electoral campaign and to ensure their support in the future. Grau's Minister of Education reputedly allocated $80,000 for their maintenance.[6]

The political gangs, in turn, provided Auténtico politicians with a small private army to act as bodyguard and control over key police forces with which to counterbalance the power of the army. They also helped to intimidate opponents of government bosses and, where intimidation failed, they murdered. The US-based Mafia controlled the brothels and casinos of Cuba and their acknowledged boss Charles 'Lucky' Luciano lived for some time in exile in the Hotel Nacional in Havana.[7] The streets of the capital came to resemble Chicago at the height of prohibition and the dailies were filled with gruesome photographs of victims. The degeneration of political life under Grau was exemplified by the prolonged gun battle on 15 September 1947 in the streets of Marianao, a satellite town of Havana, between two different police forces led by rival gangs.

The armed groups retained from the anti-Machado days a vague, redemptionist rhetoric of social justice and honest government.[8] Their leaders were mainly ex-students who had played an important role in the revolutionary period of the early 1930s. Drawn from a marginal social group without the ability to mobilise, they derived from that experience a belief in insurrection rather than class struggle as the path to power. There were few models in Cuban history suggesting that a constitutional parliamentary road to power could be successful. Despite their opposition to the United States, they were also fervent anti-Communists (though several had been members of the Party in the 1930s) partly because of the collaboration of the Cuban Communists with Batista. The onset of the Cold War in 1947 deepened this hostility. The presence in their ranks of several relatively young veterans of the Spanish Republican army brought into their already bitter quarrels the divisions and resentments of the civil war in Spain. Among the groups there was also a strong macho cult of physical heroism.

However, what divided the political gangs was not so much ideology as competition for political influence and public funds. The structure of power in Cuba, dominated by an informal corporatist system, offered few opportunities for self-advancement through legitimate democratic channels. The easiest route to political power lay through patronage. Auténtico bosses were ready to grant privileges to pay for the services of the armed groups or to buy off their potential opposition. In order to raise additional funds beyond government pay-offs, the gangs turned to extortion rackets as well. In a country with a high rate of graduate unemployment, graft and extortion became a way of life for dozens of middle-class youths. Having encouraged the armed groups from the outset, the Auténticos found themselves unable to control them. Gang rivalry became so intense that Grau's successor, Prío Socarrás, arranged a truce between the groups in 1949, offering over 2,000 sinecures in the government as a price of peace.[9]

When Castro entered Havana University, student politics was permeated by the rivalry between two groups, the Movimiento Socialista Revolucionario (MSR) and the Unión Insurreccional Revolucionaria (UIR). The Communist-led student movement of the 1930s had been displaced by a strong-arm group financed by the Auténticos and this in turn had been driven out by the MSR, which now controlled the student union. Both organisations held important positions outside the university (the MSR, for example, was awarded the post of chief of the secret police by Grau) but extended their organisation into the campus because domination of the student movement was a source of political power in itself. Situated on a hill in the middle of Havana, the campus was constitutionally a no-go area for both the police and the army. It was possible therefore to store weapons in its precincts and on several occasions gunfire was exchanged in its halls and squares and on the immense flight of steps leading up to the entrance of the university. The student electoral system was dominated by whichever group happened to be paramount physically, and in turn this organisation controlled life in the university, handling the sale of textbooks, for example, and even of stolen exam papers.

It was difficult for a politically ambitious student like Castro not to become caught up in one faction or another, and, indeed, he had a brief association with the UIR during which he may have been involved in a number of violent actions. Many years later, he gave the armed factions the following epitaph: 'those young people were not to blame. Driven by natural longings and by the legend of a heroic epoch, they wanted to carry out a revolution that had not been fulfilled at a time when it could not be made. Many of those that died as gangsters, the victims of an illusion, would today be heroes.'[10]

In view of Castro's own political activity in the university, however, it seems a somewhat generous judgement. He soon distinguished himself on the campus as a talented organiser and orator rather than a man of violence.

His initial preoccupation with student politics gave way during his second year to a broader concern with national problems. Unlike many of the activists in the university, however, Castro had had no political grounding. Neither his provincial upbringing nor his privileged education had helped him to define any clear political philosophy. Instead, he seems to have been concerned from the outset of his career with the problem of achieving power in the service of a rather vague ideal of nationalist regeneration. The earliest political contacts he made in the university reveal a pragmatism that would become a feature of his subsequent political career; among his new friends were the university leader of the MSR and president of the Students' Union, and a leading student member of Juventud Socialista, the Communist Party's youth organisation. What they shared was the anger of their generation at the betrayal of Cuba's nationalist ideals by its politicians, an anger that transcended student factionalism. Castro's earliest speeches as a student representative were an attack against false leaders and government corruption. In one of the first of his speeches to be mentioned in the press, he declaimed, speaking to a meeting of student representatives in July 1947, 'Let us not be borne down by the pessimism and disillusion spread over the last few years by false leaders, those merchants of the blood of the martyrs.'[11]

Castro's rise to prominence as a student activist was fraught with mortal risk. He was openly criticising the Grau government as well as the MSR, which was closely associated with prominent Auténtico politicians. Increasingly he drew the fire of the MSR. Towards the end of his first year, he was issued a warning to keep off the campus by one of the most powerful police chiefs in Havana, a client of the Auténticos and a prominent member of the MSR. 'This was a moment of great decision', he recalled later.

*Alone on the beach, facing the sea, I examined the situation. To return to the University would mean personal danger, physical risk . . . an extraordinary temerity. But not to return would be to give in to threats, to admit defeat . . . to abandon my own ideals and aspirations. I decided to return and I returned . . . with arms in my hands.*[12]

He was later to say that the years he spent in the university had been more dangerous than the guerrilla war in the Sierra.

In the spring of 1947, Castro found the opportunity to channel his energies into a new political organisation outside the university. As a youthful critic of the Grau government, he was invited to join a new party, the Partido del Pueblo Cubano, called the Ortodoxos to indicate their fidelity to the ideals of Martí. Founded by an ex-student leader of the 1933–4

Revolution and leading Auténtico politician Eddy Chibás, the Ortodoxos were a breakaway from the government party, mainly of its youth organisation and most of its membership in the traditionally radical province of Oriente. Chibás was a passionate and somewhat unstable man, prone to rhetorical flourishes and duels of honour like many Cuban politicians of the time (not excluding Castro himself). A radio journalist, he had been lambasting the Grau administration for its venality in regular broadcasts since 1945. Chibás' brand of patriotic and populist radicalism exercised a deep influence on the young Castro for whom no other models were available among the politicians of the day. Castro was drawn to Chibás' fearless style of moral denunciation as well as the new party's vague social reformism and anti-imperialism.

However, there was a notable difference between the two in their ostensible attitude to the Communists, providing an early indication of Castro's ideological pragmatism. As the Cold War intensified in the late 1940s, Chibás became a fervent anti-Communist, reserving his bitterest criticism not for the United States but for 'a much greater danger: the threat that the totalitarian communist imperialism of Moscow, the most despotic, cruel and aggressive in History will spread across the whole world to destroy for many centuries the democratic form of government, the free will of nations, and the liberty of expression'.[13] Apart from an occasional protestation that he was not a Communist, Castro never indulged in Cold War rhetoric and was careful to avoid undue criticism of the Popular Socialist Party (PSP), the renamed Communist Party of Cuba. This was not because at this stage he secretly sympathised with their aims but because he was already concerned with uniting the opposition to the government.

Contrary to some accounts that suggest that he was drawing ever closer to Marxist-Leninist ideas, Castro, in so far as he could be said to have a defined political philosophy, was a radical nationalist with strong beliefs about social justice.[14] In any case, the PSP hardly provided the sort of political model which Castro found for a while in the Ortodoxo Party. After collaborating with the Batista government in the early 1940s, the PSP had sought to make a pact with Grau in 1945, using its influence in the labour unions to gain political leverage. The new generation of young radicals, whose spokesman Castro was increasingly becoming, spurned the politics of both the Centre and the traditional Left of the Cuban party system. Rather than a parliamentary road to power, their barely articulated political agenda envisaged populist insurrectionism at the service of radical nationalism.

Within the new Ortodoxo Party, Castro soon became a leading exponent of this more radical strategy for political change. Gathering together a number of young members of the Party, including some who had been in the UIR gang, he formed a faction called the Acción Radical Ortodoxo (or ARO). The new group sought to challenge the traditional electoral policies of Chibás and his followers and proposed a revolutionary road to power largely derived from the insurrectionary models of Cuban history. Several events between 1947 and 1948 encouraged Castro's natural inclination towards extra-parliamentary action. In the summer of 1947, he took part in an armed expedition to overthrow the Trujillo dictatorship in the nearby Dominican Republic. When the force had already gathered and had been trained on a deserted island off the eastern coast of Cuba, the expedition was aborted at the last moment by Grau, probably under pressure from the US government. The Cuban navy boarded the small ship on which the force had gathered and Castro jumped overboard and swam to the Cuban coast.[15] On his return, Castro and some followers organised a public relations stunt by taking to Havana the bell of Demajagua, which had been rung in 1868 to launch the first War of Independence, with the aim of using it as a symbolic focus of an anti-government rally. In the rally and in subsequent demonstrations, Castro's ability to organise actions and to rouse the crowd with his impassioned oratory was already evident.

Another experience that influenced the young Castro towards an extra-parliamentary strategy was his fortuitous participation in the urban riots of April 1948 in Bogotá. In trouble with the police over a false accusation that he had been involved in the murder of an MSR leader and national sports director, he had managed to get himself on the Cuban delegation to a congress of Latin American students in the Colombian capital. The congress, coinciding with the ninth Inter-American Conference, had been sponsored by Perón, whose main aim was to win support for his claims on the Falkland/Malvinas islands by organising an anti-imperialist front among student organisations. The Cuban delegation, led by the rising star of the opposition, the young Communist Alfredo Guevara, was determined to deflect the main resolution towards condemnation of American rather than European imperialism.[16] During the conference, the leader of the Colombian Liberal party, Jorge Eliecer Gaitán, was assassinated on the day that he was due to meet the Cuban delegation for a second time. Gaitán was the immensely popular leader of the Opposition, not unlike Eddy Chibás in his populist radicalism, and a politician whom Castro had admired from a distance. His murder occurred at a moment of great social unrest in Colombia and it unleashed a popular uprising. In the frenzied atmosphere that followed, Castro joined with the crowds, according to his own account, having obtained a rifle and some ammunition and a policeman's uniform. Later he became involved with a large nucleus of forces led by rebel policemen. After 48 sleepless and risk-filled hours, Castro made his way to the Cuban Embassy and from there, together with the rest of the Cuban delegation, he was flown back to Cuba.

Many years later, Castro said of his experience in Bogotá: 'The spectacle of an absolutely spontaneous popular revolution has to have exercised a great influence on me.'[17] He had witnessed at first hand the intense energies that could be released by a single event catalysing the discontent of wide sections of the population. But without any central direction to channel these energies the uprising had been uncoordinated, and the opportunities that arose for seizing power had been lost. It must have strengthened in him the belief, sanctioned by Cuban history in part, that powerful movements of popular protest could emerge spontaneously but that a tightly knit group of professional revolutionaries was also necessary to organise them. The Colombian masses, he said later, 'failed to gain power because they were betrayed by false leaders'.[18]

Castro's experience over the next four years, between 1948 and 1952, further undermined any remaining belief he held that constitutional methods could lead to political and social change. Shortly after the Bogotá riots, Grau was succeeded as President by another Auténtico politician, Carlos Prío Socarrás, who became embroiled, like his predecessor, in the politics of corruption and patronage. At this time Castro, now 22, married a young philosophy student from a wealthy Oriente family embedded in the Cuban oligarchy, Mirta Díaz-Balart, whose brother Rafael was a university friend of his. Although they had a son a year later, Castro seems to have devoted little time to his new family, his life being consumed in political activities within and outside the university. In 1949, he finally managed to shrug off the long-standing and politically damaging accusation that he was a member of the UIR by boldly denouncing the secret pact recently made between the President and the gangs whereby the latter agreed to cease their feuds in exchange for government sinecures. Castro's public denunciation earned him widespread publicity but also the wrath of the gangs, and he was forced to go into hiding and then into voluntary exile in the United States for several months until the situation appeared to cool down.

Returning later to Cuba, Castro devoted himself to his legal studies and graduated in 1950. With two other graduates, he set up a practice on a shoestring budget in a run-down district of Havana. For the next three years they took up the defence of victimised workers, slum-dwellers, detained students and poor clients in general, hardly raising enough money to pay for the rent of the office. Castro wasted little time also in pushing his way into the public arena. A frequent guest on a local radio station, Radio Álvarez, and a regular contributor to the daily newspaper *Alerta*, Castro followed the example of his mentor, the Ortodoxo senator and journalist Eddy Chibás, in berating the Prío administration for its corruption. The campaign of denunciation against the government, however, received a setback when, in a dramatic gesture, Chibás shot and killed himself at the end of a radio broadcast, having failed to produce evidence he had promised implicating the Minister of Education in acts of corruption. Chibás' suicide was the act of an unstable person but it also expressed the frustration of those who were trying to bring about change in Cuba through legitimate channels. Though Castro claimed for many years subsequently that his political programme was inspired by Chibás, he had clearly moved on to an altogether more radical strategy for change, as was evident from the internal debates among the Ortodoxos between the party leaders and his own small faction, ARO.[19] Castro learned a lot from Chibás about public relations, in particular the value of bold, emotive political broadcasting, but he was not as convinced as Chibás was that moral campaigns were enough.

For all his growing doubts about parliamentary action, Castro threw himself into the elections of 1952. Having been left off the Ortodoxo slate by a timid party leadership, Castro got himself nominated as a Congressional candidate by two poor districts. In the run-up to the elections, he conducted a vigorous campaign, sending out thousands of leaflets and delivering several speeches every day. The Ortodoxos would probably have won the elections. Castro claimed later that had he become a Congressman he would have used parliament as a 'point of departure from which I might establish a revolutionary platform and influence the masses in its favour; not as a way of fulfilling these changes directly. I was convinced then that it could only be realised by revolutionary means.'[20] In the meantime, however, Batista, who had spent the intervening years in his home in Florida without ever losing touch with Cuban politics, returned to the island to lead a new military coup. Fearing an Ortodoxo victory, he seized power before the elections could be held and proclaimed himself chief of state. The dismal experience of the governments claiming allegiance to the 1933 Revolution was thus brought to an end by the very man who had launched the Revolution in the first place.

Batista's military coup of 10 March 1952 destroyed any lingering idea Castro may have entertained that Cuba could be regenerated through parliament. The existing political system was too fragile to be the vehicle of radical reform. The endemic corruption that for decades had characterised Cuban governments was the result not just of personal greed but of the weakness of political representation in Cuba. In the absence of any institution embodying the interests of the different elites, the parties in power sought to maintain office by concession, patronage and pay-offs. The result was governmental paralysis. A reformist government, moreover, would run the risk of intervention by the only effective political force, the army, which was used to controlling the political destiny of the island. Any movement to redeem Cuba, Castro felt, would have to confront the problem of armed power.

In any case, Castro was not inclined towards the protocols of parliamentary democracy. Like many of his peers, his political ideas were inspired by the heroic and violent myths of Cuba's past. He had spent his university years organising protest actions, declaiming on the steps of the campus and dodging batons and bullets. Indeed, he grew into manhood in a culture prizing oratory and physical heroism above all. Through political models such as Guiteras, Chibás, Gaitán and Perón, he was aware of the power of populist leadership, and he had experienced the extraordinary energy of mass protest.[21] He had been drawn to the Ortodoxo programme of nationalist redemption and social justice but not to its parliamentary strategy. None of this suggests that Castro even considered himself a communist at the time. Some orthodox accounts, including his own, argue that he was moving rapidly towards Marxist ideas but can only adduce the fact that he was reading Marx and Lenin at the time and that he was harbouring extra-parliamentary strategies.[22] The core of Marxist strategy is the class struggle, and there is little evidence at this stage that Castro saw the activity of the Cuban workers as more than one element in his strategy for the seizure of power. His closest collaborators, he argued later, had 'class instincts' but not class consciousness.[23] It is true that among Castro's closest acquaintances were two Communists. Yet one has the impression from his own writings, speeches and actions in this period that he was relatively unsophisticated ideologically, drawing inspiration from many different sources, of which the most important were Cuba's nationalist traditions.

Castro also appears as a political outsider, an upstart to some, drawing grudging admiration as well as exasperation from both the Ortodoxo leadership and the Communists. A restless, ambitious, immensely self-confident young man, with a sharp eye for political opportunities, he was also moved by vague ideals of progress and justice. The Batista coup of 1952 closed the path of self-advancement for middle-class youth and brought to an end eight years of a largely ineffectual and corrupt democracy. Castro's response, as we shall see in the next chapter, was true to radical nationalist traditions, not Marxist or liberal democratic traditions.

# Notes

1  Castro, in I. Ramonet, *Fidel Castro. Biografía a dos voces* (Random House Mondadori, Mexico and Barcelona, 2006), pp. 60–1; F. Betto, *Fidel and Religion* (Weidenfeld & Nicolson, London, 1987), pp. 127–8.

2  Castro, in Ramonet, *Castro*, pp. 96 and 69–81; see also C. Franqui, *Diary of the Cuban Revolution* (Viking Press, New York, 1980), pp. 1–8.

3  Betto, *Fidel and Religion*, pp. 114–22; Franqui, *Diary*, p. 8; Ramonet, *Castro*, pp. 82–3.

4  J.I. Dominguez, *Cuba: Order and Revolution* (Harvard University Press, Cambridge, Mass., 1978), p. 555, n. 87.

5  Ibid., pp. 84–95.

6  J. Suchlicki, *University Students and Revolution in Cuba 1920–1968* (University of Miami Press, 1969), p. 49.

7  V. Skierka, *Fidel Castro: a Biography* (Polity Press, Cambridge, 2004), pp. 21–2.

8  *Bohemia*, 15 June 1947, pp. 52–5.

9  H. Thomas, *Cuba: the Pursuit of Freedom* (Harper & Row, New York, 1971), pp. 763–4.

10  M. Llerena, *The Unsuspected Revolution* (Cornell University Press, Ithaca, NY, 1978), pp. 42–3.

11  *Diario de la Marina*, 17 July 1947; see also *El Mundo*, 28 November 1946.

12  *América Libre*, 22–28 May 1961.

13  From a radio broadcast on 1 January 1951, quoted in L. Conte Agüero, *Eduardo Chibás, el Adalid de Cuba* (Jus, Mexico, 1955), p. 718.

14  Castro later defined his position first as 'Utopian socialist' and then in a more recent interview as 'utopian communist' (Ramonet, *Castro*, p. 113) while Lionel Martin and orthodox Cuban historiography see an early affinity on Castro's part with Marxist ideas.

15  According to Skierka, *Castro*, p. 26.

16  Author's conversation with Tomás Gutiérrez Alea, 29 Aug. 1988.

17  T. Szulc, *Fidel: a Critical Portrait* (Hutchinson, London, 1987), p. 123. For Castro's account of the Bogotazo, see pp. 120–3, Franqui, *Diary*, pp. 13–19 and A. Alape, *El Bogotazo: Memorias del Olvido* (Casa de las América, Havana, 1983).

18  *América Libre*, 22–28 May 1961.

19  Castro, in Ramonet, *Castro*, p. 105.

20  Castro's statement is quoted in M. Mencía, *Tiempos Precursores* (Editorial de Ciencias Sociales, Havana, 1986), pp. 77–8.

21  One of Castro's friends at the time and later a bitter opponent claims that among his favourite readings were the complete writings and speeches of Mussolini but

no other sources confirm this (J. Pardo Llada, *Fidel y el 'Che'* (Plaza y Janes, Barcelona, 1988), p. 30).

**22** Castro himself in evidence to Betto, *Fidel and Religion*, pp. 141–3; to Ramonet, *Castro*, pp. 113–17, though here Castro claimed he had been a convinced Marxist-Leninist by 1952; L. Martin, *The Early Fidel* (Lyle Stuart, Secaucus, NJ, 1978), pp. 60–4.

**23** Ramonet, *Castro*, p. 119.

# CHAPTER 3

# Rise to Power

Batista attempted to present his coup of March 1952 as a progressive measure designed to bring an end to corruption and anarchy in Cuba. To this effect, he promised to carry out a number of social reforms and eventually to hold elections; he had not lost his populist touch. The promises could not have been more cynical, for he began his new rule by suspending constitutional guarantees such as the right to strike and abolishing both Congress and political parties. Yet the political system of Cuba had been so discredited by eight years of Auténtico administration that many Cubans welcomed his coup. The Cuban business elites and the small conservative parties rallied to his side while the executive of the Cuban Labour Federation, the CTC, whose left-wing leadership had been destroyed by repression in the late 1940s, made a deal with Batista in which they agreed to collaborate in exchange for corporatist favours.[1] For its part the US government under Truman gave its seal of approval to the coup 10 days later.

The most resolute opposition came from the student movement, which staged demonstrations throughout the island. By contrast, the top Auténtico politicians chose to flee to the US while the Ortodoxo leadership dithered over what response it should make to the abolition of its party, finally issuing a call for a tame campaign of civic resistance. It took over a year for the two organisations, now in exile, to agree to a joint statement demanding the restoration of democracy, the Ortodoxo rank and file being divided over whether to enter into any pact with the Auténticos. A more serious split that led to punch-ups between members separated those who advocated peaceful resistance and others, led by Castro, who were campaigning for more violent methods. The timidity of the Ortodoxo leadership increasingly exasperated the younger activists. Castro was already organising a clandestine network and an underground press, and by the autumn of 1952 he was calling for a different leadership based on a new generation of activists. Even at this stage, his message was no longer about regenerating Cuban liberal democracy but about regenerating Cuba through vaguely articulated revolutionary means. The appeal was populist and radical nationalist not Leninist, as the retrospective gloss of official Revolutionary literature would have it. In his mimeographed paper *El Acusador*, Castro wrote,

*The present moment is revolutionary, not political. Politics is the consecration of the opportunism of those who have means and resources. The Revolution opens the way for true merit, for those who bare their chest and take up the standard. A Revolutionary Party needs a young revolutionary leadership drawn from the people in whose hands Cuba can be saved.*[2]

By mid-1953, he had organised about 1,200 followers, mostly from the Ortodoxo youth, into 150 cells, based mainly in the westernmost provinces of Havana and Pinar del Río.

Castro was not the only conspirator. In a repeat of the Machado years, several middle-class underground organisations were set up. One of these, the Movimiento Nacional Revolucionario, tried unsuccessfully to carry out a coup within the army in April 1953 with the aid of some officers who were members of its underground network. By that time, Castro had drawn up his own very different plans for armed action. Inspired by several famous incidents in Cuban history, he and his co-conspirators planned to seize a military barracks in Santiago, the capital of Oriente province, in the hope that this might encourage a mass uprising against the new dictator. The plan was rash and wishful but not as far-fetched as it might appear. Oriente was by tradition a rebellious province. It was from here that the independence movements had been launched against the Spanish colonialists, who had occupied mainly the western provinces; the spark that had set alight the rebellions had been the seizure of barracks and the distribution of their weapons.

The east–west divide in Cuba is fundamental to an understanding of its history. For centuries, the easternmost province had been largely isolated from the rest of the island by mountain ranges and ocean currents. While the western provinces had been settled by immigrants, the east became Cuba's frontier land where escaped slaves and fugitives from the law found refuge. In the late nineteenth century, Oriente had been at once the poorest and most Cuban of the island's provinces and the most rebellious against the rule of Spain. It had also been the scene of numerous slave revolts, and more recently of sugar workers' uprisings. In the early 1930s, urban guerrilla groups led by Antonio Guiteras had carried out several actions against the Machado dictatorship. In the 1950s, it was the east that suffered the highest level of unemployment on the island; Oriente accounted for almost 30 per cent of the jobless. Living standards were also considerably lower there than in the west and political dissatisfaction, consequently, was higher.

The geographical position of Oriente also offered the rebels a strategic advantage; it could be cut off from the rest of the island if the only road from the west could be blocked. Militarily, the plan was relatively simple if fraught with risks. Castro and his people were to seize the Moncada barracks and distribute arms to those people willing to join the rebellion. A separate armed group would capture the barracks at Bayamo, some 100 kilometres away, holding up the deployment of reinforcements on the road from the west. If the uprising were to fail, the rebels would retreat into the densely wooded mountains of the Sierra Maestra, there to begin a rural guerrilla campaign.

The weakness of the plan lay in its faith that the people of Oriente would rise up spontaneously in response to the exemplary action of Castro's band. The rebels had no organisation in Santiago itself; in fact, only one of them came from the Oriente capital and there was only one cell in the whole of the province.[3] Some measure of the *naïveté* of the scheme is afforded by the broadcast that the plotters hoped to put out once the barracks had been seized. Written by a young poet under the supervision of Castro and in the name of 'The Cuban Revolution', the proclamation laid claim to the traditions of Cuba's independence struggles in the year of Martí's centenary. It also called for the moral regeneration of society, promising economic development and social justice, without explaining the means whereby these were to be achieved. The manifesto was to be followed by an appeal for a national uprising, a recording of Chibás' farewell speech and heroic music, including Beethoven's *Eroica* and Chopin's A flat Polonaise.

In the event, the action failed because of a number of mistakes and mishaps. A chance encounter near the gates of the barracks with a two-man military patrol armed with machine guns alerted the garrison. Dressed in military uniform, the rebels were fired on before their leading car driven by Castro had reached the gates of the barracks. The men in the cars behind misunderstood the situation and seized a hospital nearby thinking it was part of the barracks. Two other groups of rebels were positioned above and behind the barracks to give covering fire. One, led by Castro's brother, Raúl, had occupied the roof of a nearby block, and another, led by the joint leader of the action, Abel Santamaría, had seized a hospital building at the back of the barracks. The latter group, not knowing of the failure of the assault, remained in the hospital where they were captured by soldiers and shot in cold blood or tortured to death. The two women taking part in the action witnessed the beatings inflicted on some of the prisoners; one of them, Abel Santamaría's sister Haydée, was brought her brother's gouged-out eye by a sergeant. Fleeing by car, Castro and some of the survivors made their way into the nearby Sierra to hide from the patrols that soon began to scour the hills behind Santiago.[4]

In Bayamo, the smaller group of rebels had had as little luck, failing to reach anywhere near the barracks before they were fired on and forced to abandon the assault. During the next few days, the fleeing rebels were picked up in groups or individually by the army and the rural guard. Many were summarily shot; of the 111 men who had taken part in the action, 69 died, only 8 of them killed in combat. Castro himself, with a small band of survivors, was finally captured after six rough days of flight in the mountains. Their lives were saved thanks to the black lieutenant commanding the detachment that discovered them. Concerned to avoid their cold-blooded murder, he insisted on delivering them to the city jail rather than the Moncada barracks where an irate garrison awaited them. Other rebels were saved by the intervention of the Archbishop of Santiago at the head of a group of civic leaders. The Archbishop himself drove into the mountains and prevented further shooting. Finally, the arrested rebels were taken to the large jail on the outskirts of the city to await trial.

The attempted capture of the Moncada barracks on 26 July 1953 has been presented in some orthodox Cuban accounts as the first stage in a more or less defined strategy leading to the proclamation in 1961 of a Marxist-Leninist state.[5] What evidence we have of Castro's thinking at the time suggests, on the contrary, that the object of the assault was to spark off a popular revolt leading to the installation of an Ortodoxo provisional government under radical leadership followed by general elections.[6] Nevertheless, the government programme of social reforms and nationalisations that Castro had in mind was not one which could have been acceptable to the Cuban elites or to the United States. It was likely therefore that he had already moved beyond a social democratic policy of radical reform within the existing political framework.

None of this proves, however, that Castro was inspired by Marxist ideas or Leninist strategy, as he later claimed.[7] The action and the programme of Moncada were firmly within the Cuban tradition of radical nationalism, whose main representatives were Martí and Antonio Guiteras; more so, indeed, than another hero of the Cuban revolutionary narrative, Julio Antonio Mella, who was more closely associated, as a young Communist of

the 1920s generation, with working-class internationalism. The plan to seize
the barracks derived from Cuban history, not from the Russian Revolution
(though Castro and Abel Santamaría, it seems, were reading Lenin's *State
and Revolution* at the time). It was also the desperate gesture of a marginal
social group with few links with organised workers. To claim, as some commentators have done, that the Moncada action had a proletarian character
on the basis of the occupations of the assailants is to indulge in tokenism.[8]
While most of them had a working-class background, only one or two were
from the organised labour movement; indeed, the majority were workers in
marginal or casual occupations such as delivery men, building workers,
waiters, street vendors, cooks and the like, while several were self-employed
or unemployed.[9] The vast majority were rank-and-file members of the
Ortodoxo party whose founder had been a visceral anti-Communist. The
26th July Movement, as it soon came to be called, had popular roots, unlike
all the other anti-Batista underground groups except the Communists, but it
was not a working-class organisation.

In the trial that followed in September, Castro proclaimed the programme for Cuba's regeneration which the rebels had been unable to broadcast. Castro conducted his own defence and he later reconstructed from
memory his long and skilful speech to the court, using the notes taken by a
follower during the trial; the speech was to become later the official testament of the Cuban Revolution. Standing before the judges in a borrowed
gown, Castro launched into a wide-ranging critique of the political, economic and social situation in Cuba. At pains to establish a legal justification
of the Moncada assault, he linked the action with the revolutionary traditions of Cuba, quoting Martí repeatedly, and invoked universal principles
such as the right of rebellion against despotism derived from many centuries
of history. The names of Dante, John of Salisbury, St Thomas Aquinas,
Knox, Milton, Thomas Paine and others rang out in the tiny sweltering
room of a small tropical town, and it must have bewildered the few people
allowed to be present. Castro ended his long speech on a defiant note: 'As
for me, I know that prison will be hard, harder than it has been for anyone,
filled with threats, with callous and cruel barbarity, but I do not fear it,
just as I do not fear the fury of the despicable tyrant that tore out the lives
of seventy of my brothers. Condemn me, it does not matter, history will
absolve me.'[10]

Castro's defence took the form of a manifesto to the people, *el pueblo*,
from whom he deliberately excluded 'the well-off and conservative sections
of the nation'. Although he was careful to keep within the framework of
the 1940 Constitution, Castro was proposing the regeneration of Cuban

economy, politics and society. The key word was 'new', not just a new Cuba but a new Man, whose incarnation was a young generation free from the corruption of the past. Behind the patriotic and progressive rhetoric were more radical, although barely articulated, proposals. Cuba would throw off the 'shackles' of foreign nations, of which there could only be one he had in mind, the United States. The economy would be 'renewed' on the basis of a 'synchronized plan', for which read state intervention of one sort or another, and work and money would be shared equitably, suggesting some form of egalitarian redistribution. That is, the speech contained the blueprint of the most important social and economic reforms that the new regime would attempt to carry out after the victory of the Revolution in 1959.

Many years later, Castro characterised the Moncada programme thus: 'whoever reads it carefully and analyses it in depth will see, in the first place that it was a programme of national liberation, a very advanced programme and a programme that was very close to socialism'.[11] Because of its radical nature, official accounts have portrayed the Manifesto as a Marxist document, arguing on one hand that Castro had to conceal the full extent of his revolutionary plans because the moment was not ripe and on the other that he was reinterpreting Marxist-Leninist thought to suit the special nature of the Cuban situation. They are right to point out the continuity of Castro's programme for reform. But it was above all a social democratic programme, as befitting a member of the Ortodoxo Party, and it was similar to social democratic agendas elsewhere in the Caribbean and Central America. In the same year of the Moncada assault, the reformist government of Colonel Jacobo Arbenz was carrying out the first stages of an analogous programme in an attempt to modernise the semi-feudal economy of Guatemala. Moreover, what is missing from the Moncada manifesto and 'History will absolve me' speech is the central notion of Marxism, class struggle. Castro's programme of 1953 belonged to a different tradition, that of anti-colonial, nationalist regeneration, in which radical reform and nationalisation were, in theory at least, compatible with social democracy. This is not to deny the influence of Marxist ideas on Castro's thinking. But in 1953, he was a Martí follower, *tendance* Marx, not the other way round.[12]

The Moncada action and the trial brought Castro vividly into the public eye. In a nation used to violent gestures of rebellion, the assault on the barracks evoked widespread admiration, while the much-publicised brutality of the army awakened the sympathies of many Cubans for the survivors. When Castro began his 15-year sentence on the Isle of Pines, off the western coast of Cuba, he was already something of a national figure. A year after the assault, he was paid a courtesy call in jail by the Interior Minister and two other cabinet ministers in a tacit recognition of his new status. The 19 months he and 25 of his comrades spent on the island before they were amnestied were devoted to study and discussion. There the foundations of the 26th July Movement were laid, and a new strategy for the seizure of power forged. Although he had no reason to believe he would be amnestied, Castro's optimism seemed boundless. It did not seem to desert him even when he was put into solitary confinement for organising the chanting of the 26th July hymn within earshot of Batista, who was paying an official visit to the island.

Only once did he seem to lose heart. In July 1954, he learned that his wife, Mirta Díaz-Balart, whose brother Rafael, once Castro's friend at university, was deputy to the Interior Minister in Batista's cabinet, had been accused of being on the payroll of the Ministry. The much-publicised news was deeply hurtful to Castro on both a political and a personal level. Always able to deal effectively with political attacks, he seemed to crumble for a short while before what he perceived as an assault on his private life. In a surprising transposition of a typically Castilian code of aggrieved sexual honour on to a political plane, he wrote disbelievingly to a friend: 'The prestige of my wife and my honour as a revolutionary is at stake. Do not hesitate to return the offence, and wound back to an infinite degree. Let them see me dead a thousand times rather than suffer impotently such an offence!' The accusation also brought out Castro's latent prejudice against homosexuals, a strong component of Cuban machismo at the time. Attacking the Interior Minister for his claim about Castro's wife, he wrote, 'Only an effeminate like Hermida who has sunk to the last rung of sexual degeneration could stoop to such a procedure, marked by such indecency and lack of manliness.' When it became clear that the accusation was true, Castro issued divorce proceedings against his wife. On the edge of despair, he wrote to a close friend and political collaborator: 'I consider the 26th July [Movement] far more important than my own person and the moment I know that I cannot be useful to the cause for which I have suffered so much, I will take my life without hesitation, all the more so now that I have not even a private ideal left to serve.'[13]

Meanwhile, the campaign for the freeing of the Moncada prisoners had gathered widespread support and found a sympathetic echo in the press. In May 1955, Batista, anxious to appear benevolent, signed an amnesty bill and Castro and his comrades were released unconditionally. To considerable acclaim, the young rebel returned to the political fray, launching renewed attacks on the regime. Batista was facing an upsurge of protest against his rule and responded by tightening his measures of repression.

The opportunities for agitation were narrowing every day and increasingly Castro feared he might be re-arrested or even assassinated, a fate that had befallen many other opponents of the dictator. His brother Raúl sought asylum in Mexico, and Castro himself, after taking farewell of his young son Fidelito, left Cuba for Mexico barely six weeks after his release, there to prepare for a fresh attempt to overthrow the dictator.

The new strategy was an extension of the original plans for the Moncada assault. Castro would land with a force of men on the west coast of Oriente where they would be met by around a hundred combatants of the 26th July Movement and several lorries. The combined force would seize the nearby town of Niquero and then move up the coast to capture Manzanillo. The landing would coincide with uprisings and strikes in Santiago and Guantánamo. A campaign of agitation and sabotage would follow, leading to a general strike that would topple Batista.[14] Unlike Moncada, the new plans did not rely on a single exemplary action that might spark off a spontaneous uprising. Another lesson had been learnt from the 1953 fiasco: beyond the armed groups there had to be a grass-roots organisation to provide arms, recruits and logistical support, and to agitate among workers and civic groups for the crucial general strike. As in the Moncada plan, however, the rebels would move into the Sierra Maestra to begin a rural guerrilla campaign should the original endeavour fail.

Castro had left behind in Cuba the bare bones of the new 26th July Movement. His followers on the island set to work to build the organisation from scratch. In most of the historical accounts of the Revolution, their efforts have received little attention. The Sierra campaign that began in 1957 has unjustifiably overshadowed the labour of the 26th July militants in the towns and the countryside. Their main recruiting ground was the Ortodoxo branches throughout the island, but especially in Oriente where the Movement began to lay popular roots. There was considerable support among Ortodoxo militants for Castro's strategy of armed resistance in contrast to the leadership's policy of political agitation. At a congress of Party members in August 1955, Castro's message calling for a 'revolutionary line' received a standing ovation and chants of 'Revolution'; at provincial party assemblies the same response was heard.[15] By early 1956, Castro felt sufficiently strong to break publicly with the Ortodoxo Party and declare the new movement.

The 26th July militants' work of agitation and recruitment was divided into geographical and functional sectors. In the western tip of Oriente (now called the province of Granma) where the landing of Castro's force was planned, there were separate groups of industrial workers, agricultural labourers, peasants, fishermen and students. The largest town near the projected landing place, Manzanillo, had a long tradition of labour protest among its sugar workers, dockers, shoemakers and tobacco workers. In the local union elections of 1956, militants sympathetic to the Movement came close to gaining control of the union branches but were forced to withdraw because of threats by the military.[16] Many workers drawn to the 26th July Movement were young Ortodoxo supporters impatient with the Party leadership. The Communist rank-and-file organisation, the Comités pro Defensa de las Demandas Obreras was avoided by many sections of workers because of the Party's previous collaboration with Batista; in reality, there was a strong anti-Communist sentiment among many Cuban workers.

This explains in part the care Castro took in building bridges with the anti-Batista opposition. Although he would shortly be in contact with the Communists through two top-level emissaries who visited him separately in Mexico in 1956, Castro bluntly denied any links with the Communist Party, the PSP. In jail with his fellow conspirators for several weeks in Mexico City after a police round-up, the result probably of pressure from the Cuban authorities, Castro had an article published in the weekly Cuban paper *Bohemia*, rejecting a claim by Batista in the previous issue that he was a Communist. 'Of course', he wrote, 'the accusation of being a Communist seemed absurd to all those in Cuba who know my public career, which has been without any kind of links with the Communist Party.' In a barely disguised attack on the PSP's previous collaboration with Batista, Castro went on,

*What right, on the other hand, does Batista have to speak about Communism when he was presidential candidate of the Communist Party in the 1940 elections, when his electoral posters appeared under the hammer and sickle, when he was photographed alongside Blas Roca and Lázaro Peña [two top Cuban Communists], and when half a dozen of his present ministers and close collaborators were leading members of the Communist Party?*[17]

Castro's denial was clearly meant to reassure many of his followers in Cuba who opposed the Communists. But it also marked his distance from the PSP, which was calling for a non-violent, united-front policy of opposition to the dictatorship. While he may have been drawn to certain Marxist ideas at this stage, Castro had no illusions about the Cuban Communist Party.

He took care also to spread wide his net of contacts. The planned expedition needed considerable sums of money. Besides the flow of cash from the Movement in Cuba, several large contributions were made by wealthy sympathisers; not least among them was ex-President Prío Socarrás, now in exile in Miami. Like Martí some 60 years previously, Castro went on a fund-raising tour of the Cuban communities in Florida and along the East coast of the United States, giving rousing speeches to enthusiastic audiences and raising large sums of money. In August, Castro reached an agreement with the Directorio Revolucionario, a student-based, armed, underground organisation, led by the president of the Students' Union, José Antonio Echeverría, to operate jointly in armed actions in preparation for the forthcoming landing.

By October 1956, the expeditionary force had been assembled and trained. Their instructor, Alberto Bayo, was an expert in guerrilla warfare, a veteran of the Spanish military campaign against the guerrillas of the Moroccan Rif in the 1920s and a Loyalist general during the Spanish civil war. A measure of Castro's powers of persuasion was that Bayo gave up his job and sold his business shortly after meeting him in order to train the would-be Cuban invaders in what must have appeared a madcap project. He wrote later that Castro 'subjugated me. I became intoxicated with his enthusiasm. . . . Then and there I promised Fidel to resign from my . . . [job] and to sell my business.'[18]

Among the expeditionaries was the young Argentinian doctor Ernesto Guevara, nicknamed 'Che' (the Argentinian equivalent of 'mate') by his new companions. Guevara had left Argentina in 1953, just after he had completed his training as a doctor, to begin a long journey across South America with his friend Alberto Granado. He was in Guatemala in 1954 where, according to Castro, he met several of the veterans of the Moncada attack who had fled to that country. With them he witnessed the overthrow of the reformist Arbenz government by a CIA-trained army.[19] A year later he was in Mexico and met Raúl Castro, who in turn introduced him to his brother. By all accounts, Guevara was deeply impressed by Fidel and his plans to return to Cuba to stage a new revolt against the Batista dictatorship, but contrary to legend he took a while before committing himself to the expedition towards the end of 1955. It is likely that this new venture gave a focus to Guevara's growing radicalism, nourished by the poverty he had witnessed in his travels throughout the continent and by his first-hand experience of US intervention in Latin America. Like millions of young people at the time, he was a Communist fellow-traveller and was familiar with Marxist literature, more so than Castro, but he was not a party member nor does it appear that he was particularly committed to Communism at this stage beyond an identification with the struggle against injustice and American imperialism.[20]

Disregarding the advice of both the Communists and the leader of the 26th July Movement in Oriente, Frank País, Castro decided to set sail before the end of 1956. The Communists were opposed to the idea of the expedition in itself. In a letter a few months later to the American journalist Herbert L. Matthews, the PSP President wrote, 'In these days and with reference to assaults on barracks and expeditions from abroad – taking place without relying on popular support – our position is very clear; we are against these methods.' What Cuba needed, he went on, was 'democratic elections'.[21] The Communists argued that if the expedition had to take place it should at least wait for the beginning of the cane harvest in January when it might coincide with strike activity. Less than 12 months previously, a quarter of a million sugar workers had come out on strike after their wages fell by 23 per cent following a cut in Cuba's sugar quota on the world market and the decision by the United States to increase its own production. The strike had taken on insurrectionary proportions in some places; workers had seized town halls and clashed with the army.

For his part, the young 26th July leader Frank País had insisted that the organisation in Oriente, the stronghold of the Movement, was not ready for the expedition.[22] But Castro would brook no delay. He had promised publicly that he would return to Cuba before 1958. Any postponement, moreover, might jeopardise the expedition that was now ready to set sail; the Mexican police had already been alerted to the activities of the Cuban oppositionists. Castro's decision to go ahead with the mission illustrated once again his belief in the overriding importance of public relations and his voluntarist faith in the triumph of will over logistics.

Logistically, indeed, the expedition turned out to be a disaster. Setting sail on 25 November on a yacht which was intended to carry less than half the load, the 82-man invasion ran into a storm, had mechanical break-downs, was forced to jettison supplies, lost its way and landed at the wrong place on the wrong day. Two days before the yacht *Granma* beached in a muddy estuary on 2 December, Frank País' armed group had attempted to stage an uprising in Santiago, but after some 30 hours of sporadic gunfire against the police and the army they had been forced to abandon the enterprise. Forty-eight hours later, wading painfully through a mangrove swamp, the ragged and exhausted expeditionaries finally landed on dry ground. Castro announced grandly to the first peasant they came across, 'I am Fidel Castro and we have come to liberate Cuba.' Four days later, another peasant betrayed them to Rural Guards, who were searching the area for the expeditionaries. In the devastating ambush that followed, Castro's tiny band was all but destroyed. Of the 82 men who had set out, only 16 (though legend has it that there were 12, giving a religious, mytho-logical dimension to the narrative) remained alive or free to start the war against the modern army of the Batista regime.

Some of the anecdotes of that terrible episode tell of Castro's apparently absurd optimism. After being dispersed in the ambush for several days, a demoralised Guevara with a handful of unarmed men managed to reach the main group high up in the Sierra Maestra. Seeing them arrive, Castro exclaimed, excitedly pacing up and down on a hilltop overlooking a valley, 'Batista's fucking had it now!'[23] What saved the expedition, however, was not Castro's confidence, although that must have helped to raise morale, but the peasants of the Sierra Maestra.

The agrarian structure of the rough and isolated Sierra was very different from that of other parts of Cuba's countryside. Most of the peasants were squatters who made a precarious living off small parcels of land belonging to local landlords or *latifundistas*. A continuous war was waged by the land-lords' foremen to prevent them encroaching any further on their territory. According to the colonel in charge of the operation to destroy Castro's expedi-tion, 'From these struggles there arose constant fights between the squat-ters and the foremen and their followers, with the result that sometimes a foreman or one of his men died and at other times it was a squatter who was killed or who had his hut burnt down.'[24] Several generations of peasants had fought attempts by the army or the Rural Guard to evict them; some were regarded by the authorities as nothing better than bandits. The mobility of these peasants and their intimate knowledge of the people and the terrain of the Sierra enabled Castro's band to survive and begin to grow in number. The army's brutal treatment of peasants suspected of sheltering the rebels helped to provide the first recruits of the new guerrilla force, although at first many were frightened into fleeing the area.[25]

Furthermore, Castro's policy of paying for the food provided by the peasants, of executing their most notorious persecutors and putting his men to work in the coffee harvest in the spring of 1957 turned their initial sym-pathy into active support. As Castro's unit became established and moved into new areas, it absorbed small bands of poorly armed fugitives and bandits who had fled to the remotest regions, there to fight the occasional skirmish with the Rural Guard. A guerrilla struggle in the Sierra had existed long before the arrival of Castro and his fighters.

It had not been Castro's intention to wage the war almost entirely from a rural base, nor were the peasants of the Sierra Maestra typical of the Cuban countryside as a whole. Yet as the campaign against Batista gradually centred on the Sierra, a new mythology arose about peasant rebellion and rural virtue that was later to underpin the legitimacy of the Revolution and influence the Left worldwide. In this new version of rural populism reminis-cent of the Narodniks and the Chinese Communists and articulated later by Che Guevara above all, the city was represented as a source of corruption while a somewhat idealised peasantry replaced the urban proletariat as the revolutionary class of Cuba. The mythification of the rural guerrilla campaign drew inspiration from the *cubanía rebelde* tradition. The nineteenth-century campaigns against the Spanish army were portrayed as rural campaigns against the city where the imperialists and their Cuban collaborators were based. In the final victorious moments, the *mambí* or liberation army had swept down from the mountains and forests to liberate the occupied cities and proclaim Cuban independence. The forest or *monte* also resonated with Afro-Cuban religious myths, in which vegetation was animated by the spirits.[26]

Yet the war in the Sierra could not be described in any sense as a peasant war. The guerrilla leaders were city people, although they took on the emblematic guise of the land, and many of the rank and file were volunteers recruited in the towns by the 26th July Movement. The urban underground was heavily engaged in sabotage, agitation and logistical work in support of the military campaign in the mountains. During the struggle against Batista, according to one calculation, it carried out over 30,000 acts of sabotage. Yet, as one ex-guerrilla later wrote, having abandoned Cuba after it became aligned with Moscow, 'The Comandante and his Twelve Followers were the revolution, not the city, the clandestine war, the 26th July Movement, the strikes, the sabotage, the people's boycott of Batista's elections. The revolution was the hero not the people.'[27]

The two-year campaign that led finally to the defeat of the Batista regime marked the gradual shift away from the original plan to combine sabotage, guerrilla activity and urban agitation to a strategy of full-scale engagement with the regular army. The ability of the rebels to repel military units not only eroded the morale of the rank-and-file soldiers but also strengthened the belief that the army could be defeated by military means. As the guerrilla forces consolidated their hold in the mountains, the centre of opposition to Batista increasingly became the liberated zone in the Sierra. Support from local small farmers and farmhands increased as the rebels treated them with respect, purchasing food and increasing their help with the harvests. This change of emphasis was accelerated by two things: the relative failure of anti-Batista actions in the city, and the skilful radio and press campaign carried out by Castro from his mountain fastness.

Other forces besides the 26th July Movement were attempting to topple the regime. In March 1957, the student-led underground organisation the Directorio Revolucionario made a wild bid to eliminate Batista at a stroke by attacking the National Palace. They were beaten back and many perished in the aftermath, including the popular student leader José Antonio Echevarría. In May, a guerrilla expedition financed by ex-President Prío Socarrás landed on the north coast of Oriente but was betrayed by a peasant and wiped out. In September, some officers and sailors of the naval base at Cienfuegos staged a mutiny which was to have been part of an island-wide coup by anti-Batista elements in the armed forces. The isolated mutineers were easily crushed by forces loyal to the regime. These abortive actions only served to raise Castro's stature as the leading opponent of the dictator.

The point was underlined by the public relations campaign he conducted from the Sierra. Since his student days, Castro had learnt the value of using the media to draw attention to his ideas. He had also become aware of the opportunities for agitation offered by radio broadcasting through his old mentor Eddy Chibás. Barely 10 weeks after the *Granma* landing, he staged a publicity stunt that did more for his standing than any military engagement. Under his instructions, organisers of the Movement smuggled a willing *New York Times* journalist, Herbert L. Matthews, into the depths of the Sierra to interview Castro, whom many had claimed to be dead. With a force of only 18 men, Castro managed to give the impression, by careful stage management and some talented acting on the part of his followers, that he controlled a wide area of the mountains and had considerable numbers under his command. Published in the *New York Times* and later reported in the press in Cuba, where censorship had recently been lifted, Matthews' article caused a sensation, not least because it suggested that Castro's force was invincible.

Another important media coup was the installation of a radio station in the spring of 1958 by which time the rebel forces controlled a large area of the Sierra. Radio Rebelde brought a new dimension to the guerrilla war. Castro used its airwaves with great effect to put over his programme for reforms, and the regular news bulletins featured in the broadcasts gave a conscientiously accurate report of military engagements, in marked contrast to the triumphalist fantasies of the pro-Batista media. By the end of the campaign Radio Rebelde was vying with light music frequencies for popularity.[28]

A year after they had landed, Castro's forces dominated the Sierra Maestra. Below them, the army attempted to lay siege but the flow of messengers, arms and recruits to and from the guerrilla stronghold and the city slipped through the army patrols without undue difficulty. Castro was joined by one of the Movement's most effective organisers in Oriente, Celia Sánchez, who became his companion and personal assistant from then on until her death in 1980. In the Sierra, the rebels had set up rudimentary hospitals, workshops for making light arms, ammunition and leather equipment, and a printing press in addition to the radio station. At this stage, the army, stung by a number of small defeats, chose not to make any military excursions into rebel territory, so that an uneasy truce reigned.

Divisions were emerging, however, between Castro and the leadership of the 26th July Movement on the rest of the island, the so-called *llano*, which now constituted a majority of its National Directorate. Castro's new strategy consisted of extending rural guerrilla warfare to other parts of the island, laying siege to the cities from the countryside; the general strike was the final blow that would topple Batista. Although urban sabotage and civic agitation still had an important role to play, the main function of the *llano*, in Castro's view, was to service the guerrillas.[29] The Movement's leaders outside the Sierra, on the contrary, still clung to the strategy of the urban uprising and the general strike as the main instrument of Batista's overthrow. Castro repeatedly complained that they were holding back on arms, while the *llano* organisers, according to Guevara, showed signs of 'a certain opposition to the *caudillo* who was feared [to exist] in Fidel, and the militarist faction represented by us, the people in the Sierra'.[30] Although he showed complete faith in Castro, the 26th July organiser in Oriente, Frank País, was quite prepared to reorganise the Movement, centralising its command into the hands of a few leaders and setting up new civic fronts, without consulting Castro.[31]

The idea that workers would spontaneously come out on strike against the regime was given a boost by events that followed the murder of País by the police in August 1957. Protest strikes spread from his home town of Santiago to the provinces of Camagüey and Las Villas, forcing the government to suspend constitutional rights. It was a testimony to the close links that bound the Movement in Oriente to many sections of workers in the eastern part of the island and the more radical traditions of the local labour movement. But workers in western Cuba, especially in the province of Havana where most of the labour force was concentrated, did not join the action. This was not surprising since País was hardly known there but it was also the result of the fact that the Communists, who were relatively strong among the organised rank and file, were not yet prepared to support the 26th July movement. That is why Castro was sceptical about the possibilities of an island-wide general strike. This was being urged on him by the *llano* leadership of the Movement. Nevertheless, the optimistic reports coming in about the mood among workers encouraged Castro to support their call for a general strike in the spring of 1958. In a speech on Radio Rebelde after the August strikes, Castro had said, 'the spontaneous strike that followed the murder of our comrade Frank País did not overcome the tyranny but it did point the way towards the organised strike'.[32]

Most accounts of the strike of 9 April consider it to have been a total failure. It failed to dislodge Batista and, indeed, encouraged the dictator to believe for a short while that events were moving his way once again. According to the American Ambassador, 'Batista apparently felt he was in the ascendancy.'[33] Yet it did mobilise thousands of Cuban workers. In Las Villas province, most industries and services came to a halt; the town of Sagua La Grande to the north of the province was taken over by workers and held for a while against the army and the air force. Camagüey province was swept by strike action for two days, while the towns of Oriente were paralysed by strikes and street fighting. In the west, however, only a few thousand workers came out and there were only isolated acts of sabotage.[34] In fact, it was a repeat of the strike pattern of August 1957. But the lesson that was drawn this time was the opposite one.

In a crucial meeting of the Movement leadership in the Sierra 24 days later, the *llano* leaders were attacked for failing to organise the strike sufficiently, for relying on spontaneity and not involving workers in its preparation, indeed for the very assumptions that had underlain Castro's strategy for Moncada. The strike had been prepared in secret by the small network of Movement supporters among the workers, the National Workers' Front (FON), and depended on an appeal by radio to workers to down tools. It seems also that the Movement's labour organisers refused to involve the Communists in the preparations because they and the *llano* leadership as a whole shared a long-standing distrust of them.[35] But a more important explanation for the relative failure of the strike, apart from the distinction between the labour movement in the east and west, lay in the fact that it did not occur at a moment of generalised labour protest, nor was it clear that Batista's regime was on the brink of collapse. Nevertheless, the conclusion drawn by the meeting was that it had not succeeded because of the short-comings of the *llano* leadership and that, although the perspective of a general strike should be maintained, the main emphasis from then on would be on the military campaign.[36]

The action of 9 April was a watershed in the anti-Batista struggle. It strengthened Castro's leadership of the 26th July Movement, and discredited the *llano* organisers. The National Directorate was transferred to the Sierra and Castro became the supreme commander of the Movement. His faith in the labour and civic fronts in the towns was rudely shaken. In a bitter letter to Celia Sánchez he wrote:

*No one will ever be able to make me trust the organization again. . . . I am the supposed leader of this Movement, and in the eyes of history I must take*

*responsibility for the stupidity of others, and I am a shit who can decide on*
*nothing at all. With the excuse of opposing caudillism, each one attempts more*
*and more to do what he feels like doing. I am not such a fool that I don't realise*
*this, nor am I a man given to seeing visions and phantoms. I will not give up my*
*critical spirit and intuition and especially, now, when I have more responsibilities*
*than ever in my life.*

*I don't believe a schism is developing in the Movement, nor would it be helpful*
*for the Revolution, but in the future, we ourselves will resolve our own problems.*[37]

The event also marked the beginning of a rapprochement between the
PSP and himself. Without a trustworthy base among workers, Castro would
need to cultivate allies in the one party that seemed to have some reliable
grass-roots support. The PSP, conscious of Castro's growing stature, was also
keen to establish closer contact and by September 1958 had a top-level
member permanently in the Sierra. The failure of the 9 April general strike,
finally, reinforced the moral hegemony of the rural guerrilla over the city.
The campaigns in the urban centres of Cuba, whether they were sabotage,
demonstrations, propaganda or strike action, fatally weakened the Batista
regime. Without the support of the llano organisation, the guerrillas would
have been semi-starved of arms and money.[38] The city may have its share of
martyrs in the mythology of the Revolution yet it is the war in the mountains that furnishes the national epic of contemporary Cuba.

Indeed, the Sierra campaign was the mould that shaped the future Revolution. The rebel army came to be seen by Castro and his closest followers
not only as the source of power in the new state but also as the instrument
of social change. As the so-called liberated zones in the mountains were
extended, the commanders began to carry out expropriations and enact
laws that would be the basis of agrarian reform in the coming Revolution.
First-hand experience of the conditions suffered by the poorest land labourers
in Cuba no doubt strengthened the determination to end rural exploitation.
The official ethic of the future society, honouring self-sacrifice, solidarity,
military discipline and loyalty, was forged among the soldiers of the rebel
army. The Sierra campaign provided the tightly knit group that would form
the core of the Revolution's leadership; for decades some of Castro's closest
confidants were veterans of the *Granma* expedition, whereas only one *llano*
organiser held a position of any importance in the regime.

It seems likely, then, that the future course of the Revolution was delineated sometime between the consolidation of the guerrillas towards the end
of 1957 and the summer of 1958, in the aftermath of the events of 9 April.
In official accounts, Castro appears to have had it all worked out since

Moncada. Those who broke with the new Revolution after its triumph, on the other hand, claimed he had changed course and betrayed its ideals. It was clear that he had a programme which could not be carried out in the framework of the traditional party system in Cuba. The betrayal thesis rests on a failure of imagination. Cuba could not undergo such radical changes without a transformation of its internal political system and even a re-alignment of its foreign relations.[39] At the same time, it is difficult to believe that before the consolidation of the rebel army Castro had a clear picture of the direction that the future Revolution would take. He had a radical programme of reforms but not a well-defined political model. One has the sense that throughout the 1950s he was feeling his way politically and strategically. In the Sierra, the road map became more defined. In the rebel army he had built a concrete power base to carry out the structural changes he envisaged for Cuba. After the strike of 9 April he began to turn to the Communist Party as a source of organised support.

Above all, his political ideas became more clearly shaped under the influence of his two closest advisers, his brother Raúl Castro and Che Guevara. Both men were unorthodox Communists, the first because he had supported Fidel in what the PSP considered pure adventurism, and the second because he was impelled more by a Pan-American, anti-US imperialism than by support for Moscow. But both appeared to have been more familiar with Marxist ideas than Castro, whatever their retrospective self-justifications. Guevara, as we have mentioned, had witnessed the destruction by the CIA of a government that had tried to carry out a programme of reforms similar to that planned by Castro. The primary lesson of this experience was that social democracy was too fragile an instrument of change. In the Sierra, they were the only rebels of any political sophistication and both had the opportunity to discuss the future course of the Revolution at length with Castro. Under their influence, the idea of a Cuban version of 'socialism in one country' may have begun to take shape in Castro's mind as a model for the future development of Cuba independent of the United States. There is no reason to doubt the painstakingly honest Guevara when he wrote in December 1957 to Frank País' successor in the 26th July Movement:

*Because of my ideological background, I belong to those who believe that the solution of the world's problems lies behind the so-called iron curtain, and I see this Movement as one of the many inspired by the bourgeoisie's desire to free themselves from the economic chains of imperialism. I always thought of Fidel as an authentic leader of the leftist bourgeoisie, although his image is enhanced by personal qualities of extraordinary brilliance that set him above his class.[40]*

Whatever his political definition at the time, Castro was taking care to avoid raising suspicions among the anti-Batista opposition and in the United States that he wanted to go beyond the framework of a restored democratic system in Cuba. While Batista remained in power, he needed the support of the opposition. But he was quick to denounce any rival claims to the leadership of the anti-Batista movement. Unknown to him, the Movement's representatives in Miami had signed an agreement in the autumn of 1957 with a new united front of the opposition, the Junta de Liberación Cubana, whereby Castro's forces would be incorporated into the regular armed forces once Batista had been overthrown. Learning of this unauthorised move that would have deprived him of his armed power base, Castro broke from the Junta.[41] His rebel army was beginning to score victories against Batista's army while the organisations of the opposition had failed in their attempts to storm the Presidential Palace or to stage a mutiny in the armed forces.

However, after the abortive April strike and the start of an all-out offensive by the army in May, Castro was forced to moderate his position. In July, he issued a manifesto known as the Caracas Pact, the second such manifesto since February 1957, which was signed jointly with all opposition forces with the exception of the Communist Party. In it there was no mention of a radical agenda except agrarian reform. Instead, the document referred to the restoration of constitutional and democratic rights and made a vaguely worded promise of economic and social progress that could have issued from the Auténticos themselves.

It was no coincidence that Castro's search for unity with moderate and conservative opponents of Batista occurred as the army launched a mass offensive against the guerrilla stronghold. Since the rebel forces had established themselves in the Sierra Maestra, the army had made several unsuccessful attempts to dislodge them. By March 1958 Castro had felt confident enough to establish new fronts in Oriente. Raúl, for instance, had gone with a column to the Sierra Cristal in the eastern part of the province, where the rebels began to enact a wide-ranging programme of social reform in the newly liberated zone. The failure of the April 1958 strike, however, had encouraged Batista to believe he could rout the rebel army. Twelve thousand troops, backed by the air force, had been sent to destroy the rebel forces in both Sierras.

The failure of the offensive was the story not so much of the military strength of the guerrillas as of the demoralisation of the regular army. Already unpopular among large sections of the population for their association with the dictatorship, many officers and soldiers had little stomach for fighting. Several units had gone over to the rebels and there had been many desertions.[42] In contrast, the guerrillas were a highly disciplined body. An influential moderate supporter of the Movement later recalled that during a visit to the rebel hideout the scene

*was like something out of the movies, watching them coming, taking positions all around, and all in complete silence. Everything there was said in whispers. I spent a month speaking in whispers: it was their discipline, the difference between the Rebel Army and the Batista army. The Batista army always arrived shouting, and it was easy to surprise them because it was known they were there.*[43]

By September, Castro was ready to move the main force of guerrillas out of the Sierra Maestra and towards Santiago, the capital of Oriente. He was almost certainly aware of the risk that Batista might be overthrown by a reformist coup in the military or that the United States might try to mediate to impose a moderate government. It was important, therefore, to occupy as much of the island as possible to forestall any frustration of his planned revolution. Shortly afterwards, he sent Guevara and Camilo Cienfuegos, a young worker from Havana and veteran of the *Granma* expedition, on an epic march to the centre of the island at the head of two separate columns. For these operations and for the final offensive, Castro needed money and political support. His new moderation was designed to attract the backing of wider sections of the population than those sympathetic to the 26th July Movement. And indeed, money began to flow in, no longer only from the civic and labour fronts of the Movement but now also from sugar-mill owners, sugar farmers, cattle ranchers, bankers and industrialists, especially in Oriente.[44]

What led increasing numbers of businessmen to support the rebels was not just the growing unpopularity of Batista but also Castro's call for national regeneration. Restricted by the US sugar quota and increasingly under pressure from North American sugar-beet producers, the Cuban sugar barons, for example, were responsive to appeals for a reform of Cuba's economic policy and political system. Castro's interviews for American journals between February and April 1958 were intended to reassure the business elite that they had nothing to fear from the Revolution and much to gain. Speaking in February to a journalist from *Look* magazine, who had been led by guides for four days and nights along mountain trails to the guerrilla headquarters, he declared, 'I know revolution sounds like bitter medicine to many businessmen. But after the first shock, they will find it a boon – no more thieving tax collectors, no plundering army chieftains or bribe-hungry officials to bleed them white. Our revolution is as much a moral as a political one.'[45]

Having beaten back the army, the rebel forces launched their own general offensive. Castro's column from the west and his brother's from the east advanced into the heart of Oriente, capturing town after town until they surrounded Santiago. Guevara's and Cienfuegos's units cut the island in half, preventing the flow of reinforcements from the west, and then moved on Havana. With his army rapidly disintegrating, Batista made preparations to leave Cuba. Meanwhile, a group of senior army officers was plotting to replace him with a mixed civilian and military junta, which, they were assured, would be recognised by the US government. On New Year's Day Batista fled to the Dominican Republic. The junta that replaced him enjoyed only a brief moment of power. From his headquarters just outside Santiago, Castro issued a call for a general strike to overthrow the military coup and was answered by the vast mass of workers. By the evening of 1 January, the junta had collapsed. The next day, Castro entered Santiago in triumph and shortly afterwards, to widespread jubilation, Guevara and Cienfuegos took control of Havana.

Batista's regime fell above all because it was corrupt and barbarous. The dictator plundered the state coffers and sanctioned the torture and murder of thousands of his opponents. But it also fell, just as it had risen to power in 1934 and 1952, because it did not represent any social elites. Even the military was sharply divided, as the Cienfuegos naval mutiny had shown. Batista's closest advisers were officers who had risen from the ranks with him in the 1933 Revolution. Their power and privilege were resented by the more professional officer elite drawn from Cuba's middle class, among whom conspiracies had multiplied. The tacit consensus among sections of the population that had underpinned Batista's regime at first had crumbled because he proved unable to deal with any of the problems that concerned them. Corruption was still rampant, the poor were still as poor. Batista's support among the organised working class had withered. Unemployment in 1958 had risen from 8.9 per cent in January to 18 per cent in December. Only the top layer of the union bureaucracy still identified with the regime because it had nowhere else to go.

Thus Batista had lost his populist base but he had not endeared himself either to the indigenous elites that controlled much of Cuba's wealth. His coup in 1952 had not brought violence to an end, as many Cubans had hoped, but, on the contrary, had engendered yet more. To the instability of the Cuban political system was added a growing sense of material insecurity among the middle class. Although they enjoyed one of the highest living standards in Latin America, their income had suffered a decline in the 1950s owing to rising inflation and a steady fall in the price of sugar on the international market. Per capita income in Cuba had fallen by 18 per cent in the two years following the coup and by 1958 had dropped to its 1947 level. Between 1956 and 1957, meanwhile, the prices of basic foodstuffs had risen by up to 40 per cent.[46] A new economic downturn in the second half of 1958 created a generalised discontent while the tightening of economic competition and control from the United States encouraged sections of the middle class and the bourgeoisie to look favourably on the assertive nationalist policy promised by Castro. Like the rebel army itself, the climate of unrest spread from the east of the island, where traditions of rebellion were stronger, until it engulfed the west.

Batista's regime failed also because it was illegitimate. He had seized power on the eve of general elections that favoured another candidate and had maintained his rule through repression; the two presidential elections of 1954 and 1958 were fraudulent exercises in democracy. But his dictatorship had not been thorough because he was too preoccupied with the search for an elusive consensus of the kind he had enjoyed in the 1940s. While curbing the freedom of the press, he had also allowed it to criticise his regime when he had felt more secure. Castro managed to get no less than 25 denunciations of Batista published in Cuban periodicals. Indeed, the dictator had underestimated his most determined opponent, setting him free after he had served less than two years of a 15-year sentence, and minimising the threat posed by the rebel forces until it was too late. His army, without any effective counter-insurgency aid from the United States, conducted a campaign notable for its brutality and bungling; when the United States belatedly declared an arms embargo it was more of a psychological than a material blow.

Of the traditional political forces in Cuba, the military had been the only one that commanded any national authority. The elites that owned most of the island's wealth had proved incapable of uniting around a national project. The conservative parties had been too fragmented to be a focus of representation, while the Auténticos were discredited, having consistently reneged on their promises to end corruption. The only party with any substantial electoral support had been the Ortodoxos, but they lacked a well-defined ideology as well as an organisation and, besides, their popular leader was dead. The failure of the political system was due to a great extent to the contradictions engendered by Cuba's uneven and dependent development. A relatively well-developed society, Cuba could not carry through any much-needed and desired structural reforms while it was trapped by its sugar monoculture. Any attempt to do so threatened to incur the displeasure of the United States, whose military or merely diplomatic interventions had largely determined the course of Cuban politics in the past.

Castro thus stepped into a power vacuum that was not entirely of his making. He had skilfully seized the opportunities offered by a conjunction of historical conditions that were unique to Cuba. His success, moreover, owed as much to his imaginative use of the mass media as to the guerrilla campaign. Through newspapers and radio, in particular the guerrilla army's Radio Rebelde, he had attracted widespread admiration for his patriotic oratory and his denunciations of injustice and oppression. He took advantage of the modern mass communications system already in place in Cuba. The rebel leaders of the Movement were able to project their struggle on to the wide screen of Cuba's historical narrative, the unfulfilled revolution of Martí and other national heroes. That claim to a historical mission seized the imagination of many Cubans, starved of heroic models among the politicians of the day.[47] By 1959 Castro had become the repository of many disparate hopes for Cuba's regeneration. As he made his slow triumphal way by road from Santiago to Havana, he was treated as the last in the long line of Cuban heroes – the last, because, unlike the others, he had survived and prevailed.

## Notes

1 M. Mencía, *El Grito de Moncada* (Política, Havana, 1986), vol. 1, pp. 110–14.

2 *El Acusador*, no. 3, 16 Aug. 1952, quoted in Mencía, *El Grito*, p. 250; for Mencía's 'Leninist' claim see p. 248.

3 M. Mencía, *Tiempos Precursores* (Editorial de Ciencias Sociales, Havana, 1986), p. 123.

4 This account is based on a number of sources including R. Merle, *Moncada. Premier Combat de Fidel Castro* (Robert Laffont, Paris, 1965); Mencía, *Tiempos Precursores*; T. Szulc, *Fidel: a Critical Portrait* (Hutchinson, London, 1987), pp. 174–209; and Castro's own recollections in I. Ramonet, *Fidel Castro. Biografía a dos voces* (Random House Mondadori, Mexico and Barcelona, 2006), pp. 117–46.

5 For example, in O. Fernández Ríos, *Formación y desarrollo del estado socialista en Cuba* (Ciencias Sociales, Havana, 1988) and Mencía, *El Grito*.

6 Castro's letter to Conte Agüero on 12 Dec. 1953, in L. Conte Agüero, *Cartas del Presidio* (Lex, Havana, 1959), p. 21.

7 See Castro's speech to the Caroline University of Prague in Ministerio de Educación Superior, *La Revolución Cubana 1953–1980* (Havana, 1983), vol. 1,

pp. 245–9; see also in the same book, Mirta Aguirre's article 'El Leninismo en la Historia me absolverá', pp. 251–79. On the other hand, Castro also later claimed 'We weren't thinking of the USSR or anything like that. That came afterwards' (Ramonet, *Castro*, p. 155).

**8** For example, L. Martin, *The Early Fidel: Roots of Castro's Communism* (Lyle Stuart, Secaucus, NJ, 1978), p. 116.

**9** Mencía, *El Grito*, vol. 2, pp. 472–3.

**10** Ministerio de Educación Superior, *La Revolución Cubana*, p. 244.

**11** F. Castro, *Fidel Castro habla con Barbara Walters* (Carlos Valencia, Colombia, 1977), p. 30.

**12** Cf. Martin, *Early Fidel*, p. 122.

**13** Letters to Luis Conte Agüero, 17 and 31 July 1954, in Conte Agüero, *Cartas*, pp. 46 and 52.

**14** Faustino Pérez in *Bohemia*, 11 Jan. 1959 p. 38; also 'Los Sucesos del 30 de Noviembre de 1956', in *Bohemia*, 6 Dec. 1959, pp. 48–51 and 121–3.

**15** F. Castro, 'El Movimiento 26 de Julio', *Bohemia*, 1 April 1956.

**16** Testimony of Celia Sánchez in Museo de la Clandestinidad, Santiago.

**17** *Bohemia*, 15 July 1956, pp. 63 and 84–5.

**18** Szulc, *Fidel*, pp. 250–1.

**19** Ramonet, *Castro*, p. 160.

**20** J.G. Castañeda, *La vida en rojo. Una biografía del Che Guevara* (Espasa Calpe, Argentina, 1997), pp. 117–30. Evidence amassed by Castañeda suggests that the much-repeated claim that Guevara committed himself to the expedition after a night-long dialogue with Castro is something of a myth. For his part, R.E. Quirk, in *Fidel Castro* (Norton, New York, 1994), pp. 92–8, relies too much on Guevara's estranged wife Hilda Gadea for evidence and his account of Guevara's sudden espousal of a revolutionary cause is somewhat implausible.

**21** H.L. Matthews, *The Cuban Story* (Braziller, New York, 1961), pp. 51–2.

**22** Mencía, *Tiempos Precursores*, pp. 309–10.

**23** In the original, 'Ahora sí, Batista se jodió'; as Guevara recounted (author's conversation with Tomás Gutiérrez Alea, 29 Aug. 1988).

**24** Colonel Pedro A. Barrera Pérez, quoted in J. García Montés and A. Alonso Avila, *Historia del Partido Comunista de Cuba* (Universal, Miami, 1970), pp. 553–4, n. 5.

**25** E. Guevara, 'Un año de lucha armada', *Verde Olivo*, 5 Jan. 1964.

**26** A. Kapcia, *Cuba: Island of Dreams* (Berg, Oxford, 2000), pp. 181–3.

**27** C. Franqui, *Diary of the Cuban Revolution* (Viking Press, New York, 1980), p. 509 and *Family Portrait with Fidel* (Jonathan Cape, London, 1983), p. 35.

**28** F. Castro, *Fidel en Radio Rebelde* (Gente Nueva, Havana, 1973).

**29**  See, for example, Castro's letter to Celia Sánchez on 11 Aug. 1957, in Franqui, *Diary*, pp. 220–1.

**30**  Quoted in Szulc, *Fidel*, p. 350.

**31**  País' letter to Castro, 7 July 1957, in Franqui, *Diary*, pp. 202–5.

**32**  M. Winocur, *Las clases olvidadas en la revolución Cubana* (Grijalbo, Barcelona, 1979), p. 100. For Castro's scepticism, see Ramonet, *Castro*, p.179.

**33**  E.T. Smith, *The Fourth Floor* (Random House, New York, 1962), p. 128.

**34**  Details from *Carta Semanal*, 23 April 1958, quoted in *Hoy*, 9 April 1964.

**35**  See 'Una reunión decisiva', in E. Guevara, *Obra Revolucionaria* (2nd edn, Era, Mexico, 1968), p. 237 and in *Obras 1957–67* (2 vols, Maspéro, Paris, 1970), vol. 2, p. 98.

**36**  *Hoy*, 9 April 1964.

**37**  Letter to Celia Sánchez, 16 April 1958, quoted in Franqui, *Diary*, pp. 300–1.

**38**  This was the *llano* organizer Carlos Franqui's considered and more convincing view, given the evidence, as opposed to Guevara's belief in the overwhelming predominance of guerrilla warfare in the victory. See Franqui's reconstruction of their discussion in C. Franqui, *Retrato de familia con Fidel* (Seix Barral, Barcelona, 1981), pp. 458–9 (their exchange of opinion is not fully reproduced in the 1983 English edition).

**39**  M. Pérez-Stable, *The Cuban Revolution* (Oxford University Press, New York, 1993), p. 59.

**40**  Franqui, *Diary*, p. 269.

**41**  Ibid., pp. 265–7.

**42**  L.A. Pérez Jr, *Army Politics in Cuba 1898–1958* (University of Pittsburgh Press, 1976), pp. 153–5.

**43**  Raúl Chibás to Tad Szulc, in Szulc, *Fidel*, p. 333.

**44**  J.I. Domínguez, *Cuba: Order and Revolution* (Harvard University, Cambridge, Mass., 1978), pp. 128–9.

**45**  *Look*, 4 Feb. 1958.

**46**  L.A. Pérez Jr, *Cuba: Between Reform and Revolution* (Oxford University Press, New York, 1988).

**47**  See, for example, the correspondence between Castro and Frank País and Celia Sánchez, in Franqui, *Diary*.

# CHAPTER 4

# Defying the Colossus

'When I saw the rockets that they fired on Mario's house, I swore that the Americans are going to pay dearly for what they're doing. When this war is over, I'll start a much longer and bigger war of my own: the war I'm going to fight against them. I realize that will be my true destiny'.

Fidel Castro in a letter to Celia Sánchez, 5 June 1958, after US-supplied missiles had destroyed the house of a peasant supporter of the Castro movement[1]

When Castro reached Havana on 8 January 1959 after his triumphal procession across Cuba, his Moncada programme was no longer the wish list it had been in 1953. Although evidence of his thinking at the time is slim and he was careful to keep his plans close to his chest, the measures he took over the following months suggest that he had already developed a road map for political and economic change in Cuba that was not compatible with liberal capitalism or social democracy. The new balance of power in Cuba gave him the opportunity to attempt to realise what had once been a largely rhetorical utopian project: to bring about modernity and social justice through nationalisation and radical reform. The main agency of this regeneration would be the core elite formed under his leadership and purged by prison and battle, drawn mainly from middle-class professionals or intellectuals used to working with the machinery of the state. The peculiar nature of the 1959 Revolution encouraged the belief that Cuba could be transformed from the commanding heights of a centralised state.

In this he and his closest collaborators shared the conviction of many of the post-colonial leaders in the Third World during the 1950s that only central planning could ensure economic, social and cultural development. Only thus would it be possible also to guarantee that the benefits of economic growth were distributed equitably. These radical processes would flow from above because the new regime had come about not through social but through political revolution and its power derived from the military victory of the rebel army operating on the margins of society, even if it enjoyed the support of the majority of Cubans.

The obstacles Castro and his core elite faced were formidable. In order to carry out their plans for a sweeping transformation of the island they had to dismantle the old order, keep their disparate political allies on board or neutralise them, and confront the economic interests, both domestic and foreign, that controlled Cuba's wealth. Above all, they had to face the potential wrath of the United States, whose administration was that which had helped to destroy the reformist Arbenz regime in Guatemala less than six years previously. The United States, the colossus to the north, had exercised an almost proprietorial relationship with the island, shaping its economy, intervening repeatedly in its administration ever since it achieved independence and occupying Cuban territory in Guantánamo Bay, for which it paid a pittance in rent.

For all his overriding sense of confidence, Castro proceeded cautiously at first, testing the political waters. Among the cadre there were few with any political experience. The rebel army, semi-literate if disciplined, was hardly a source of administrative skills. He had to reconcile, at least for the time being, the widely differing ideologies among the anti-Batista coalition, from moderate democrats within the 26th July Movement to Stalinists within the PSP.[2] Popular enthusiasm for political change also needed to be organised. During the Sierra campaign Castro had been careful to create the widest possible consensus among the anti-Batista opposition. While he had made it clear he was seeking to regenerate Cuba, he had also issued calls for a return to liberal democracy through parliamentary elections and respect for private property. True to populist traditions, he was able to use his apparent political indefinition to some effect. Even fairly close collaborators were unsure where he was going. The *llano* organiser Carlos Franqui, once head of propaganda for the Movement and responsible for both *Revolución* and Radio Rebelde, wrote much later, after he had broken with the Revolution, that everyone knew what Castro was, the undisputed caudillo of the revolution. But no one knew what he was thinking. 'In ideological terms, nothing is clear. Fidel, an enigma for everyone.'[3] From his Sierra stronghold, Castro had named a widely esteemed judge sympathetic to the Movement, Manuel Urrutia Lleó, as President of the post-Batista provisional government. Upon

Batista's fall, Urrutia nominated a cabinet drawn from moderate members of the Movement while Castro himself was confirmed as Commander-in-Chief of the new armed forces. It was a government acceptable to most sections of public opinion in Cuba and the United States.

It soon became no more than a token administration, however. In a move that would become characteristic of his political style, Castro set up an unofficial committee of his closest advisers, including his brother Raúl and Che Guevara, and it was this Office of Revolutionary Plans and Co-ordination that in reality set the agenda of the Revolution.[4] Whether they were conscious of it or not, the Cuban revolutionaries were following a dual power strategy that Lenin and Mao had employed with some success. Following earlier contacts during the war, Castro began discreet negotiations at the same time with leading members of the Communist Party, which still regarded his Movement as petty bourgeois. He hoped thereby to fuse the Communists with the radical wing of the Movement, using the experience and the organised base of the PSP to help create the new institutions of the Revolution on his own terms.

In May, the National Institute of Agrarian Reform (INRA) was set up with Castro as its President. Its two objectives were to administer the Agrarian Reform Act, the centrepiece of legislation in the early days of the Revolu-tion, and carry out the first interventions in industry. During the months that followed, INRA, by absorbing the Office of Revolutionary Plans and Co-ordination, became an unofficial parallel government staffed by Castro's closest advisers. It is clear from Castro's own most recent account that the administration of INRA was somewhat chaotic and there were differences of opinion among the revolutionary leaders over the extent of agrarian reform. Castro claimed he had been more radical over land expropriations than Guevara, who became head of INRA's department of industry.[5]

The pace of Castro's reforms was determined partly by how confident he felt that the resulting tensions could be controlled. From his first day in Havana he had demonstrated his power of popular mobilisation. When the rival urban guerrilla organisation, the Directorio Revolucionario (DR), had shown a reluctance to give up their arms to the rebel army, he had turned the crowd against them and they had capitulated. His plans for reform were also helped by the lack of cohesion among the economic elites in Cuba. The Agrarian Reform Act, for example, envisaged the nationalisation of landholdings of more than 1,000 acres, with a higher limit of just over 3,000 acres for foreign companies, as well as those Cuban sugar and rice planta-tions with high yields. According to the terms of the Act, the expropriated holdings, amounting to some 40 per cent of cultivated land, were to be distributed to plantation workers and small farmers or converted into state farms (later to become cooperatives), all with the purpose of diversifying away from the virtual sugar monoculture of Cuban agriculture as well as mopping up unemployment and landlessness in the countryside. While the expropriations were fiercely opposed by the big landowners and US companies, they were welcomed by finance and industrial capital together with wide sections of the middle class. The economic nationalism expected of the new government raised the hopes of private enterprise in Cuba that it could thereby capture a bigger slice of business.[6] Thus fragmented, the domestic opposition to the gradual nationalisation of the economy presented only a weak challenge.

By mid-February, Castro had felt sufficiently confident to take over as prime minister with new, wide-ranging powers, bringing to an end the uneasy period of dual power. The cabinet increasingly became a rubber stamp for policies decided by Castro and his closest advisers. Media unsympathetic to the radical measures being enacted by the government were closed down and critical voices silenced. In the summer of 1959, Castro moved against the moderates in the cabinet, provoked in part by Urrutia's public statements against the infiltration of Communists into the administration. Summoning the crowds once again, Castro forced Urrutia's resignation, naming a close supporter, Osvaldo Dorticós, as President in his place. The tensions within the Movement over the increasing influence of the Communists reached a head with the resignation in October of the governor of Camagüey province Huber Matos, a leading veteran of the Sierra Maestra. Matos sent his resignation letter, in which he complained about the infiltration of Communists into the government, directly to Castro two days after the appointment of Raúl Castro as Minister of the Armed Forces. Matos and other like-minded officers in his command were put on trial and Matos was sentenced to 20 years in prison for rebellion.[7] The Revolution was beginning to devour its sons.

Once again, Castro was able to use the crisis to consolidate his power, this time by announcing the creation of the armed militias. These became part of the unfolding structure of revolutionary power, consisting of the Armed Forces and their counter-intelligence department, the political police and the intelligence services of the Ministry of the Interior, all of which enabled Castro to establish a balance of power within the institutions of the new state. He also intervened in the November Congress of the Cuban Labour Federation to insist on unity between delegates of the PSP and the anti-Communist representatives of his Movement.[8] By the end of the year, the honeymoon between the liberal and radical wings of the Movement was over.

Another source of tension was the growing opposition of the Church hierarchy to the radical turn of the new regime. There had been many Catholics in the anti-Batista movement and initially the Church had welcomed the Revolution. Traditionally, however, it had been a conservative force in Cuban society. The hierarchy had supported Spain during the Independence Wars, and later it espoused the cause of Francoism in the Spanish Civil War. When the new government began to secularise education and downgrade the institutional role of the Church in national affairs, the Catholic hierarchy joined with the anti-Castro opposition in mobilising a huge protest movement.

However, it was the increasingly virulent reaction of the US administration to Cuban reforms that accelerated the radical drift of the government. Castro had been concerned from the beginning to try to maintain relations with Washington without compromising his programme of internal reforms. In an effort to improve communications, he devoted some time during the first months of the Revolution to improving his English, which he spoke imperfectly and with a heavy Cuban accent. But there is no reason to doubt Castro's evaluation of Cuban–American relations in 1960–1, which he made many years later in a private conversation with an American diplomat.

*I came to power with some preconceived ideas about the United States and about Cuba's relationship with her. In retrospect, I can see a number of things I wish I had done differently. We would not in any event have ended up as close friends. The US had dominated us too long. The Cuban Revolution was determined to end that domination. There was, then, an inherent conflict of interests. Still, even adversaries find it useful to maintain bridges between them. Perhaps I burned some of these bridges precipitately; there were times when I may have been more abrupt, more aggressive, than was called for by the situation. We were all younger then; we made the mistakes of youth.*[9]

This unusually mild and self-critical reference to Cuban policy towards the United States belongs to a much later period when Castro was keen to renew relations with Washington, but it does point to two important aspects of the US–Cuban conflict. The first is the extent to which the Cuban Revolution was driven by a barely contained historical antagonism towards the United States. Secondly, the revolutionary leaders knew that an accommodation was unlikely because the reforms they were planning would be unacceptable to Washington. So Castro's earliest public pronouncements after 1 January 1959 on relations with the United States were a smokescreen. In the first three months of the Revolution he repeatedly articulated the reformist programme of the 26th July Movement whereby Cuba would have a mixed economy in which American private investment and US government aid would continue to play an important role. However, he was already drawing up plans for state intervention in public utilities, mining and sugar, in all of which American interests were prominent. We also know now that as early as March 1959, when Urrutia's moderate government was still nominally in power, the US National Security Council under Eisenhower was considering armed action against Cuba.[10]

In fact, relations between Cuba and the United States were fuelled from the beginning by mutual suspicion and misunderstanding. The initial sympathy for the Revolution among wide circles of Americans gave way to disquiet once the show trials and executions of Batista personnel involved in torture and killings began shortly after the victory. The trials, in which Castro sometimes took a leading role as prosecutor, were a more formal version of the revolutionary justice meted out to those deemed guilty of victimising peasant families during the guerrilla campaign in the Sierra. The most notorious of Batista's henchmen were tried in the national sports stadium in front of hundreds of spectators, provoking much international criticism. Castro admitted many years later that the form in which these trials were held had been wrong. However, he also pointed out that unlike many other post-dictatorships, there had been no breakdown in law and order and therefore no popular atrocities against the perpetrators of Batista's repression.[11]

Similarly, when Castro announced the suspension of elections during his visit to the United States in April, few Americans could understand the extent to which parliamentary democracy in Cuba had become discredited by the corruption of the politicians of the past, with the passive acquiescence of the US government. This was followed by the expropriation of large US-owned sugar farms under the agrarian reform law, made even more unpalatable to the American companies because the compensation offered by the Cuban state was based on the low value they had placed on the land for tax purposes. The military and trade agreement signed between Cuba and the Soviet Union in February 1960 only heightened fears in the US administration that the island was turning Communist. CIA reports in subsequent months revealed that Soviet arms were beginning to flow to Cuba and Castro was supporting revolutionaries in Central America and the Caribbean.[12] It should be remembered also that because of its strategic position and its historical links with the United States, Cuba had been viewed by generations of American policy-makers as a part of the defence of the southern flank of the United States, as well as a key asset in the control of the Caribbean and the shipping lanes to and from the Panama Canal. To this traditional sensitivity about security in its backyard was added the Cold War obsession with the menace of Communism which tended to obscure the essentially nationalistic roots of leftist movements in the area and in other parts of the Third World.

Suspicions on the Cuban side that the United States was aiding counter-revolutionaries came to a head when a French merchant ship carrying Belgian arms for Cuba blew up in Havana harbour on 4 March 1960, inflicting many casualties. The US administration had already made it difficult for Cuba to purchase arms from American allies and the Cuban perception was that the explosion was the result of sabotage by counter-revolutionaries sponsored by the CIA.[13] In a mass rally that followed, Castro warned of the danger of an invasion by the enemies of the Cuban Revolution, issuing for the first time the famous slogan *Patria o Muerte, Venceremos*. Indeed, less than a fortnight later, the US administration under Eisenhower secretly instructed the CIA to prepare a paramilitary force for action against the Cuban government.[14] The verbal dispute between the two countries descended into a spiral of measures and counter-measures, which Castro was able to exploit to consolidate his power and hurry the pace of the Revolution.

When the Cuban government nationalised foreign-owned petrol refineries at the end of June 1960 after they had refused to process crude oil bought from the Soviets, Eisenhower reduced US imports of sugar from Cuba. The Cubans responded by seizing the larger American companies operating on the island. The United States followed in October with a partial economic embargo on trade to Cuba. Diplomatic relations were broken off in January 1961 and a year later, in February 1962, the new US President John F. Kennedy imposed a full economic and financial embargo.

The dynamic of the US–Cuban conflict led the revolutionary government to speed up the process of political and economic centralisation. Castro judged that the looming confrontation with the United States made it possible to carry out sooner what had been in effect a much longer-term strategy. His own assessment many years later of the events of 1960–1 is persuasive:

*We were carrying out our programme little by little. All these [United States] aggressions accelerated the revolutionary process. Were they the cause? No, this would be an error. . . . In Cuba we were going to construct socialism in the most orderly possible manner, within a reasonable period of time, with the least amount of trauma and problems, but the aggressions of imperialism accelerated the revolutionary process.[15]*

The crisis in relations between Cuba and the United States deepened the growing polarisation in Cuban society. From mid-1960 the first big wave of emigrants abandoned Cuba for a life of exile in the United States. Since they were drawn largely from Cuba's business and professional elites, their departure removed a potential source of opposition to the new regime and thereby helped to accelerate the process of political centralisation.

Finally, in April 1961, the long-expected invasion force of Cuban exiles set sail from Nicaragua under US navy escort. The new American President, John F. Kennedy, had approved in principle the invasion project of the outgoing Eisenhower administration but had modified it considerably and harboured doubts about its feasibility. The new operation, drawn up by the CIA and codenamed Zapata, no longer involved the use of US forces in combat because Kennedy was worried that any open American offensive against Cuba might provoke a Soviet move against Berlin.[16] The landings took place on two beaches, one called Playa Girón, situated in the Bay of Pigs in the remote, swampy region of southern Matanzas. Ironically, it was an area Castro had recently explored at length while investigating a personal project to drain the marshes. The invasion was preceded by aerial attacks on the island's air force bases by American bombers manned by exiled Cuban pilots. However, they failed to put out of action all of Cuba's tiny air force. This proved fatal to the invaders. Without authorisation to make any further air strikes and thus deprived of air support, the invading force was harassed by Cuban planes. Two freighters were sunk, the CIA command ship was struck and the rest of the fleet fled, leaving 1,300 men stranded on the two beaches. The Cuban forces moved quickly into the area under the energetic command of Castro. A photograph of the time shows him leaping off a Cuban tank in the war zone. After two days of fierce fighting, during which air strikes newly authorised by the US administration inflicted heavy casualties on the Cuban militia, the invaders were overcome.

The victory at Playa Girón was celebrated amid national euphoria. It was as if the United States had finally received its comeuppance after a century of meddling in the affairs of Cuba. Castro's prestige among the population would never be higher. Shortly before the landings, as the crisis unfolded, he had been sufficiently confident of his mass support to declare for the first time that the Revolution was a socialist revolution. Later the same year, he declared on television that he was a Marxist and that the Cuban Revolution would have a 'Marxist-Leninist' programme. The words of a popular song of the post-Playa Girón days, 'Cuba Sí, Yanquis No', suggest how collective faith in Castro seemed to override the residue of old ideologies; if Fidel was in charge, they implied, it did not matter which direction the Revolution went:

*Si las cosas de Fidel*
*son cosas de buen marxista*
*que me pongan en la lista*
*que estoy de acuerdo con él.*
*(If Fidel's 'concerns' are those of a good Marxist, put me down on the list, for I*
*agree with him.)*

The Playa Girón incident not only helped to define the official ideology of the Revolution but also speeded up its institutionalisation. Three months later, Castro announced the fusion of the anti-Batista organisations, his own 26th July Movement, the Directorio Revolucionario and the Communists into the Organizaciones Integradas Revolucionarias as a first step towards the creation of a new Communist Party. It also led the Cuban leadership to seek closer ties with the Soviet Union. There was little doubt in their minds that the United States would attempt a new invasion, this time with the US marines. Official US documents declassified in the late 1990s reveal that the Kennedy administration was not only carrying out a programme of covert operations against Cuba with Cuban exiles, known as Operation Mongoose, but had also drawn up plans for US military intervention, Operation Northwoods.[17] Operation Mongoose involved sabotage, paramilitary raids, continued support for guerrilla activities, counterfeit money, contamination of Cuban products and so on, funded out of a budget of some $100 million and all controlled from a massive operations centre on the University of Miami campus. Operation Northwoods, on the other hand, envisaged an amphibious invasion of Cuba with a quarter of a million American soldiers, marines and airmen, backed by full aerial and naval support.[18]

Castro had established a close rapport with Khrushchev in September 1960 during a United Nations General Assembly in New York; the famous embrace between the two men, the short and pudgy Soviet leader and the towering Cuban, seemed to represent a genuine mutual sympathy. Shortly afterwards a commercial and military pact had been signed between the two countries. The Soviet Union was experiencing rapid economic growth and the new sense of confidence that it gave led the Kremlin to seek to improve its position in the world balance of power by providing economic and military aid to radical Third World states. A pro-Soviet Cuba represented for Khrushchev a double opportunity: to check the growing influence of China in the Third World and above all to exert pressure on the United States. For his part, Castro was anxious to obtain substantial Soviet military aid after the Bay of Pigs victory in order to deter the United States from a second invasion attempt. Moreover, the domestic situation in 1962 was unstable.

Anti-government guerrillas were active in the Escambray mountains where the DR had operated during the war against Batista, the economy was floundering and tensions had arisen in the new party between Castroists and some of the old Communists.

The idea of installing Soviet medium-range missiles on Cuban soil came, according to most accounts, from Khrushchev himself.[19] The Soviet Premier hoped thereby to strengthen his bargaining hand with Washington at a stroke. It was a move dictated by pure opportunism because the balance of nuclear deterrence at the time lay with the United States, which was hardly likely to accept the presence of nuclear warheads in its backyard. Kept in the dark about the ratio of strike power between the two superpowers, Castro evidently believed that Cuba could be drawn in under the nuclear umbrella of the Soviet Union without unleashing a world war.[20] Out of this he hoped to achieve at the least a guarantee that the United States would not invade Cuba. Furthermore, there was an important principle at stake according to Castro: Cuba's right, as a sovereign nation, to defend itself as it willed.

It is now known that by October 1962, 36 nuclear warheads had been delivered to Cuba for use with intermediate-range ballistic missiles. In addition, nine short-range nuclear missiles with Luna launchers were ready to be used against Guantánamo in the east and Bahía Honda in the west where an amphibious invasion force was expected. These mobile 'Frog' missiles were under the command of local Soviet officers who had discretion to launch them in the event of an invasion without consulting the supreme command in Havana or Moscow. Cuban leaders have since stressed that they fully expected an invasion and, indeed, it was later disclosed that US troops were put on a state of high alert, while B52 bombers were prepared for an air strike and the lids of long-range missiles targeted on the Soviet Union were lifted. Moreover, some 42,000 Soviet troops were on the island, backing the 240,000 Cubans under arms.[21] Information given by the CIA Soviet agent Colonel Oleg Penkovsky about the location of the missiles was confirmed by photographs taken by American U2 spy planes revealing the presence of the intermediate-range missiles. In reply to Kennedy's urgent queries, Khrushchev claimed they were only defensive weapons, a response, Castro later argued, that was both politically and ethically wrong.[22]

Kennedy then demanded their withdrawal and imposed a quarantine line around the island. On 24 October, a Russian convoy including a freighter with 20 more warheads on board was steaming towards the US fleet ringing the island. The world seemed on the brink of a nuclear war. At the last moment Khrushchev pulled back. The Russian convoy turned around and headed for home. On the 27th, a US U2 plane was shot down by a Russian surface-to-air missile. But Kennedy and Khrushchev were already negotiating an end to the crisis. Without consulting Castro, the Soviet Premier agreed to remove the nuclear missiles from Cuba in exchange for the withdrawal of an ageing generation of American missiles in Turkey and a pledge that the United States would not attempt to invade Cuba.

The missile crisis of 1962 had begun as a dispute over the right of Cuba to possess offensive weapons and had ended in a superpower confrontation in which Cuba was just one of several pawns. By his own account, Castro was furious at being left out of the Soviet–American negotiations. In an interview with NBC many years later, he said this about Khrushchev's decision: 'We did not feel betrayed but we were very irritated and displeased.' More recently, he argued that had the Cubans been consulted, they might have been able to negotiate the closure of the US base in Guantánamo and the suspension of the U2 flights.[23] The resulting bad blood between Havana and Moscow was to persist throughout the 1960s. The bitterness was reflected in a secret speech Castro made to the Central Committee in January 1968 which framed the Soviet Union's withdrawal as betrayal.[24] Yet characteristically, Castro had gained some advantage from the whole affair. He had indirectly extracted a guarantee from the United States that it would not stage a military invasion of Cuba. At the same time he had ensured the sort of support from the Soviet Union that was indispensable if Cuba was to survive the American economic embargo.

There can be little argument now that the actions of the US government forced Castro into a deeper military and economic reliance on the Soviet Union than he would have wished. The whole thrust of the Cuban Revolution was towards the pursuit of independence and modernisation; it was above all a nationalist movement whose roots lay in anti-colonial struggle. No subsequent declarations of the friendliness of relations between the two countries were enough to disguise Cuba's dependence on its new ally. The Cuban economy began to be locked into that of the Comecon countries as effectively as it had been embedded in that of the United States, even though the form that this dependency took was very different.

Yet it was not merely the search to survive US hostility that led Castro to commit Cuba to the Soviets. In view of the bitterness of anti-US feelings among the Cuban leadership it was logical that they should feel empathy towards the USSR as a vociferous defender of all opposition to American imperialism and neocolonialism. But there was also an ideological component in the Cuban government's turn towards Soviet-type socialism and it is this aspect that has often been misunderstood. Quite apart from its token adherence to socialist values, the Soviet Union offered the Cuban leaders a model of modernisation through a command economy that suited their strategy. After the 1917 Revolution had failed to spread to the more modernised countries of Europe, the Soviet state under Stalin had abandoned the internationalist strategy of the old Bolshevik leadership and turned inwards towards autarky; the theory that socialism in one country was possible became the new orthodoxy. Through a brutal process of industrialisation, the USSR had grown into a powerful, state-run economy. This transformation was carried out independently of most of the rest of the world under the centralised direction of the Communist Party.

Castro felt some sympathy towards Stalin, though he could hardly be described as a Stalinist himself. In an interview with an American journalist, he declared, 'Stalin had . . . great merits, extraordinary merits without a doubt, in the period of industrialization of the USSR, and at the head of the Soviet state in the difficult days of the Nazi attack.' But in a later interview Castro admitted that Stalin 'committed the errors we all know about, repression, the purges and all that', and he attacked the Stalinist legacy in Communist parties such as the Cuban PSP of 'exclusion', 'ghetto mentality', obsessive 'control' and sectarian 'infiltration'.[25] There were other models of centralised development under a one-party system that the Cuban leaders looked to, such as North Korea and China. Castro believed that his revolutionary programme of reforms required a similar degree of political and economic control. A return to private enterprise or even a mixed economy would mean encouraging political pluralism; and even if this were possible in the 'siege' conditions imposed by the United States, it would slow down or prevent the longed-for transformation of Cuban society. But Soviet Communism was not a model that Castro wished to implant into Cuba; he preferred rather to adapt it to the peculiar conditions of Cuban society. 'We must not ignore experience', he said in a speech in 1966, referring to the Soviets, 'but we must also guard against a mechanical copying of formulas.'[26]

In fact, Castro was too restless and the Cuban Revolution too idiosyncratic for Soviet orthodoxy. Even after Castro's declaration of socialism on the eve of the Bay of Pigs invasion, it had taken the Soviet leaders a year to warm to his leadership. Instead, it was a group of pre-Revolutionary Communists who seemed to have the Kremlin's support. Since their secret negotiations with Castro soon after the revolutionary triumph, Communist leaders had begun to occupy prominent positions in the embryonic new state. Among them were many who were able to adjust to the wildly unorthodox leadership of Castro and his followers; the increasing rapprochement with the Soviet Union no doubt smoothed the passage. But there were others who remained uneasy about Castroism and had attempted to use their position to place reliable Communists at the head of the rank-and-file organisations of the new party. In March 1962, Castro asserted his own authority by launching into a vitriolic attack against the most prominent member of this faction, Aníbal Escalante. He accused him of packing the party with relatives and fellow members; now that Cuba was officially socialist, Escalante was using his prestige as a Communist, according to Castro, to undermine the authority of its true leaders.[27]

In an earlier incident, during a commemoration of those who died in an attempt to storm the presidential palace in 1957, including the student leader José Antonio Echeverría, the chairman had read out Echeverría's testament, omitting, under instructions from members of the faction, a passage indicating his religiosity. Castro had been following the text of the testament and leaped up to make an impassioned speech denouncing the censorship as a 'short-sighted, sectarian, stupid and defective conception, negating History'. It was, he went on, 'a miserable, cowardly, mutilated symptom or current of those who have no faith in Marxism, of those who have no faith in the Revolution, of those who have no faith in its ideas'.[28] In attacking the group of pre-Revolutionary Communists, Castro was also asserting his independence from Moscow orthodoxy. The Russian ambassador, who had been implicated in the Escalante affair, was removed on Castro's request and replaced by a man of his own choice. Henceforth, the Kremlin would have to recognise that there was only one supreme authority in Cuba.

Over the following decades, Castro's policies were to fluctuate between orthodoxy and heterodoxy according to domestic and international circumstances. There were elements of Soviet orthodoxy that suited the conditions in Cuba as Castro saw them: the need for state control, a disciplined workforce, the subordination of consumption to production. Marxism-Leninism was a worldwide ideological church whose bête-noire was American imperialism; it was therefore a community of belief that Castro, Guevara and others could feel part of. Moreover, notions of freedom, equality and the right of self-determination that figured prominently in the official doctrine of the Soviet Union were values sanctified by the Cuban radical tradition.

Yet if the Marxist-Leninist movement was a 'church' it was one with many heresies already. Lenin had already challenged classical Marxism in *Imperialism: The Highest Stage of Capitalism* by arguing that imperialism created the conditions in which it was possible for revolution to take place in semi-developed societies like czarist Russia where the industrial working class was a small minority of the population. He had also claimed in *What is to be Done?* that only a revolutionary vanguard of intellectuals could lead the socialist revolution because workers were too imbued in a trade unionism compatible with capitalism. Both seminal works served to give a Marxist-Leninist imprimatur to the Cuban Revolution and its structure of leadership; it is significant that Castro mentions these two books as formative influences in his thinking in the early 1950s.[29]

For all the attempts of Cuban historians and politicians, however, the Revolution cannot be squeezed into the mould of European revolutionary socialism, just as the Soviet Union under Stalin broke with Marxist-Leninist traditions. The Revolution was not directly the result of the class struggle, nor did the organised working class emerge as the new hegemonic force in Cuban society. Rather, the Revolution belongs to the movements of national liberation that swept the Third World in the post-war period. As in Cuba, they were usually led by disaffected sections of the middle class who won power on a populist and nationalist programme, often using the name of socialism to describe the nationalised economy, the egalitarian policies and centralised state that substituted for those of the old regime.

However, the genesis of the Cuban Revolution was unlike that of any other Third World revolution. The most striking difference was the ease of Castro's victory. Compared to the long and bloody struggles in China, Algeria and Vietnam, for example, the Cuban Revolution was a relatively simple business. This was due to the peculiar structural conditions of Cuban society: the political fragility of the Batista regime, the dependence of the Cuban economic elites on the United States, the small size of the island, its relatively developed urban society. It was to a great extent the facility of Castro's victory that seized the imagination of millions of people in Latin America and Europe, for whom it became a repository of hopes and fantasies that had little to do with Cuban realities. Far from being a universal prototype, the Revolution was a Cuban affair that could not be duplicated elsewhere, as the revolutionary leaders were to find out to their cost. The Revolution drew its inspiration from Cuban history, and the shape that its institutions took derived from the imperatives of economic growth and social reform in the conditions of economic embargo imposed by the United States. It was to these two fundamental issues that Castro turned in the first decade of his Revolution.

## Notes

1  C. Franqui, *Diary of the Cuban Revolution* (Viking Press, New York, 1980), p. 338; original letter in the Oficina de Asuntos Históricos, Havana.

2  Castro, in I. Ramonet, *Fidel Castro. Biografía a dos voces* (Random House Mondadori, Mexico and Barcelona, 2006), p. 200.

3  Franqui, *Diary*, pp. 39–401; S. Farber, *The Origins of the Cuban Revolution Reconsidered* (University of North Carolina Press, Chapel Hill, 2006), pp. 61–7.

4  T. Szulc, *Fidel: a Critical Portrait* (Hutchinson, London, 1987), pp. 369–73.

5  Ramonet, *Castro*, pp. 223–6.

6  J.I. Domínguez, *Cuba: Order and Revolution* (Harvard University, Cambridge, Mass., 1978), p. 195.

7  Castro's retrospective judgement of Matos, like his evaluation of many others who ended up disagreeing with the direction of the Revolution, was ungenerous to say the least. Rather than acknowledge ideological or political difference, Castro accused him of personal failings, such as arrogance and ambition. Similarly he dismissed Urrutia as opportunistic and mediocre (Ramonet, *Castro*, p. 519).

8  *Bohemia*, 29 Nov. 1959; *Revolución*, 23 Nov. 1959; V. Skierka, *Fidel Castro: a Biography* (Polity Press, Cambridge, 2004), pp. 86–7.

9  W.S. Smith, *The Closest of Enemies* (Norton, New York, 1987), pp. 144–5.

10  Szulc, *Fidel*, p. 384.

11  Ramonet, *Castro*, pp. 202–5.

12  M.R. Beschloss, *Kennedy v. Khrushchev: The Crisis Years 1960–63* (Faber and Faber, London, 1991), p. 104.

13  Ramonet, *Castro*, pp. 230, 244.

14  The document authorising the invasion, 'A Program for Covert Action Against the Castro Regime, 16 March 1960', was declassified on 9 April 1998 (Department of State, *Foreign Relations of the United States 1958–1960*, vol. VI, Cuba, 1960).

15  Szulc, *Fidel*, p. 384.

16  Beschloss, *Kennedy v, Khrushchev*, pp. 105–8.

17  A. Kasten Nelson, 'Operation Northwoods and the covert war against Cuba 1961–1963', *Cuban Studies*, 32 (2001), pp. 145–54.

18  E.R. May and P.D. Zelikow (eds), *The Kennedy Tapes: Inside the White House during the Cuban Missile Crisis* (Harvard University Press, Cambridge, Mass.,1997), pp. 26–7, 91.

19  N. Khrushchev, *Khrushchev Remembers* (Penguin, Harmondsworth, 1971), vol. 1, pp. 526–7. This was confirmed by Castro in his speech to the Havana Conference on the Missile Crisis in January 1992. See also Beschloss, *Kennedy v. Khrushchev*, pp. 382–3.

20  See his conversation with Szulc, in Szulc, *Fidel*, pp. 470–4.

21  J.G. Blight and D.A. Welch, *On the Brink: Americans and Soviets Reexamine the Cuban Missile Crisis* (Noonday Press, New York, 1990); Brown University, *Tripartite Conference on the October Crisis of 1962 (Havana 8–13 Jan. 1992)*; author's interview with Colonel Casteneiros, March 1992.

22  Ramonet, *Castro*, pp. 249–50.

23  Ibid., p. 252; *Granma Weekly Review*, 13 March 1988.

24  Extracts from the speech and debate in the Central Committee are published in an English translation in J.H. Blight and P. Brenner, *Sad and Luminous Days: Cuba's Struggle with the Superpowers after the Missile Crisis* (Rowman and Littlefield, Lanham, Md., 2002), pp. 35–71.

25  Ramonet, *Castro*, pp. 201 and 351; F. Castro, *Fidel Castro habla con Barbara Walters* (Carlos Valencia, Colombia, 1977), p. 69.

26  Quoted in R. Dumont, *Is Cuba Socialist?* (Viking Press, New York, 1974), p. 39.

27  *Cuba Socialista*, May 1962.

28  *Cuba Socialista*, April 1962.

29  In Ramonet, *Castro*, p. 105.

# CHAPTER 5

# The Grand Illusion

The Cuban Revolution had all the appearance of a triumph of individual heroism. Castro's achievement in overthrowing the Batista regime and defying the United States encouraged a millenarian belief in the capacity of the will to overcome all obstacles. The relative ease of the Revolution and the enthusiasm it aroused among millions of Cubans led Castro and his followers to believe that with the same determination and political flair the Cubans could be mobilised to triumph over the intractable problem of underdevelopment. The handicaps were immense: Cuba was a small, only partially developed island that seemed trapped by its sugar monoculture and dependent on Soviet support for the survival of the Revolution. Nevertheless, the battle for modernisation and economic sovereignty, fought under the banner of socialism, became Castro's central preoccupation as soon as he had won power. The swings in his policies during the first decade of his rule can only be understood in the light of this grand illusion.

At the same time, Castro's prodigious role in the Revolution led many Cubans to believe, to his dismay, that he was infallible. Over the coming years, he would devote much time in his speeches to the crowds unfolding some of his own mistakes to public scrutiny. Even those liberals who chose to go into exile when the Revolution swung to the left could only explain events in terms of charisma, or what one of them called 'the mesmerising talents of a unique leader'.[1] Against Castro's own wishes, a cult of personality developed around his figure, but of a milder and more endearing kind than that associated with leaders of other Communist regimes. There were relatively few icons celebrating the living heroes of the Revolution, and the congenial public image of Castro was far from the granite deification of Stalin or Kim Il Sung. Wherever he went, he was buttonholed by people. He was comrade, *caudillo* and benefactor rolled into one.

The basis of Castro's popularity was undoubtedly his unique relationship with the public, whether on the television screen or in public meetings. By all accounts, he had been a good orator in his university days but his style changed radically after the Revolution. In his youth, he was prone to use the inflated rhetoric shared by politicians of the day and common to Cuban and Hispanic traditions. This grandiloquent style of oratory was filled with biblical and literary allusions, and relied for its effect on a crescendo of antitheses and resonant epithets to rouse the crowd to action. His post-Revolutionary speeches were no less profuse and were considerably longer, at times almost interminable, but their purpose was generally didactic rather than agitational, reflecting Castro's new role as leader. In these speeches, Castro would strike an immediate rapport with the crowd and a kind of dialogue would ensue, in which he responded to the mood of the audience and improvised answers to comments shouted from below. Delivered at a pitch surprisingly high for such a large figure, his speeches covered a broad range of issues and he made painstaking efforts to explain his views in popular terms, alternating facts and lengthy statistics with jokes and everyday images close to the experience of ordinary people. In a speech to metal workers in 1967, for instance, he used the example of the famous state-produced Coppelia ice cream to illustrate his belief in the superiority of socialist over capitalist production. Capitalism, he admitted, produces better-made goods initially but later tends to lower the quality. Socialism, on the other hand, strives constantly to improve quality. Thus, he went on, the Coppelia ice cream factory had never ceased in its efforts to increase its range of flavours and there were now twenty.[2]

He also used the public forum as the occasion to launch campaigns against elites or individuals in the regime against whom he had turned. To the delight of the audience, he would fire off gigantic broadsides, naming his victims or alluding to unnamed individuals or groups or government departments until their political reputation lay in tatters. The importance of public speech-making to Castro's exercise of power can be judged by the fact that until his health problems in the 1990s he made an average of one speech every four days of a length that varied from about one hour to half a day according to the political exigencies of the time. The shortest speeches were made in the 1970s when Castro consciously played a less prominent part in the government of Cuba.

Throughout the 1960s, Castro devoted himself above all to the task of rousing the Cuban people for the Herculean (or was it Sisyphean?) task of modernisation. The problems they faced, according to the Cuban leadership, were not just material but also psychological. Conquering underdevelopment meant creating the New Man. In a typical Castroist reversal of Stalinist determinism, the New Man would be forged in order to raise the productive forces rather than as a consequence of their development. Indeed, this new man was supposed to be already present in the figures of the Revolutionary leaders, both men and women (though the New Woman was given considerably less prominence). The official ethic of the Revolution was an extension into everyday life of that of the Sierra campaign. The new virtues that Cubans were encouraged to adopt were austerity, discipline, selflessness and comradeship. In a speech to workers' delegates towards the end of 1959 Castro declaimed: 'In the army of the workers there must be discipline, there must be comradeship, there must be unity; you are the officers of this army, you are the leaders.'[3]

The ethic of the Revolution was misunderstood by many of those on the Left abroad who saw Cuba as a model. The emphasis on austerity and discipline did not mark the birth of a new society, as they thought, but rather a return to the primitive accumulation of capital managed by the state. As Castro would reiterate for decades, the Cubans had to work doubly hard, subordinating private consumption to production in order to overcome the legacy of the past. 'We want to work hard', said Castro in a speech much later, 'because we must work hard, because we're a Third World Country, because we lost centuries under colonialism, nearly sixty years under neo-colonialism, and we've also lost a few years under the Revolution. We must make up for lost time!'[4] The regime of austerity was made all the harsher by the economic embargo of the United States and the need to divert scarce resources to national defence. The new ideology, therefore, made a virtue out of necessity.

Even more than economic reform, Castro's greatest preoccupation was to provide the human and social resources that he saw as vital to economic take-off, in particular education, health and housing. Soon after the victory, he organised thousands of young volunteers into brigades and sent them into the countryside to teach the many illiterate people among the rural population how to read and write. This campaign became one of the Revolution's great epics because it virtually wiped out illiteracy in Cuba in a few years; it also served to socialise many Cubans in the cities and the countryside to the new values of the Revolution. State provision of a free and modern health service, an efficient educational system and cheap new housing was seen as a political as well as an economic imperative. Providing for the basic needs of the population, so it was believed, lessened the importance of wages and reduced the demand for consumer goods.

The countryside benefited more than the cities from this state investment. The rural areas had been profoundly deprived before the Revolution. Only 15 per cent of rural inhabitants had running water compared with 80 per cent of the urban population, and only 9 per cent of households in the countryside had electricity. Agricultural workers had earned less than $80 a month on average (compared to the $120 that had been the average monthly industrial wage) yet they had also been chronically underemployed. State funds were now ploughed into the rural areas to provide jobs and infrastructure. Havana, on the other hand, was relatively neglected, its façades fading and peeling in the damp, salty air.

Underpinning the social reforms and the moral campaign of austerity lay the belief among Castro and his closest supporters that they could force the stages of development and create in a short while the conditions for a Communist society, one in which each person received according to his or her needs and gave according to his or her capacity. Orthodox Marxism insisted that without the development of productive forces on a massive scale not even socialism was possible; underdevelopment or semi-development meant the persistence of capitalist relations of production in one guise or another, whatever the degree of nationalisation of the economy. Che Guevara, the most articulate exponent among the Castroists of the belief in socialism here and now, argued on the contrary that Cuba's alignment with the developed Soviet bloc made it possible to jump stages in the transition towards socialism.[5]

The Bolshevik leaders had faced a similar dilemma in 1924. Surrounded on all sides by hostile states and confronted with the resistance of the mass of peasants to any socialist measures, they had engaged in a bitter polemic about how to save the Revolution. One wing had argued for a policy of rapid industrialisation, accumulating the capital to carry this out by subordinating consumption to production and eroding private rural capital. Fearing the collapse of agriculture and a counter-revolution led by the richer peasantry, another wing of the Bolsheviks favoured a policy of allowing the peasants to grow wealthy and thus of using private enterprise to reconstruct Russia. Stalin had supported the second option at first, and once he had seized power put the first into operation by destroying the peasantry.

The Cuban leaders believed they faced none of these problems; economic alliance with the Soviet bloc allowed industrialisation to take place without trauma, while the Cuban peasantry actually supported socialist land reform. Under the direction of Che Guevara as Minister for Industry, ambitious plans were drawn up to industrialise Cuba without sacrificing the living standards of the Cubans. Indeed, the first two years saw a rise in consumption as the poorer sections of the population gained access to better food and housing. This redistribution was possible in part because of the smooth passage of the Revolution; the economy had not been damaged by civil war, the factories were well-stocked and equipped, foreign reserves from previous exports were still available. But it soon became clear that the economy could not sustain such relatively high levels of consumption; stocks were running out, cattle were being destroyed to be eaten and the American economic embargo could not be circumvented entirely by trade with the Soviet bloc. In March 1962, rationing was introduced for the first time; Cubans would have to live with it from then on.

At the same time, the hope that the Cuban economy could somehow be plugged into that of the Comecon countries was eroded by two major problems: the sheer physical distance involved, and the incompatibility of Cuba's industry and infrastructure, until then geared to the US economy, with those of the Soviet bloc. Moreover, neither Comecon technology nor its technicians were up to the same standard as those of the United States. A combination of inexperience and poor quality of raw materials and machines led to many failures in the programme of industrialisation. Despite the wildly optimistic forecasts of Castro and others, industry grew by only 0.4 per cent in 1962 and actually declined by 1.5 per cent in the following year. Agriculture suffered even more, not only as a result of the emphasis on industrialisation but also because of massive and not always successful attempts to diversify produce. The sugar industry, already in a parlous state under Batista, had been hit by the loss of many of its managers and technicians who had begun to emigrate to the United States a year or so after the Revolutionary triumph. Moreover, in the rush to diversify agriculture, many canefields had been burnt down; the 1963 harvest turned out to be the worst since the Second World War. According to government statistics, sugar production dropped from a post-Revolutionary peak of 6,876,000 metric tons in 1961 to 3,883,000 in 1963, while the index of total agricultural production fell to its lowest level since the 1940s and industrial production suffered a steep decline.[6] These problems were compounded by the economic disruption caused by structural change as well as the diversion of resources towards defence. By the middle of 1963, the Cuban economy was heading for a slump.

The crisis brought out latent divisions within the Cuban leadership. Both Castro and Guevara had been exponents of the Stalinist model of industrialisation and agricultural diversification. This process of economic modernisation was to be managed entirely by a centralised leadership allocating targets and controlling budgets. At the head of this vast operation as Minister of Industry, Guevara spent most of the day and night receiving reports, launching schemes, handling accounts, poring over technical books, acting in his new role much as he had done as a guerrilla in the Sierra. Similarly, Castro tirelessly roamed the Cuban countryside, setting up ambitious agricultural projects, getting labour and machinery moved around, animating and lecturing his people wherever he went. The French agronomist René Dumont, who spent a short time with Castro as an adviser, wrote about his experience: 'Travelling with Castro I sometimes had the impression that I was visiting Cuba with its owner, who was showing off its fields and pastures, its cows if not its men.'[7] For the old Communists, the whole style of the Revolutionary leadership must have seemed chaotic. Moreover, reformist breezes were beginning to blow from Eastern Europe counselling a very different economic management to the one practised by the Castroists.

The internal debate that ensued in Cuba was similar to that among Bolshevik leaders in 1925 and among the Chinese Communists in 1958–9 after the débâcle of the Great Leap Forward. It took the form of a clash between two very different discourses of economic development: on the one hand, an exogenous model drawing its inspiration from Lenin's New Economic Policy, based on applying market mechanisms, decentralisation and material incentives to competing state enterprises, and on the other, an endogenous model stressing central planning, moral incentives and social need.[8] The pre-Revolutionary Communists and their allies in economic policy argued for the first model on the grounds that a primitive accumulation of capital was only possible on the basis of a large increase in sugar production. Only the mass export of sugar and a better use of its derivatives, in their opinion, could create the platform for economic take-off. At the same time, they favoured the new reforms sweeping Eastern Europe, which provided for internal economic autonomy and a greater stress on profitability and material incentives. Their polemical statements were tacitly directed against Guevara as the most conspicuous backer of the endogenous model of economic policy, yet they knew that Castro supported Guevara's ideas.[9] Frequently the pragmatist, Castro gave way in the face of the economic setbacks of 1963. On a long trip to the Soviet Union without Guevara in the spring of 1963, he signed numerous agreements that effectively confined Cuba to the production of its traditional raw materials within the socialist division of labour. The bitter pill was coated by the Soviet leaders with the guarantee of a market for Cuban sugar at a high fixed price that allowed for long-term planning. Guevara's ministry was split up, resources were diverted from industry to agriculture, and a bloodletting began of officials in the bureaucracy.

As they would continue to do in the coming decades, the Cuban leaders sought to blame individuals rather than policies or the policy-making mechanisms for the collapse of the industrialisation venture. It was clear that the plans of Castro, Guevara and their closest followers had been over-ambitious. Reflecting on this period many years later, Castro confessed, 'At that time we had many ideas that were well-intentioned, but they were not very realistic; we wanted to jump stages.'[10] One problem was that the political success of the Revolution had created a faith that revolutionary consciousness or *conciencia* could move mountains. In a characteristically honest vein, Guevara concluded, 'We did not base our arguments on statistical facts, nor on historical experience. We dealt with nature in a subjective manner, as if by talking to it we could persuade it.'[11] Cuban workers and technicians were willing, indeed almost too willing, but on the whole they lacked the necessary experience and technical knowledge. Another problem was the extreme centralisation of decision-making, as a result of which the Cuban economy suffered severe dislocations. In this Castro was as much to blame as Guevara, since he was responsible for launching numerous agricultural initiatives like military offensives which, by his own later admission, failed to take cost-effectiveness or appropriate technology into account.[12]

Nevertheless, it was Guevara who bore the consequences of the débâcle, though he remained for a short while as close as ever to Castro. Eighteen months after the decision to overhaul economic policy was announced, Guevara left for a tour of African and Asian countries. On his return he resigned his government positions, gave up his Cuban citizenship and left for Africa in April 1965. Guevara's departure from Cuba has been the subject of much discussion. It is possible that he left simply because there was no obvious role for him once his policy of industrialisation had failed. He was not sacked, nor is it likely that he had any fundamental disagreement with Castro since the latter was shortly to revive many of Guevara's most cherished policies. Besides, it was typical of Castro's leadership to move aside rather than to fire any leading exponent of a policy that had officially been declared a failure.

However, Guevara's unorthodox methods and his growing criticism of the Soviet Union's policies in the Third World ill-suited the delicate process of rapprochement with Moscow made necessary by the economic crisis. Guevara's speech at a meeting of the Afro-American Solidarity in Algiers in February 1965, during which he had accused the Soviet bloc of complicity with imperialism, was not calculated to endear him to the Soviet Union.

Indeed, it is rumoured that on his return from Algiers he had had a long and heated exchange with Fidel and Raúl Castro and President Dorticós in which he restated his opposition to convergence with Soviet international policy and departed from Cuba without taking leave of Castro.[13] He was joined by a small force of veterans of the Sierra campaign to assist the Katangese rebels against the Congolese government. From there, according to Castro, he went to Prague in March 1966 and four months later returned to Cuba on a clandestine visit to train 15 more veterans for a new guerrilla campaign in Bolivia, undergoing plastic surgery to transform his appearance. During this visit he was in touch with Castro and other Cuban leaders.[14] By October he had set up camp in the Bolivian highlands. Guevara had always made clear that his overriding commitment was to revolution in the South American continent. The example of the Cuban Revolution offered the hope that similar guerrilla actions could succeed elsewhere. The new mood of rebellion stirring in the Third World in the mid-1960s, stimulated by the resistance of the Vietnamese against the United States, further encouraged his grand vision. This was probably his most important motive for leaving Cuba.

Guevara's disappearance and the collapse of the industrialisation campaign strengthened the hand of the orthodox, pro-Soviet elements in the middle stratum of the Cuban leadership. Indeed, it seemed for a while as if Castro was bowing to greater pressure. The price of renewed Soviet support was a certain decentralisation of economic decision-making and the introduction of a limited range of market mechanisms. At the same time, the Cuban leaders hastened the process of creating an orthodox institutional framework urged by the Kremlin, and in October 1965, the single party of the Revolution, the Cuban Communist Party (PCC), was formed out of the organisations that had emerged from the victory.

Yet Castro had not abandoned the twin objectives of the Revolution: to create a Communist society on the basis of a developed economy, and to secure a lasting independence for Cuba. Soviet policies since the missile crisis increasingly seemed to threaten the achievement of these objectives. On a domestic plane, the new economic reforms in the Soviet Union were incompatible with the model propounded by Castro of a society struggling to survive and develop. In his eyes, the central task of the Cubans was to accumulate resources under the direction of the Revolutionary elite, who would cream off the surplus to pay for defence and industrial investment and maintain essential social services such as health and education. Through the introduction of material incentives, the reforms threatened to undermine the egalitarian principles of the Revolution and divert the efforts of Cubans towards personal material goals rather than national accumulation. In any case, monetary rewards made little sense in a domestic economy offering few consumer goods and a relatively high social wage. The Soviet reforms also threatened to confine the Cuban economy to a specialised niche within the Comecon system, producing sugar and tropical products in exchange for industrial goods; this would merely renew a neocolonial relationship long familiar to Cuba, though in a different guise. The new economic model recently adopted by the Soviet Union also laid open the Cuban political system to emerging elites in the bureaucracy and among workers who would not only create inequalities but stand between the leadership and the people.[15]

Internationally, the Soviet Union's policies also seemed to pose serious difficulties for the Cuban Revolution. The twentieth Congress of the Soviet Communist Party in 1956 had declared that the new balance of power between East and West created the conditions for a peaceful emergence of socialism in the West in ways determined by the local characteristics of each country. Communist Parties had thus been given the green light to take the parliamentary road to socialism. This meant the adoption of a new form of Popular Frontism; that is, an alliance with forces ranged against local oligarchies stretching from social democrats to reformist generals. It also entailed the development of a new relationship with Third World countries characterised by a greater concern for commercial viability and less for the political colour of governments. The decision had marked the beginning of a new era of peaceful coexistence with the West, disrupted briefly by the missile crisis of 1962.

Both the Chinese and the Cuban leadership disliked the policy of peaceful coexistence and the parliamentary road to socialism. For over half a century constitutional methods had failed to bring about reform in Cuba. When elected governments in Latin America had attempted to introduce social and economic changes, they had been threatened and, in Guatemala's case, destroyed by US-sponsored counter-revolution. According to Revolutionary mythology, both the Chinese and the Cuban Revolutions had been the result of guerrilla campaigns that had started in the countryside and spread to the cities. For the Castroists conditions were ripe in Latin America for such actions, which, they were confident, would culminate in a continent-wide revolution. In a barely disguised attack on the Latin American Communist Parties, Castro declared in 1966 that guerrilla struggle was the only revolutionary road that most countries in that continent could take. 'What we are convinced about is that in the immense majority of Latin American nations conditions exist for making the Revolution that are far superior to those that existed in Cuba, and that if those revolutions are not being made in those countries it is because many who call themselves revolutionaries lack conviction.'[16]

The international situation in the mid-1960s suggested to the Cuban leaders that this course was essential for the survival of the Revolution. Castro was dismayed by the Sino-Soviet dispute which served only to weaken the socialist bloc. 'Not even the attacks on North Vietnam [by the United States]', he said in a speech in March 1965, 'have helped to overcome the divisions within the socialist family. . . . Who benefits from these disputes other than our enemies?'[17] Cuba's close proximity to the United States made it extremely vulnerable, and the Cubans were not confident about the assurances given to Moscow at the end of the missile crisis that the United States would not try to invade the island. According to Castro the Sino-Soviet split, added to the new moderation of the Soviet Union especially after the fall of Khrushchev in 1965, appeared only to encourage the United States to greater aggression, of which its growing intervention in Vietnam was the clearest sign. Moscow could not be relied on to defend the Cuban Revolution; this had been the traumatic lesson of 1962. Besides, the Soviet Union seemed increasingly conciliatory towards the United States. The Cuban Revolution needed Soviet aid but it could only survive in the long run through the massive efforts of its people to create the material basis for development and through the export of its model to Latin America where, it was hoped, new revolutions would come to the aid of the beleaguered island.

For Castro, therefore, the Soviet Union's policies in the mid-1960s represented neither a guarantee of defence against the United States nor a model of economic development. At the same time he could not afford to lose the support of Moscow. This dilemma lay behind the swings in his policy in the second half of the 1960s. From 1965, Castro began to distance himself from the Soviet Union and openly to criticise its foreign policy in terms even harsher than those used by Guevara. While in the early years of the Revolution he had defied the Eagle, he could be said now to be baiting the Bear. At home, he launched a new offensive to tackle the problem of underdevelopment once and for all, sweeping aside the faint-hearted, the nonconformists and above all the residual pro-Soviet opposition within the PCC. The two campaigns were part of the same overall objective: to defend the Revolution, to assert Cuban independence and to mobilise the people for the task of modernisation. The failure of the industrialisation programme made the whole project all the more urgent.

Castro's assertiveness towards Moscow derived from a new sense of confidence. While the Sino-Soviet dispute had indeed weakened the socialist bloc it also gave Cuba a certain leverage over the Soviet Union, which was anxious to keep Cuba on its side of the divide. Castro was careful, however, to keep his distance from the Chinese, who were trying to exploit the differences between Havana and Moscow.[18] The lukewarm support given to North Vietnam by both the Chinese and the Soviet Union raised the possibility of a third alignment of socialist forces embracing Hanoi, the Vietcong, the Cubans and North Korea. The resistance of the North Vietnamese under the onslaught of American bombs must have been a source of immense encouragement to the Cuban leaders. Moreover, Cuba enjoyed the sort of prestige among Third World nations and in many sections of public opinion in the West that Moscow could hardly ignore.

But Castro's confidence rested above all on his faith in the strategy of guerrilla warfare in Latin America. In the early 1960s it seemed as if the Cuban example could be exported. There was widespread agitation among peasants in Central America and in the Andean region. Guerrilla groups had sprung up in Colombia, Venezuela, Peru and Guatemala. And in Bolivia, the poorest, roughest and most central nation in South America, Guevara was preparing to launch a guerrilla war calculated to spread to neighbouring Argentina, Brazil, Peru and beyond. His presence in the Bolivian jungle with a select group of veterans of the Sierra campaign led to exaggerated hopes of a revolutionary wave in the sub-continent that would end Cuba's isolation and lessen its dependence on the Soviet Union. Even Castro seemed to have succumbed to the myth, reinforced by the Cuban Revolution, that heroism or revolutionary faith could triumph over all odds. The Cuban Revolution would not have taken place, he said in a speech in 1966, if account had been taken of objective conditions. 'As for subjective conditions', he went on, 'there were possibly no more than twenty, at first no more than ten, people who believed that a revolution was possible . . . what was important was not the individuals involved but conviction; merit lies not in the individuals but in conviction.'[19]

Castro's barely disguised attacks on the Soviet Union between 1965 and 1968 can only be understood in the light of this confidence that a new revolutionary axis was taking shape, led by Cuba, Vietnam and North Korea, and soon embracing newly liberated Latin American countries and several Third World nations. It was to be a new Communist front that would turn the tide of American imperialism to which the Soviets and their orthodox followers seemed to have capitulated. This was the hidden agenda of the Tricontinental Conference of revolutionary organisations from Africa, Asia and Latin America held in Havana in January 1966, during which a message from Guevara was read out calling on Latin American revolutionaries to set up 'two, three, many Vietnams'. Some 18 months later, this was followed by a Cuban-sponsored meeting of Latin American revolutionary organisations in which a new front was set up, the Latin American Solidarity Organisation (the acronym in Spanish, OLAS, means 'waves'). Against the votes of the few orthodox Communist Parties that attended the meeting, OLAS approved the strategy of guerrilla warfare and elected the absent Guevara, at the time deep in the Bolivian highlands, as honorary president. During the conference, Castro launched into an attack on the Venezuelan Party for sabotaging the guerrilla movement in that country and for intriguing against Cuba. He also indirectly criticised the Soviet Union and Comecon countries for delivering petrol and granting credit to countries that had imposed a trade boycott on Cuba.[20]

Moscow reacted to its increasingly wayward and captious protégé by delaying the signing of trade agreements, and eventually cutting back on urgent supplies of oil to Cuba. A declassified East German document suggests that the Soviet Union and its allies were considering whether to continue the relationship with Cuba at all.[21] Soviet–Cuban relations reached a low point when Castro refused to attend the celebration of the fiftieth anniversary of the Russian Revolution in autumn 1967. Three months later, he delivered his most stinging attack on Communist orthodoxy. At an international conference of intellectuals in Havana, he proclaimed,

*there can be nothing so anti-Marxist as dogma, there can be nothing so anti-Marxist as the petrification of ideas. And there are ideas that are even put forward in the name of Marxism that seem real fossils . . . Marxism needs to develop, overcome a certain sclerosis, interpret the realities of the present in an objective and scientific way, behave like a revolutionary force and not like a pseudo-revolutionary church.*[22]

This audacious message, however, was directed mainly at those in the ranks of the Party in Cuba who had misgivings about the radical direction which the Revolution was taking. In February 1968, shortly after Castro's speech, the leading exponents of Soviet orthodoxy were put on trial accused of factionalism. The report of the Central Committee outlining the charges was introduced by Raúl Castro and lasted 12 hours. It unfolded a lurid tableau of secret gatherings among pro-Soviet Communists and clandestine rendezvous with Soviet and Eastern European officials.[23] That the so-called 'microfaction' affair amounted to a serious conspiracy is doubtful but it exposed the continuing tensions between the two wings of the Cuban Revolution, the pre-Revolutionary Communists and the 26th July Movement.

The trial also served to warn the Soviets that they would not be allowed to indulge in internal lobbying.

The crackdown against the pro-Soviet Communists was part of a broader offensive launched in 1968 by Castro to bend the will of the Cubans to the task of accumulation. Since the reorganisation of the economic ministries in 1965, he had taken over the reins of the economy as President of INRA, personally approving and directing scores of ambitious projects. The East European model of five-year central planning was abandoned in favour of regional or sectoral plans orchestrated by individual leaders such as Castro himself. By the beginning of 1968, however, there were ominous signs that the economy was heading for a crisis once again. The Soviet Union was tightening the screw by drastically reducing its supply of fuel and gas oil to Cuba. Many of the economic plans had failed to live up to expectations owing to inadequate planning or lack of technical expertise.[24] Castro was particularly irked by the operations of small farmers and traders who were taking advantage of rationing and commodity shortages to run a black market. Their presence was not politically expedient at a time when he was calling for universal sacrifice nor did it correspond to the society that he was attempting to build. 'We did not make a revolution', he exclaimed, 'in order to establish the right to trade.' Seizing with vivid detail on the example of street stallholders who sold fried egg sandwiches, he warned of the danger of allowing small-scale private capitalism to expand.[25] In March, he launched a Revolutionary Offensive to mop up the last vestiges of the private sector, nationalising over 55,000 small businesses accounting for around a third of Cuba's retail sales.[26]

The harsher political climate was reflected in the growing campaign against Cubans who did not conform to the spirit of discipline urged by Castro. In a strongly machista society, that discipline extended to sexual orientations as well. As early as 1965 the army had begun forcibly to recruit homosexuals into separate work battalions, alongside conscientious objectors and men with low educational levels. Privately, Castro had been known for sharing the typically Cuban male prejudice against homosexuals. An ex-Castroist recounts hearing the two Castro brothers laughing at a joke about a Czech homosexual-detection machine.[27] But after a plea by the Writers' and Artists' Union, several of whose members had been press-ganged into these battalions, Castro had ordered them to be disbanded in 1967, though this did not halt discrimination in many other fields of activity.[28]

Revolutionary discipline also extended to intellectuals and creative artists. Castro had originally defined the role of the intellectual in the Cuban Revolution at a meeting with artists and writers in 1961 in which he had established the principle that everything was permissible within the Revolution but nothing against it.[29] In the light of subsequent events, it was clear that what he meant by 'within the Revolution' was more to do with how revolutionary orthodoxy was defined at any moment by the leadership than with a distinct set of norms and values. *Lunes*, the iconoclastic cultural supplement of the official newspaper *Revolución*, had been closed down in 1961 when the Playa Girón events appeared to necessitate 'revolutionary unity'.

On the other hand, the 'Third Worldist' turn of the Revolution after 1965 had led to the closure in 1967 of the Schools of Revolutionary Instruction that were teaching orthodox Soviet Marxism, while the intellectuals around the journal *Pensamiento Crítico* and the Philosophy Department of Havana University were encouraged to develop the Guevarist discourse of the New Man and the 'Cuban Way'. This helped to generate a wave of solidarity from the New Left in Europe and America, culminating in a spectacular cultural congress in 1968 attended by intellectuals from many parts of the globe. Yet by the end of that year, writers and artists were coming under fire, in particular from the military, for failing to produce exemplary works rather in the style laid down by Stalin's Minister of Culture Zhdanov. This new cycle of repression against intellectuals was exemplified by the campaign of Raúl Castro and the army from late 1968 against *Pensamiento Crítico*.[30] Being within the Revolution was increasingly interpreted in the late 1960s by a growing band of neo-Stalinists in the bureaucracy and military as ruling out anything but Soviet Marxist orthodoxy and socialist realism. Artists and writers who appeared to express doubts about the Revolution or whose creative activity ignored political correctness began to find it progressively harder to have their work approved. By the end of the decade, when the regime was forced to turn once again towards Soviet orthodoxy because of the failure of the Guevarist Third World strategy and the economic need for Soviet support, a number of intellectuals had been forced into exile while others had been jailed or compelled publicly to confess their 'counter-revolutionary views'. One such case was that of the poet Herberto Padilla, which aroused solidarity among many foreign intellectuals who had supported the Revolution, such as García Márquez and Sartre. Eventually, *Pensamiento Crítico* was closed down in 1971 and the Department of Philosophy of Havana University purged.[31]

It is difficult to establish Castro's precise attitude towards the persecution of 'wayward' intellectuals. He may not have approved of the over-zealous application of socialist realism, and many years later he joined in the retrospective criticism of the cultural line of the late 1960s and early 1970s.[32] But there could be little doubt concerning his general position in the debate about cultural and educational policies. In the early days of the new regime, there had been differences among teachers, intellectuals and cultural officials about the nature of Revolutionary art and education. For some, the Revolution represented the liberation of the creative and critical spirit; for others, art and education had to serve political priorities. For Castro, the intellectual had to be at the service of the 'people', subordinating his or her own individuality to the needs of the Revolution. Castro may have shared this neo-Zhdanovism with the old Cuban Stalinists who had now gained influence in the regime but in his case it sprang perhaps from different sources. The years of conspiratorial activity and guerrilla struggle had imbued him with a militaristic distrust of ideological or cultural pluralism. Because of his own social background, he had never identified with the cosmopolitan culture of many of his fellow students in Havana. Moreover in his own personal relations, Castro had shown a strong vein of prudishness. During his stay in Mexico, according to a close friend and supporter, he had got engaged briefly to a beautiful Cuban girl and, infuriated by the fact that she wore a bikini when swimming, he insisted that she wear a bathing costume that he bought especially for her.[33] This underlying puritanism extended to political and cultural matters as well, taking the guise of an unavoidable austerity. Castro's speeches in the late 1960s argued that the very survival of the Revolution depended on the total commitment of every Cuban to its immediate objectives; any other attitude, he implied, was a dangerous diversion. This message was spelt out in September 1968 in a speech to the local Committees for the Defence of the Revolution. Reviewing the difficult economic situation he exhorted:

*And we repeat: no liberalism! No softening! A revolutionary nation, an organised nation, a combative nation, a strong nation, because these are the virtues that are required these days. And everything else is pure illusion, it would be to underestimate the task, underestimate the enemy, underestimate the historic importance of this period, underestimate the struggle that lies ahead of us.[34]*

The urgent tone of his speech reflected the fact that by 1968 Castro's options were narrowing. On one hand, the guerrilla movements in Latin America were collapsing. In October 1967, after a harrowing time in the Bolivian mountains, Guevara and his group had been captured and murdered by American-trained Bolivian Rangers, helped by a CIA unit which may have profited from the advice of the fugitive Nazi war criminal Klaus Barbie.[35] His death was a double blow to Castro. Aside from his personal grief at the loss of a close friend and comrade, the failure of the Bolivian

venture cast doubt on the possibility of exporting the Cuban model of guerrilla warfare to the South American continent. Despite Castro's words that it
was ideas not individuals that counted, the death of Guevara was all the
more a defeat for the guerrilla strategy because of the mystique of invulner-
ability that surrounded the living heroes of the Cuban Revolution.

Castro laid much of the blame for Guevara's death on the shoulders
of the Bolivian Communist Party, whose leaders he accused of sabotaging
the guerrilla operation.[36] Yet this only underlined the difficulty of working
independently of the orthodox Parties which in several countries controlled
resources vital to the success of the guerrillas. Moreover, at the end of the
1960s the policies of the popular front advocated by the Communist Parties
seemed about to be vindicated. In Peru, a reformist, anti-oligarchic, military
junta took control in 1968 and began to nationalise US multinational companies. A year later, the new democratic government of Bolivia expropriated
the Gulf Oil corporation, while in Chile a broad front of parties of the left
and centre-left, Popular Unity, was formed to contest the 1970 Presidential
elections. In short, events in Latin America at the end of the decade seemed
in themselves to counsel a return to Soviet orthodoxy in international relations on the part of the Cuban regime.

However, it was above all economic pressures that drove Castro to seek
a rapprochement with the Soviet Union. Apart from Moscow's increasing
restriction of oil supplies, the Cuban economy was in massive debt to the
Soviet bloc. In the trade agreements between the two countries, the Soviet
Union bought Cuban sugar at a price usually higher than that of the world
market while Cuba used the non-convertible currency with which the sugar
was paid for to buy Comecon oil and industrial goods. Any surplus of sugar
could then be sold on the world market to raise the foreign currency vital
for the purchase of technology and goods unavailable in the socialist
bloc. Throughout the 1960s, however, Cuban exports of sugar to the Soviet
Union had been well below its imports of Comecon goods and Moscow had
so far been willing to finance these trade deficits. By 1969, Cuba was about
7.5 million tons in arrears and Castro declared it to be the Year of Decisive
Endeavour during which the efforts of all Cubans would be devoted to producing a harvest of 10 million tons of sugar. Whether such a record harvest
could be achieved or not, Castro could no longer afford to antagonise
the Soviet Union. The Warsaw Pact intervention in Czechoslovakia on
21 August 1968 gave him an unusual opportunity to begin rebuilding
bridges with Moscow.

Castro's address to the Cuban nation 48 hours after the invasion was
awaited with great expectation. A group of top Cuban officials on a visit to

Europe promised the French journalist K.S. Karol that it 'would open a new page in the history of the international labour movement'.[37] Quite apart from Castro's growing quarrel with the Soviet Union since 1965, the Warsaw Pact invasion cannot fall to have evoked parallels with the United States' continual intervention in Cuban affairs since the island won its independence in 1902. A similar doctrine of collective security and 'spheres of influence' was being used to justify the violation of Czechoslovakia's sovereignty and it could be invoked in a reactive invasion of Cuba by the United States. In a secret speech to the Central Committee only seven months previously, Castro had bitterly attacked the Soviet Union for its unilateral desertion of Cuba in 1962.[38]

Indeed, Castro began his address by dismissing the Soviet Union's claims that the intervention was legally justified. 'What cannot be denied here', he said, 'is that the sovereignty of the Czechoslovak State was violated. . . . And the violation was, in fact, of a flagrant nature.' Nevertheless, he insisted, the intervention was a necessary evil: 'we had no doubt that the political situation in Czechoslovakia was deteriorating and going downhill on its way back to capitalism and that it was inexorably going to fall into the arms of imperialism'. In the name of the law he described as even more sacred to Communists than international law – that is, the 'people's struggle against imperialism' – the socialist bloc had been obliged to step in.

Yet Castro also used the occasion to make two tacit demands of the Soviet Union: an end to the market economy reforms in the socialist bloc, and a commitment that it would come to the defence of other socialist countries such as Cuba should they be threatened by imperialism. These demands took the form of questions:

*Does this [the intervention] by chance mean that the Soviet Union is also going to curb certain currents in the field of economy that are in favour of putting increasingly greater emphasis on mercantile relations . . . ? . . . We ask ourselves . . . will they send the divisions of the Warsaw Pact to Cuba if the Yankee imperialists attack our country, or even in the case of the threat of a Yankee imperialist attack on our country, if our country requests it?*[39]

Castro's qualified approval of the Czechoslovak invasion confused or disappointed many on the Left abroad who had welcomed first the Cuban Revolution and then the Prague Spring as the same break with post-Stalinist orthodoxy. It was seen then and is still seen by many commentators as a piece of *realpolitik* dictated by Soviet pressure.[40] But if it is viewed in the light of the Cuban regime's domestic problems, Castro's support for the invasion takes on a new dimension. The Czech leaders' reforms, as Castro himself argued, were an intensification of the decentralising measures and market mechanisms introduced by the Soviet Union during the mid-1960s. The 'microfaction' trial had been directed precisely against the local proponents of such measures while the Revolutionary Offensive of March had set out to eliminate the residual private sector and the budding black market that threatened to reintroduce market values by the back door.

In Castro's eyes, no relaxation of central control and social discipline was possible in the midst of economic crisis and imperialist encirclement, as his speech at the time had made clear. The Prague Spring, luxuriating in alternative cultures, was the antithesis of his model for a besieged Cuba. The reformist measures of Dubcek and his allies had raised too many expectations and had been followed by a wave of strikes. Castro's inclination, as he was to show repeatedly over the coming years, was not to ignore social discontent but to appropriate it, to channel it in the direction he chose, to use it to undermine or displace those he believed stood in the way of the changing priorities of the Revolution. His distrust of the Prague Spring was all the deeper because its leading lights – students, artists and intellectuals – were from the same social elite that in Cuba during the late 1960s was being criticised for harbouring bourgeois liberal tendencies. Castro's lack of sympathy or understanding for the aims of the reform movement in Czechoslovakia was summed up in his dismissive remark, 'And for the thousands of millions of human beings who . . . are still living without hope under conditions of starvation and extreme want there are questions in which they are more interested than the problem of whether or not to let their hair grow.'[41]

Castro had his own reasons, therefore, for supporting the Warsaw Pact invasion. Much as he had criticised the Soviets' foreign policy, he clearly felt encouraged by their new determination to prevent any further divisions within the socialist bloc that would leave Cuba dangerously exposed. At the same time, he welcomed the intervention in so far as it restored political cohesion in Eastern Europe and brought to an end a disruptive experiment in economic reform originating in the Soviet Union. In any case, Castro had little option other than to support the Soviet action. Increasingly isolated abroad, its guerrilla strategy in tatters and saddled with a massive trade deficit, the Cuban regime could not afford to lose Soviet support.

In these circumstances, the 1969–70 campaign to produce a sugar harvest of 10 million tons became for Castro and the Revolutionary leadership a last, almost desperate attempt to accumulate the resources to develop the island and to retain a measure of independence in the formulation of their policies. In the words of the leading pre-Revolutionary Communist and head of foreign relations Carlos Rafael Rodríguez, 'The ten million ton harvest will guarantee our country's second liberation.'[42] The campaign was also to be the apotheosis of Castro's model of mobilisation, proof that moral determination could move mountains. On its success, he staked his own reputation and that of the state. The whole nation was roused for the task, and all other economic activity was subordinated to its achievement. Indeed, the 10 million ton harvest became a political rather than an economic goal. In a speech on 18 October 1969, Castro declared,

*The ten million ton harvest represents far more than tons of sugar, far more than an economic victory; it is a test, a moral commitment for this country. And precisely because it is a test and a moral commitment we cannot fall short by even a single gram of these ten million tons. . . . Ten million tons less a single pound – we declare it before all the world – will be a defeat, not a victory.*[43]

The campaign was also designed to raise the morale of the Cubans at a time when the strains of work and rationing were beginning to surface. Workers increasingly had had to forgo the wage benefits they had won at the beginning of the Revolution in exchange for a limited range of free state services. Unpaid overtime or 'voluntary labour' had become compulsory, while material incentives were being replaced by moral incentives such as the privileges extended to exemplary workers who formed part of the Advanced Workers' Movement. Productivity was not rising but absenteeism was. It seemed as though Castro was hoping that the great sugar campaign would reawaken the Playa Girón spirit and make hardship bearable.

In his customary style, Castro set an example to the nation by spending four hours a day during harvest time cutting cane. The planting and harvesting season was extended to increase the yield, and the celebration of Christmas was postponed. But as the months advanced it became clear that the target would not be reached. In May 1970, Castro conceded that the harvest would fall short of the 10 million tons. In the event, the sugar yield reached a record level of around 8.5 million tons. This was indeed a remarkable achievement, almost double the amount harvested in the previous year. The failure to reach the target had been due not to a lack of willingness on the part of Cubans but to insufficient planning and inadequate technical resources. But because Castro had made the campaign a test of the credibility of the regime, the shortfall was a terrible defeat for his leadership. To make matters worse, the concentration on the harvest had resulted in severe dislocations of an economy already in crisis. Over 21 per cent of industrial and agricultural goods and more than 41 per cent of forestry products registered their worst year since the Revolution.[44]

On 26 July 1970, the anniversary of the Moncada action, Castro rose before an immense crowd to deliver one of the most important speeches of his career. Without preamble, he launched into an astonishing criticism of the management of Cuban society over the previous decade. Referring to the regime's attempt simultaneously to raise living standards and accumulate capital, he said,

*we proved incapable of waging what we called the simultaneous battle. And in effect, the heroic effort to raise production, to raise our purchasing power resulted in dislocations in the economy, in a fall in production in other sectors, and in general in an increase in our difficulties.*

After running through a long list of economic indices, Castro continued, 'We are going to begin by pointing out the responsibility of all of us [leaders] and mine in particular for all these problems.' He then made a rather rhetorical proposal that the Cuban people should look for a new leadership, to which the crowd predictably shouted their dissent, and, as if ashamed by this demagogic lapse, Castro admitted that it would be hypocritical on his part to pretend he wished to resign.

Nevertheless, he went on,

*I believe that we, the leaders of this Revolution, have cost too much in our apprenticeship. And unfortunately, our problem is . . . the result of our own ignorance. . . . Most of the time we fell into the error of minimising the complexity of the problems facing us. We must renew [the leadership] because it's only logical that there are comrades who are worn out, burnt out; they have lost their energy, they can no longer carry the burden on their shoulders.*

Having criticised the leadership, Castro then went on to outline the changes he wanted to see. He called for more democratic consultation at a rank-and-file level. He also argued for a greater delegation of powers among the Party leadership and a profound re-examination of the whole direction of the Revolution. Recalling the assault on Moncada, the guerrilla war and the Playa Girón invasion, he remarked,

*It is easier to win twenty wars than win the battle of development. The fight today is not against people – unless they are ourselves – we are fighting against objective factors; we are fighting against the past, we are fighting with the continued presence of this past in the present, we are fighting against limitations of all kinds. But sincerely this is the greatest challenge that we have had in our lives and the greatest challenge the Revolution has ever faced.*[45]

Castro's speech was a tour de force, at once highly personal, didactic and normative. There can have been few other examples of a head of state who has so explicitly revealed his own shortcomings and failures. By doing so, Castro was able to turn a defeat almost into a virtue. But his speech also marked the end of an era. It was significant that he had to return to the rostrum just after he had finished speaking because he had forgotten that part of his speech dealing with the memory of Che Guevara. Indeed, the whole Guevarist model of 'burning' the stages of growth through moral mobilisation to which Castro had returned in the mid-1960s was now being quietly buried. Its failure was not so much the consequence of the abortive sugar campaign or of Soviet pressure but of a growing crisis within Cuban society. Despite the crowd's adulation of Castro, there were signs of discontent about the direction the Revolution was taking.

The clearest indication that something was wrong was the epidemic of absenteeism throughout the country; Castro himself noted that in August and September 1970 some 20 per cent of the workforce were absent on any given day, while in Oriente in August 1970 52 per cent of agricultural workers failed to show up for work.[46] It was clear that Castro's oratorical relationship with the masses and his almost daily contact with ordinary people were no substitute for an organised system of consultation. The low levels of productivity indicated also that moral incentives were not working and that many workers no longer responded to constant appeals to patriotism. There was an evident disjuncture between the great campaigns such as the 10 million ton harvest to which the Cubans had responded wholeheartedly and the daily effort of productivity. Moreover, it appeared that the free services which the regime now provided in health care, education, transport, social security and even local telephone calls were not enough to compensate for the lack of goods in the shops and the discomforts of everyday life.

The failure of the sugar campaign also eroded the widespread myth of Castro's infallibility. For the first time, he was seen to be vulnerable to error. Characteristically, he was able to turn this to good account by encouraging the Cubans to look for collective solutions rather than heroes and scapegoats. 'It would be an unforgivable deception of the people', he said in his July 1970 speech, 'if we tried to pretend that the problems we have are problems here of individuals. . . . We believe that this is a problem involving the whole people!'[47] But Castro himself was to a great extent to blame for the personalism that so dominated the Cuban political system. In his frequent criticisms of bureaucracy and production problems, as well as his attacks on refractory elements in the regime, he had fostered the idea that it was individuals who were at fault and not systems or decision-making processes.

More importantly, he had encouraged the notion of emulation, high-lighting the exemplary role of the heroes of the Revolution. He himself had chosen to play a pre-eminent role in Cuban affairs, not out of thirst for power, as most detractors of the Revolution would have us believe, but out of elitism. Implicit in many of his speeches was the idea that to carry out the great task of development the Cubans could not be left to their own devices because they had been conditioned by decades of neocolonialism, not to say centuries of underdevelopment and dependency. This mentality of under-development was what Castro meant when he referred in his July speech to the 'continued presence of the past in the present'. The need for exemplary leadership rather than delegation of power had been all the more acute in his eyes because the Revolution was under siege. It was rather more unusual, however, for Castro to admit that he was himself part of that tradition. In his speech to the First Congress of the Cuban Communist Party in 1975, he would concede, 'The embryo of chauvinism and of the petty-bourgeois spirit affecting those of us who reached the road of revolution by a merely intellectual way develops, sometimes unconsciously, certain attitudes that may be regarded as self-sufficiency and excessive self-esteem.'[48]

By the end of the decade the Cuban Revolution faced an impasse. The economy was in a crisis, the Cubans were restless and the regime was isolated outside the socialist bloc, increasingly reliant on Soviet support. A new road towards development and independence had to be constructed. Characteristically, Castro bent to the task, somewhat chastened by the failures of the 1960s to judge by his speeches, but with the same will and pragmatism that he had displayed on numerous occasions in the past.

## Notes

1  M. Llerena, *The Unsuspected Revolution* (Cornell University Press, Ithaca, NY, 1978), p. 200.

2  *Verde Olivo*, 5 March 1967.

3  *Revolución*, 20 Nov. 1959.

4  *Granma Weekly Review (GWR)*, 13 Dec. 1987.

5  'La Planificación Socialista, su Significado', in E. Guevara, *Obra Revolucionaria* (2nd edn, Era, Mexico, 1968), pp. 602–10.

6  J.I. Domínguez, *Cuba: Order and Revolution* (Harvard University, Cambridge, Mass., 1978), pp. 174–8.

7  R. Dumont, *Is Cuba Socialist?* (Viking Press, New York, 1974), p. 57.

8  A. Kapcia, *Cuba: Island of Dreams* (Berg, Oxford, 2000), pp. 133–8.

9  *Nueva Industria*, 3 Oct. 1963; C. Brundenius, *Economic Growth, Basic Needs and Income Distribution in Revolutionary Cuba* (University of Lund, 1981), pp. 71–5; Castro confirms this in I. Ramonet, *Fidel Castro. Biografía a dos voces* (Random House Mondadori, Mexico and Barcelona, 2006), p. 228; see also J.G. Castañeda, *La vida en rojo. Una biografía del Che Guevara* (Espasa Calpe, Argentina, 1997), Chap VIII.

10  *Granma*, 12 Feb. 1985.

11  Quoted in Brundenius, *Economic Growth*, p. 71.

12  *Granma*, 27 July 1970.

13  V. Skierka, *Fidel Castro: a Biography* (Polity Press, Cambridge, 2004), pp. 170–5. For a detailed analysis of Guevara's state of mind and his plans, see Castañeda, *La vida en rojo*, Chap VIII.

14  Ramonet, *Castro*, pp. 266–8.

15  A. Suárez, *Cuba: Castroism and Communism, 1959–1966* (MIT Press, Cambridge, Mass., 1967).

16  *Granma*, 27 July 1966.

17  *Revolución*, 15 March 1965.

18  Domínguez, *Cuba*, p. 161; Brundenius, *Economic Growth*, p. 78; Castro's speech of 1979, 'Vietnam is not alone', in M. Taber (ed.), *Fidel Castro Speeches: Cuba's Internationalist Foreign Policy 1975–80* (Pathfinder, New York, 1981), p. 142.

19  *Granma*, 27 July 1966.

20  http://www.cuba.cu/gobierno/discursos/1967/esp/f100867e.html (last accessed 2 June 2008).

21  Skierka, *Castro*, pp. 190–1.

22  *Granma*, 13 Jan. 1968.

23  R. Castro, *Desenmascaran la microfacción* (Hoy, Minas (Uruguay), 1968).

24  Dumont, *Is Cuba Socialist?*, pp. 41–7, 61–2, 71–95.

25  *GWR*, 24 March 1968.

26  Brundenius, *Economic Growth*, p. 79.

27  C. Franqui, *Family Portrait with Fidel* (Jonathan Cape, London, 1983), p. 140.

28  Author's conversation with Pablo Armando Fernández, Aug. 1988. Castro admitted later that there had been a lot of discrimination at the time on racial, gender and sexual grounds but claimed he had not been prejudiced himself (Ramonet, *Castro*, pp. 204–7).

29  F. Castro, *Palabras a los intelectuales* (Havana, 1961).

30  One of the leading media criticising intellectuals was *Verde Olivo*. See, for example, the 20 and 27 October 1968 issues.

**31**  K. Artaraz, 'El Ejercicio de Pensar: the rise and fall of *Pensamiento Crítico*', *Bulletin of Latin American Research*, 24(3) (July 2005), pp. 348–66.

**32**  For example, in the fourth Congress of UNEAC reported in *Cuba Socialista*, no. 32 (March–April 1988).

**33**  Teresa Casuso, quoted in T. Szulc, *Fidel: a Critical Portrait* (Hutchinson, London, 1987), p. 274.

**34**  *Verde Olivo*, 6 Oct. 1968, p. 62.

**35**  The allegation of Barbie's involvement is made in a documentary film by Kevin Macdonald, *My Enemy's Enemy* (*The Observer*, 23 December 2007).

**36**  See Castro's introduction to E. Guevara, *El Diario del Che en Bolivia* (Instituto del Libro, Havana, 1968), pp. vii–viii.

**37**  K.S. Karol, *Guerrillas in Power: the Course of the Cuban Revolution* (Hill & Wang, New York, 1970), p. 506.

**38**  J.H. Blight and P. Brenner, *Sad and Luminous Days: Cuba's Struggle with the Superpowers after the Missile Crisis* (Rowman and Littlefield, Lanham, Md., 2002), pp. 35–71.

**39**  *GWR*, 25 Aug. 1968. This important speech is not available on the *Granma* website of Castro's speeches, suggesting that it remains a controversial and sensitive issue.

**40**  For example, P. Bourne, *Castro: a Biography of Fidel Castro* (Macmillan, London, 1987), p. 271 and to some extent Szulc, *Fidel*, pp. 504–5.

**41**  *GWR*, 25 Aug. 1968.

**42**  *Bohemia*, 13 June 1969.

**43**  *GWR*, 26 Oct. 1969.

**44**  Domínguez, *Cuba*, pp. 177–8.

**45**  *Granma*, 27 July 1970.

**46**  Domínguez, *Cuba*, pp. 275–6.

**47**  *Granma*, 27 July 1970.

**48**  *GWR*, 4 Jan. 1976.

# CHAPTER 6

# The Revolutionary Godfather

The abortive sugar harvest campaign of 1969–70 marked the end of a cycle of efforts by the Cuban state to break out of the iron circle of dependency and distorted development through ideological appeal to the Cuban people. At the same time, the exaggerated hopes that the Revolution could be exported to Latin America were dashed by the destruction of most of the continent's guerrilla groups by the end of the decade. From the beginning of the 1970s, the Cuban leaders sought to redirect their foreign policy and reshape Cuba's economic and political structures to accommodate them to the new constraints. One of the most important of these was the increasing dependence on the Soviet Union, without whose aid and trade the Revolution could hardly survive. The deepening economic crisis facing Cuba after the campaign made the leadership all the more sensitive to Soviet pressure for internal reform and a realignment of its foreign policy.

The reforms that followed in the first half of the decade brought Cuba's economic and political institutions into line with those of the Soviet Union. With the cooperation of numerous Soviet advisers, Cuba's economic agencies and enterprises were restructured. A Soviet–Cuban Commission was set up in December 1970 to coordinate the use of Soviet aid, and two years later Cuba became a fully integrated member of the Soviet bloc common market, the Comecon or Council for Mutual Economic Assistance (CMEA). A new system of economic management was gradually evolved and was in operation by the end of the decade. It provided for a certain measure of financial accountability, profitability and materials flow among enterprises, as well as the introduction of a wide range of material incentives. On the political front, a new constitution largely modelled on that of the Soviet Union was approved in a referendum in 1976. It established three pyramids of power, the Council of Ministers or government, the Communist Party headed by the Politburo, and the Organs of People's Power (OPP), an institutional innovation with no obvious parallel in the Soviet system, providing for elected assemblies on a municipal level and indirect suffrage on a provincial level leading to a National Assembly and a Council of State to which the Council of Ministers was accountable.

Some commentators have defined this process of institutionalisation as the 'Sovietisation' of Cuba, ascribing the changes to the influence of Moscow.[1] The Soviet Union under Brezhnev did indeed have several reasons for wishing to bring the island into its fold: Cuba would pose less of a threat to the process of détente with the United States and the cost of supporting the Cuban economy could be spread among other socialist bloc countries. The Kremlin was also in a position to insist on a reorganisation of Cuba's economic institutions as a price of any further underwriting of its economy. Yet it could be argued that the institutional reforms were the result more of the internal dynamic of the Revolution than of Soviet pressure. Throughout the 1960s, Cuba had been governed by a cabinet led by Castro, in which all legislative and executive powers were vested. The Cuban Communist Party, established in 1965, had not functioned as a mass party and indeed would hold its first congress only in 1976. Of the mass organisations, only the Committees for the Defence of the Revolution had grown any popular roots. The Revolutionary leadership had believed that the highly centralised system of government of the 1960s was necessary to ensure the survival of the Revolution in the face of American hostility and to rouse Cuba's workers for the task of development while it guaranteed social equity. Castro and his closest followers saw themselves as the trustees of the Revolution acting on behalf of the Cuban people until they were ready to assume the responsibilities of self-government in a socialist society. As Guevara had written, 'Our aspiration is that the party becomes a mass one, but only when the masses reach the level of development of the vanguard, that is, when they are educated for communism.'[2]

By 1970, however, it was clear that this political model was not functioning well. The most obvious sign, as we have seen, was the widespread absenteeism and the low levels of productivity registered in the summer and autumn. In elections to the Advanced Workers' Movement in the same period, many of the existing holders of the privileged status of exemplary worker were voted out in a tacit display of criticism of this Cuban version of Stakhanovism. Castro was quick to respond to the growing crisis of confidence among Cuban workers. He held a 12-hour debate with workers' representatives in Havana province in September, insisting on the presence of three of his top men, including the Minister of Labour. During the meeting the leaders were treated to a barrage of detailed complaints about the inefficiency of management at all levels. In tune with the new mood of self-criticism, Castro was not sparing in his attacks on excessive centralisation in economic planning, referring to the problem of 'diabolical centralisations'. He took Cuba's technocrats to task, describing them as 'Well-prepared but unrealistic people. That is, they have technological training, they have learnt a bit of mathematics, but they are very underdeveloped as far as the realities of life are concerned.'

However, his most significant criticism was directed against the whole model of accumulation through moral mobilisation that had dominated the policy of the Revolutionary leadership in the 1960s. Using a typically military metaphor, he declared,

*we have to become conscious of the fact that in a time of crisis . . . the Revolution . . . has perhaps advanced too far. It is even perhaps like an army that penetrated too far into the enemy ranks, with troops that were not sufficiently well trained, with soldiers that were still insufficiently warrior-like, and with some very bad commanders. . . . Perhaps our greatest illusion [idealismo] was to have believed that a society that has only just come out of its shell in a world that has been subjected for years to the law of the strongest . . . could become, at a stroke, a society in which everyone behaved in an ethical and moral fashion.[3]*

The process of institutional and economic reform in the 1970s was intended in part to overcome the crisis in the labour movement that had arisen during the sugar campaign. In the 1960s, labour had been viewed as an army, subject to a hierarchy of command. Now Castro was calling for its democratisation. In his concluding speech to the meeting of the Havana province branch of the Confederation of Cuban Workers (CTC), he urged, 'The number one contribution of workers is to democratize themselves, to constitute a strong and powerful labour movement.'[4] The new tone was in sharp contrast to Castro's censoriousness towards workers' representatives during the first congress of the CTC after the Revolution on 18 November 1959. Reprimanding them for the 'shameless spectacle' they had presented when divisions between anti-Communist workers of the 26th July Movement and PSP representatives had risen to the surface, he had exclaimed,

*I had the impression that you were playing with a revolution you held in your hands; I had the sensation – a hard, disagreeable sensation – as of a mass of men, of leaders, in fact, who were not behaving in a responsible way . . . if, indeed, the working-class or its representatives know what they are doing. . . . We have said: the revolution demands that the workers be organized like an army.[5]*

Castro's call for greater democracy in the labour movement, however, was not the expression of a new-found conviction about the virtues of pluralism. Rather, it arose from the urgent need to raise productivity and improve efficiency on the shop floor. Exhortations from the leadership to work harder were no longer enough; new mechanisms were needed to boost production. The labour unions had always been viewed by the leadership not as the defenders of workers' wages and conditions but, in Raúl Castro's words, 'as vehicles for orientation, directives and goals which the revolutionary power must convey to the working masses'.[6] In the late 1960s, the CTC had not been encouraged to grow by the leadership and it had been the Advanced Workers' Movement that had received official publicity.[7] After 1970, in contrast, CTC branches were set up in thousands of workplaces and delegate congresses began to be held regularly. The CTC itself was relaunched in November 1973 with a new structure and statutes. That the call for democracy was more to do with tightening labour discipline than giving rein to rank-and-file demands was borne out by the simultaneous campaign against absenteeism and 'loafing' launched by Castro. From the platform, he railed at the widespread slackness at work, turning his stern gaze on individual workplaces. Issue after issue of the official paper *Granma* in autumn 1970 contained slogans linking democratisation to the campaign against absenteeism, and in the following year an 'anti-loafing' law was passed providing for a range of sanctions against supposedly 'work-shy' people.

Bolstering the labour unions was also intended to enable a new system of work organisation to be introduced as part of the package of economic reforms. The new strategy represented a return to the more orthodox policies essayed briefly between 1963 and 1966. Higher productivity could only come about by offering material incentives to workers and establishing work norms.[8] Castro's call for greater democracy in the labour movement was designed partly to prepare workers for a more rigorous system of control over their work. Describing the round of discussions with workers' representatives in the autumn of 1970, he said that debate and participation would create the appropriate 'mood' for the introduction of new schemes of organization and work norms.[9]

The new emphasis on such things as work quotas, clocking-in and material incentives represented a setback for those in the leadership, not least for Castro himself, who had believed they could infuse the labour movement with a new ethic of patriotic selflessness. The compulsive drive for accumulation had to be slowed down because many workers were not responding to moral appeals. Although Castro calculated that only 20 per cent of workers were 'shirkers', the high rate of absenteeism and the low level of productivity at the turn of the decade suggested that dissatisfaction among workers was more widespread than he acknowledged publicly.[10] The new labour strategy, however, did not mean abandoning moral incentives altogether but finding a different balance between monetary and moral rewards. In a speech on 26 July 1973, Castro defined it thus:

*Together with moral incentive, we must also use material incentive, without abusing either one, because the former would lead us to idealism, while the latter would lead to individual selfishness. We must act in such a way that economic incentives will not become the exclusive motivation of man, nor moral incentives serve to have some live off the work of the rest.*[11]

The reform of the unions was part of a wider restructuring of the political and economic system in Cuba in the 1970s. Like the changes in work practices, the reforms were more a response to the failure of the campaigns of the late 1960s and to the pressures from below that they generated than the result of Soviet pressure. Their interlocking objectives were to decentralise to some extent the administration of government and the management of the economy in order to make them more efficient, and to give the mass of Cubans a greater say in the running of local affairs so that criticism at the base could rise to the top. This was in contrast to the radical period of the late 1960s when, in Castro's words, the idea had prevailed that 'critical comments and the denunciations of errors were playing into the hands of the enemy'.[12] Neither of these aims, however, was intended to lessen the political control of the Party and the Revolutionary leadership.

The three fundamental measures of this institutionalisation were the creation of the OPP as well as the implementation of the new system of management described earlier (*Sistema de Dirección y Planificación de la Economía*) and the reorganisation of the top government posts. The establishment of the OPP devolved many of the bureaucratic functions hitherto performed by the regional administrative bodies to locally elected assemblies at municipal and provincial levels. The new structure allowed a certain measure of democratic control over local affairs. It also represented for the leadership a more reliable system of consultation and assessment of public opinion than the informal procedures they had adopted throughout the 1960s. At a higher level, however, the Communist Party had considerable control over the nomination of candidates to the provincial assemblies and the supreme body of the OPP, the National Assembly. In keeping with the elitist tradition of the Revolution, the higher echelons of the OPP were not intended to represent public opinion but were to be manned by the most active and reliable cadres, who were invariably Party members.

The reorganisation of the government was also a reaction to the policy failures of the 1960s. Until 1972, the most important functions had been concentrated in the hands of a small cabinet consisting of Castro and a handful of leaders of the Revolution. Beneath them, government administration had also been highly centralised: planning and execution of policy had been dealt with centrally in Havana and decisions were passed down through a hierarchy of administration at different levels. Throughout the 1960s, Castro had acted as the Revolution's troubleshooter, ombudsman and animator. Wandering restlessly across Cuba, he had sorted out local problems and launched a multitude of projects that often bypassed or even clashed with plans drawn up by the central Planning Board, *Juceplan*, and the ministries. The French agronomist René Dumont, who accompanied him on several of his trips around the island, observed later: 'Castro's personal ideas constitute another official programme at least as imperative as the first [that of the Planning Board and ministries]. Attempts are therefore made to do everything and what happens is that only a little of everything is done.' Castro's enormous prestige allied to his overriding self-confidence had made it difficult to contradict or reverse his frequent initiatives. Castro, Dumont continued, 'follows his own ideas, convinced that they are the best. Thus he assumes unchecked personal power and this fosters a courtier-like approach in those around him. When he throws his beret on the ground and flies into one of his rages everybody quakes and fears reprisals.'[13]

Although many of Castro's projects were successful, there were others that had negative consequences, diverting precious resources towards abortive experiments. His most costly initiative, as we have seen, had been the sugar campaign of 1969–70. Its result had been not just the dislocation of the economy but a fall in confidence among many Cubans about the direction of the Revolution. The 1970 crisis led to a restructuring of the government to attempt a more rational organisation of the economy. In 1972 the cabinet was enlarged to include an executive committee consisting of a new layer of deputy ministers charged with a range of responsibilities hitherto held by Castro and a handful of his ministers. Alongside the deputy ministers were the heads of the central organisations, such as *Juceplan* and the National Bank. Directly responsible to this newly enlarged cabinet were a number of state organisations of non-ministerial rank and beneath them were provincial and regional boards entrusted with coordinating and executing government decisions.[14] Cuba's administrative structures were further reorganised in 1976 to bring them into line with those of the Soviet bloc. As for Castro, although by 1976 he was at the head of the Party, the Armed Forces and the government (he replaced Dorticós as President on

24 February), he gradually shed direct ministerial responsibilities as the decade progressed.

The administrative reforms thus allowed a greater degree of delegation and specialisation in the higher ranks of the government. The economy was thereby protected from the sometimes disruptive interventions of Castro. But they also helped to shield the President himself from the consequences of policy failures. The officially declared shift from individual to collective leadership helped to give the regime greater stability in the years following the trauma of the abortive sugar campaign. The change in emphasis was signalled by Castro's speech on 26 July 1973. Greatly underplaying his own role in the late 1960s he declared, with reference to the foundation of the Communist Party in 1965,

*we began to advance along the new path, without caudillos, without personalisms, without factions, in a country in which historically division and personality conflict were the cause of great political defeats. . . . If in the uncertain times of the 26th July and in the first years of the Revolution, individuals played a decisive role, that role is now carried out by the Party. Men die, the Party is immortal.*[15]

The reorganisation of government may have put Castro at one remove from many centres of administrative decision-making, but his position at the head of the Revolution, now confirmed in the Constitution, was unquestioned. There is little evidence to suggest that the failure of the sugar campaign seriously undermined his authority, as some commentators have argued.[16] Admittedly, it represented a defeat for his strategy of austerity and patriotic mobilisation, while it strengthened the voice of those calling for more orthodox policies who had been elbowed aside in the radical period of the late 1960s. The return to prominence of notable pre-Revolutionary Communists such as Carlos Rafael Rodríguez, previously Minister Without Portfolio and now chair of the new Soviet–Cuban Commission and Deputy Prime Minister in 1972, indicated an important shift in the balance of interests among the leadership. In a sense, it was a new, more extreme version of the crisis of 1963 when the Revolutionary leadership had been obliged to abandon their drive to industrialise Cuba by forced march. But it would appear now that Castro, as in 1964, was able to regain the initiative by becoming the most eloquent advocate of the new policy. He was also able to recover his prestige through foreign policy initiatives, the most spectacular of which was the campaign in Angola (see Chapter 7). There is no question that Castro was still regarded with affection and respect by most Cubans on the island; as *líder máximo* of the Revolution, he was, for the time being, irreplaceable.

Power relations in the Cuban state, however, were difficult to judge because the internal debates among the leadership were not made available. As a result, any account of relations within the regime has to rely on inference. Some writers on post-1970 Cuba claim on this basis to have identified cleavages among the Revolutionary elite around political and economic tendencies.[17] Yet it is more reasonable to assume that, in contrast to the 1960s when the ideological differences among the supporters of the Revolution had risen to the surface and had been hammered out, the Revolutionary leadership remained a relatively cohesive force in the 1970s. For one thing, the economic base for the emergence of autonomous elites did not exist in Cuba. The new decentralising measures introduced in the 1970s did not reduce the prerogative of the state as the centre of planning and resource allocation. Whereas enterprise managers were given greater powers of decision-making at the level of individual firms, for example, they were still subject to the overall control of the state. Second, all posts of any authority in the Revolutionary institutions, from military officers to government administrators, were subject to the discipline of the Communist Party whose system of democratic centralism ensured that once party policy had been decided it had to be carried out by members regardless of their position in the debate leading to the decision. Moreover, the growth of functional divisions within the regime was limited to some extent by the overlapping roles played by the different institutions. The military, for example, traditionally a relatively independent force in Latin America, was in Cuba strongly represented in the single party of the state and was entrusted at the same time with wide-reaching civilian tasks, ranging from public works engineering to providing unskilled labour for cane-cutting.

In the mid-1970s, 18 people belonging to the top institutions of the state could be described as the most important decision-makers in Cuba. Apart from Castro and his brother Raúl, they were made up of veterans of the rebel army, civilian members of the 26th July Movement and ex-members of the PSP, some of whom had been dropped from prominent public office during the radical period of the late 1960s. Though their political origins were not necessarily important in determining their positions of power, it was significant that the majority had been close collaborators of Castro since at least the beginning of the guerrilla campaign, suggesting that loyalty to the leader of the Revolution was still perceived as an important criterion of political merit. Of the full central committee members elected in the first Congress of the Party in 1976, almost a third were military men, over 28 per cent were Party officials and just under 18 per cent were from the ranks of the administration.[18] Castro's replacement of Dorticós as President, a role he had carried out unofficially from the beginning, meant that as Commander-in-Chief of the Armed Forces, First Secretary of the Party, and President of the Council of State and the Council of Ministers, he was owed allegiance by the military, Party and government officials alike.

There is some limited evidence of political differences in the 1970s among the leadership and within the central committee but these do not seem to have taken organisational form in the same way as the pro-Soviet pre-Revolutionary Communist lobby of the early 1960s. One of the most important sources of tension was the balance between economic and socio-political factors in economic planning. The shift in emphasis after 1970 from social and political values to cost-effectiveness in economic decision-making was bound to give rise to strains not only among the middle-ranking officials charged with carrying out policy but also within the leadership. Although the new line was sanctioned by Castro, he had been, with Guevara, the most vociferous exponent of the primacy of politics over economics. Indeed, he would intervene once again in the mid-1980s, as we shall see, to correct the balance which, in his opinion, had gone too far towards purely quantitative calculations.

For the time being, it was the adherents of a more technical approach to economic planning who spoke out in criticism of the policies of the 1960s. Undoubtedly they included some of the pre-Revolutionary Communists who had frowned on Guevara's ideas in the 1960s and had been excluded from positions of power. But there were also critics within the government. In a speech at Havana University in 1972 Dorticós, an ex-PSP Communist and still President of Cuba, launched into an attack on the economic planners of the 1960s that could well have applied in part to Castro himself: 'during all these years', he said,

*one of the most devalued indicators in our economic planning has been that of costs. It is frequent, it has been frequent up to now . . . to talk at most about having reached such and such a production figure, having accomplished such and such a percentage, or having surpassed the plan. But when you asked one of these officials, or almost all of them, what the costs were, at what cost, with what use of material, human, and financial resources, none of them knew the answer. And this indicated a high degree of irresponsibility . . . as if cost was something of a metaphysical entity.*[19]

Another source of tension among the different interest groups within the regime was budget allocation. The military, in particular, was creaming off a large amount of Cuba's surplus (over 5 per cent of GNP during the

1970s and 1980s) indicating the importance of national defence since the Revolution and of military involvement abroad from the mid-1970s. But this also reflected the key role the military played in the Cuban economy. As the most powerful and professional elite in the state, the military might have become the focus of a separate political tendency were it not for its close involvement in almost all aspects of life in Cuba. The top officials of the military were not only members of the Communist Party subject to its discipline but were also participants in executing economic plans. The dominant feature of the Revolutionary leadership was the interlocking nature of their civic and military functions, best exemplified by the two Castro brothers. Rather than a separate institution, the military was part and parcel of a 'nation in arms'.

Nevertheless, the institutional reforms of the 1970s gave rise to a greater functional separation within the Revolutionary establishment. The continued priority given to the military provoked the occasional complaints of civilian agencies. For example, when Cuba became involved in the war over Angolan independence in 1975, attempts were made by some enterprise managers to resist the compulsory enlistment of skilled workers to the military reserve. Their recalcitrance was made evident in a speech by Castro in which he said that it was necessary 'to combat the occasionally exaggerated criteria as to who cannot be dispensed with in production'.[20]

Yet for all the tensions that existed in the top echelons of the regime in the 1970s, the Cuban leadership remained relatively united. The transition from the centralised and hierarchical model of the 1960s to the more collective government of the mid-1970s onwards was achieved without bloodletting, though not without disagreements. The broader structures of power created in the early 1970s not only enabled the older generation of pre-Revolutionary Communists to return to positions of influence within the regime but also gave access to a new generation of administrators, technicians, officers and party organisers. In fact, the more significant differences within the regime in the years that followed tended to be generational, as we shall examine later. No radical changes of personnel took place in the top echelons of the party and the state during the 1970s that might suggest any shift in the internal balance of power. Demotions occurred as a result of policy failures or supposed incompetence, while promotions tended to reward success, such as the appointment to the Council of State of two generals prominent in the Angolan operations of 1975.

With the reforms of the early 1970s, the leadership of the Revolution thus resembled something of an extended family whose inner nucleus was formed by the veterans of the *Granma* expedition and the Sierra campaign.[21] No longer directly responsible for all its activities, Fidel Castro now assumed the role of godfather to the Revolutionary family. Although he remained the ultimate source of authority and the arbiter of disputes, he was no longer in a position easily to impose policy against any branch of the family. The new constraints on his autonomy derived in part from the renewed influence of the Soviet Union. The integration of Cuba into Comecon and the massive military aid provided by Moscow combined to create strong institutional links between Cuban economic and military personnel and their Soviet and East European counterparts. Consequently, although Castro had been able to act decisively against the pro-Soviet group in 1962 and 1968, the cost of challenging top administrators close to Soviet officials became much higher in the 1970s.[22]

The new institutional framework also made it more difficult for Castro to intervene in areas of responsibility that had been devolved to lower levels of administration. In the mid-1960s, he had launched an anti-bureaucratic drive, declaring, 'the future progress of the Revolution will be measured by the fall each year in the number of administrative employees . . . and by the rise in the number of metal-workers each year in our country'. In the 1970s, on the contrary, he was calling for the strengthening of the state apparatus on the grounds that the excessive weight of the Party in the previous decade had led to inefficiency.[23] As political control over economic agencies receded, the top personnel of the ministries were given greater latitude to run their own affairs within the framework of national planning. Moreover, the new economic organisation espoused by the regime did not require Castro to act any longer as guide and model. He no longer appeared at every opportunity to launch a fresh scheme or explain a new policy, to berate and inspire the Cubans. The shift in Castro's role was expressed in his changing appearance. The image of the young athletic man in battle fatigues with a cigar clenched between his teeth tearing about the countryside in a jeep gave way, as the 1970s progressed, to that of a dignified rather portly statesman in bemedalled army uniform, his beard going grey, presiding over ceremonies for foreign heads of state.

No simple picture, therefore, can be drawn of the structure of power in Cuba in the 1970s. Castro did not pull all the strings, as some Western commentators have argued, but nor was his power confined purely to the functions assigned to him by the Constitution, as official Cuban statements assert. The institutional reforms enshrined his authority as supreme leader but it created new centres of power that Castro could not ignore. Internal policy was thus shaped by a complex interaction between the various branches of the Revolutionary family. It was also strongly influenced by pressures outside the immediate family circle. Not least among these was public opinion, expressed informally or through the mass organisations of the Revolution; after all, it had been the workers' declining enthusiasm for productivity goals that had hastened the reorganisation of the political system in Cuba. Other powerful pressures from outside were the political and economic constraints that accompanied Cuba's increasing integration with the Soviet bloc.

Thus Castro no longer enjoyed the virtually unlimited autonomy to define policy that he had had in the 1960s. It is likely that the policies which he formulated as head of state were the result more of a consensus within the highest ranks of the regime than of the imposition of his own authority. Yet he continued to wield enormous influence on these decisions. In any disagreement, the balance of power was tilted in his direction because he could call on an immense power outside the debating chamber. Castro's ability to override opinions that contradicted his own was at its most limited in the early 1970s. Only when some of these policies faltered, as in the mid-1980s, would he seize the opportunity once again to redirect the course of the Revolution personally.

By his own admission, Castro played little part in the process of institutional reforms. That he was not entirely happy with the way it was done was revealed many years later in an interview with the Italian journalist Gianni Minà. Referring to the change in policy from the radicalism of the late 1960s to the orthodoxy of the early 1970s, he confessed, 'We had gone through a period of self-sufficiency during which we believed we knew more than other people and could do things better than them, and we moved on to another phase, in which I was not personally involved, in which a tendency developed to copy. I believed we copied bad things well and good things badly.'[24] Instead, Castro's energies in the 1970s were consumed in foreign policy. This was not because he was bored by the drab scene confronting him in Cuba, as one biographer suggests.[25] Nor was it merely because the new division of labour within the Cuban government released him from an immediate commitment to the running of the economy. His intense involvement in external relations in the 1970s was the direct result of a shift in Cuba's foreign strategy that accompanied the transformation of internal policy. And in his foreign as in his domestic policies, Castro demonstrated once again his flair for making the best of the opportunities that came his way to raise his own standing and that of the Revolution.

# Notes

1  For example, C. Mesa-Lago, *Cuba in the 1970s: Pragmatism and Institutionalization* (University of New Mexico Press, Albuquerque, 1974); also J.I. Domínguez, *Cuba: Order and Revolution* (Harvard University Press, Cambridge, Mass., 1978).

2  E. Guevara, *Man and Socialism in Cuba* (Book Institute, Havana, 1967).

3  *Granma*, 8 Sept. 1970.

4  *Granma*, 10 Sept. 1970.

5  Quoted in C. Franqui, *Family Portrait with Fidel* (Jonathan Cape, London, 1983), pp. 230–2. The official version of the speech in the online collection of Castro's speeches in *Granma Internacional* does not contain this quote.

6  *Granma Weekly Review (GWR)*, 26 Sept. 1974.

7  *GWR*, 4 Oct. 1970.

8  H. Pérez, *Sobre las dificultades objetivas de la revolución. Lo que el pueblo debe saber* (Política, Havana, 1979).

9  *Granma*, 25 Jan. 1971.

10  *Granma*, 8 Sept. 1970.

11  *GWR*, 5 Aug. 1973.

12  G. Minà, *Il racconto di Fidel* (Mondadori, Milan, 1988), pp. 153–4.

13  R. Dumont, *Is Cuba Socialist?* (Viking Press, New York, 1974), pp. 107 and 111.

14  *Granma*, 25 Nov. 1972.

15  *GWR*, 5 Aug. 1973.

16  For example, Mesa-Lago, *Cuba in the 1970s* and E. González, 'Institutionalization, political elites and foreign policies', in C. Blasier and C. Mesa-Lago (eds), *Cuba in the World* (University of Pittsburgh Press, 1979), pp. 3–36.

17  Mesa-Lago, *Cuba in the 1970s*; González, 'Institutionalization'; Domínguez, *Cuba*. For a critique of these various accounts of power in post-1970 Cuba, see A. Zimbalist (ed.), *Cuban Political Economy: Controversies in Cubanology* (Westview, Boulder, Col. and London, 1988).

18  Domínguez, *Cuba*, pp. 307–15.

19  *Economía y Desarrollo*, May–June 1972, pp. 30–1.

20  *GWR*, 4 Jan. 1976, quoted in Domínguez, *Cuba*, p. 355.

21  The simile has been used in E. González, 'Political succession in Cuba', *Studies in Comparative Communism*, 9 (1 and 2) (Spring–Summer 1976), pp. 80–107, but much of his speculation about tendencies within the leadership is questionable (see C. Bengelsdorf, 'Cubanology and crises: the mainstream looks at institutionalization', in Zimbalist, *Cuban Political Economy*, pp. 212–25).

22  Domínguez, *Cuba*, p. 382.

23  *Verde Olivo*, 5 March 1967, and *GWR*, 4 Jan. 1976.

24  Minà, *Il racconto di Fidel*, p. 142.

25  'He refused to settle for any kind of status quo, and in the second half of 1970 turned away from the depressing domestic scene and its economic problems, to international problems and controversies on which he thrived' (T. Szulc, *Fidel: a Critical Portrait* (Hutchinson, London, 1987), p. 511).

# CHAPTER 7

# The World Statesman

Towards the end of the 1960s, Cuba had stood virtually alone in the world, harassed by the United States, ostracised by most Latin American countries and increasingly frowned on by the Soviet Union. Ten years later, in contrast, the island enjoyed an unprecedented international prestige. Cuba was chosen as the host country for the Sixth Conference of the Non-Aligned Movement in 1979, with Castro as chairman for a four-year period. Thirty-five countries were receiving military and civil aid from Cuba, and like an elder statesman, Castro was giving advice to new revolutionary regimes in different parts of the world.

Cuba's new international influence derived in part from the transformation of the Third World's standing in the 1970s. Three events in particular contributed to this change in the balance of power: the oil crisis, the Vietnam War, and the fall of the Portuguese empire in Africa. The cartel of mainly Third World oil-producing nations took advantage of the growing reliance of industrialised economies on oil to push up the price of crude in 1973, provoking the first major crisis in Western capitalism since the Second World War. The defeat of the United States at the hands of the Vietcong and North Vietnam represented an important psychological boost to the cause of Third World nationalism, diminishing the threat of American intervention overseas. Apart from the Vietnamese and the Cambodians, the Cubans were the ones to benefit most, having felt the marines breathing down their necks for a decade. Thirdly, the 1974 military coup in Portugal led to the dismantling in Africa of the last of the old European colonies and the rise of three new nations. The mood of self-confidence now prevailing in the South encouraged the Cuban leadership to play a new assertive role in world affairs. As David to the American Goliath, Cuba commanded respect in much of the Third World.

The ability of the Cuban regime to influence international events was due in great measure to the Soviet connection. The return of Cuba to the fold of Moscow's loyal allies after 1968 renewed the flow of oil and capital goods from the Eastern bloc as well as military aid and training. It also opened many diplomatic doors. Impelled by a more pragmatic foreign policy than in the 1960s, the Cuban leaders found new allies in the Third World who looked to the Revolution for inspiration and welcomed its foreign aid. But Cuba's intense involvement overseas flowed above all from the immense energies released by the Revolution. Thousands of volunteers poured out of the island on medical, educational, technical and military missions abroad. This diversion of scarce domestic resources towards foreign aid can only be explained by the support of the Cuban people for the internationalist aims proclaimed by the Revolution.

The diplomatic successes of Cuba in the 1970s also owed much to Castro. Freed from the direct management of domestic affairs by the reorganisation of the government, he plunged into an intense schedule of state visits abroad and talks with visiting heads of state in Cuba itself. Castro's visits were not merely ceremonial events but often served to initiate or build closer economic and military ties with allies abroad. While he conducted top-level talks, more concrete bilateral negotiations were dealt with by the next layer of Cuba's leaders – Osvaldo Dorticós, while he was still President, Raúl Castro as Minister of the Armed Forces and the much-respected senior politician Carlos Rafael Rodríguez, who was in charge of economic and diplomatic foreign relations. Beneath these lay the ministries and alongside them the powerful planning and military commissions linking Cuba and the Soviet bloc.

Although he had to work within these institutional constraints, Castro enjoyed more autonomy in the formulation of foreign policy than in domestic affairs, not merely because he was directly responsible for external relations as head of state but also because he had always been the most decided advocate of the Revolution's international vocation. Although all policy was presented as the fruit of collective decision, a number of typically Castroist features can be identified in Cuba's foreign policy that suggest he exercised a decisive influence over its development. The most important of these was the stress on international solidarity. The primacy of politics over economics was one of Castro's enduring principles in domestic affairs: the same ideological component can be found in Cuban foreign policy in the 1970s and 1980s. Puzzled by the apparent absence of self-interest in much of Cuba's international involvement, some commentators have seen it as an expensive idiosyncrasy; others explain it away by arguing that Cuba was merely acting as the Soviet Union's surrogate abroad.[1] Castro himself claimed that Cuban foreign policy was motivated by the highest principles. In a conversation with foreign correspondents in 1983, he declared,

*we are not very nationalistic; we are patriots . . . and we are resolutely faithful to our political principles. Many times we have known how to sacrifice our national interests for the sake of the principles of our revolution and our internationalist principles. North Americans do not understand that, it puzzles them . . . our homeland is not just Cuba; our homeland is also humanity. We are learning to think in terms of humanity.*[2]

Yet it can be argued that Castro's foreign policy responded to a more concrete objective than human solidarity and a more nationalistic role than that of the Soviet Union's agent abroad. In the 1960s, he had sought unsuccessfully to consolidate the Revolution by spreading it abroad and creating a solid economy at home. His foreign policy in the 1970s, on the other hand, was the pursuit of independence by mainly diplomatic means. Castro's long-term strategy was to forge unity between Third World countries, in particular in Latin America, in order to alter the unfavourable terms of trade between developed and underdeveloped nations. In numerous speeches and interviews, he suggested that the fundamental division in the world was between the underdeveloped South and the industrialised North.[3] Like the Maoists he saw the world as a collection of competing nations organised politically into blocs but separated by a more important division between rich and poor countries, or capitalist and proletarian nations. Although solidarity towards the exploited of all lands was repeatedly stressed, it was nation or people rather than class that defined policy. From this perspective, anti-imperialism was more important than anti-capitalism, and the attitude adopted towards the United States defined friend or foe. Hence Castro supported the Dergue, the pro-Soviet military regime in Ethiopia, and later defended General Noriega of Panama and the Argentine military junta during the Malvinas or Falklands War.[4]

Castro's diplomatic ventures served a dual purpose: to raise Cuba's standing in the world and to consolidate the regime at home. His renewed popularity in Cuba in the 1970s, after the crisis of 1969–70, owed a lot to his ostentatious display of world statesmanship. He continued to be admired as the man who had restored national pride by taking on the United States; now, increasingly, he was also seen as an international statesman who was giving Cuba a new standing in the world community. It was a diplomatic circus to compensate for the lack of bread, although it was also a cause that Castro felt strongly about. Much prominence was given to his travels abroad and to the state visits of Third World leaders who came in growing numbers to Cuba. Castro's expansive gestures, embracing foreign statesmen, berating Cuba's enemies on international platforms and giving lengthy interviews to a stream of fascinated foreign correspondents and politicians, were meant as much for domestic as for international consumption.

Cuba's new foreign policy in the 1970s was the result not of Soviet pressure so much as a re-evaluation of existing policy in the light of changing circumstances abroad. Three objectives may be singled out. First, Castro and the Cuban leaders continued to seek new alliances in the Third World through military missions and foreign aid programmes whose dual purpose was to end Cuba's isolation in the international community and lessen its dependence on the Soviet Union. At the same time, they aimed to increase their leverage over the Soviet Union by becoming its indispensable ally in the Third World. By doing so, they hoped to give themselves greater autonomy in the formulation of domestic and foreign policy while ensuring the continued economic support of the Soviet Union. Thirdly, they made repeated attempts to open a dialogue with Washington in order to ease the pressure of the embargo that the United States continued to impose on Cuba. These three objectives were not always compatible, and throughout the 1970s Castro's skill as a politician was employed to squeeze the maximum advantage out of Cuba's foreign involvement without undermining them.[5]

Although Cuban foreign policy in the 1960s had asserted Cuba's own revolutionary experience as a model for Latin America, the new strategy recognised that there were different paths towards national emancipation depending on local circumstances. Castro's pronouncements in the two Declarations of Havana in the early 1960s had acknowledged that both the military and the Catholic Church could play a progressive role in the struggle for national assertion and reform in Latin America. The rise on the continent of a reformist current in the armed forces, exemplified by the military regime in Peru, and the emergence of a new movement in the Latin American Church placing stress on the struggle for social justice strengthened the belief that change would come about through an alliance of different social forces and no longer principally through guerrilla action.[6] The victory of the Popular Front in Chile under Salvador Allende seemed to vindicate the parliamentary road to socialism propounded by the Soviet Union and the orthodox Communist parties. Castro's own experience in the early 1950s had led him to the opposite conclusion that only armed action could bring about radical change. The history of Cuba suggested that the electoral process could too easily be perverted by corruption or destroyed by the military. Yet Castro was now cautiously acknowledging that in certain circumstances elections could be the centrepiece of a revolutionary strategy.

Castro articulated his new position during his three-week trip to Chile in November 1971. It was his first visit abroad for several years and it was a triumph. Received with open arms by the new President Allende and greeted everywhere by enthusiastic crowds, he toured the length of the narrow land, addressing students, copper and coal miners, nitrate workers, farm labourers and mass audiences gathered in stadiums. With his characteristic blend of didacticism and vivid detail he expounded his views on a multiplicity of themes, displaying his ability to remember technical minutiae and to marshal statistics. He was asked repeatedly if he supported the Chilean path to socialism considering that it contradicted the Cuban experience. 'Not only did we find no contradiction', he said in answer to a question from a trade-union leader,

*but we also had seen a possibility concerning the concrete and real conditions that existed at the time of the elections [in Chile]. And this is the way we will always look with satisfaction on every new variation that may appear. And let every variation in the world make its appearance! If all roads lead to Rome, we can only wish for thousands of roads to lead to Revolutionary Rome!*[7]

Yet Castro was still not convinced about the possibility of a peaceful road to socialism. Nor had he lost his instinctive grasp of the relations of power. While he praised Allende's victory, he implicitly criticised the Chilean President's failure to mobilise popular organisations against the growing menace of the Right. Almost two years after his visit, on the eve of the September 1973 military coup, he wrote to Allende urging him to use the organised strength of the working class to halt the impending coup. Two weeks after the military had seized power, he declared in a mass rally in Cuba, 'The Chilean example teaches us the lesson that it is impossible to make the revolution with the people alone: arms are also necessary! And that arms alone aren't enough to make a revolution: people are also necessary.'[8]

He was not advocating social revolution, however. In his words to Chilean workers he continually stressed that they should subordinate their demands to the 'national interest'. Indeed, he implied that any battle they waged to improve their conditions would be a diversion from the war against imperialism. In other words, the struggle for the rights of workers or any other section of society was not part of the struggle against imperialism and indeed could undermine it. Thus Castro reminded the copper workers of the damage they could do to the Chilean economy by coming out on strike. Instead, he advocated the broadest possible alliance of classes, from workers to the 'progressive sectors of the national bourgeoisie', to combat US imperialism. The inherent contradiction in his argument was that in practice social and political struggles could not be separated; to dampen workers' struggles was also to demobilise the most powerful obstacle against a military coup. Moreover, it was a typical section of the petty bourgeoisie, the Chilean lorry-owners who provoked the crisis that led to the military takeover in 1973.

Castro's stress on the importance of national unity in Chile revealed that beneath his profession of proletarian internationalism lay a more powerful undercurrent of Pan-American nationalism that drew its inspiration from Bolívar and Martí. This vision assumed an underlying unity between all sections of society in Latin America except the most reactionary and oligarchic forces who, he argued, would not survive without the support of imperialism. 'For America to be united and become Our America, the America Martí spoke of, it will be necessary to eradicate the very last vestige of those reactionaries who want the peoples to be weak so they can hold them in oppression and in subjection to foreign monopolies.'

During his tour, Castro painted a picture of a free and united Latin America that would organise the exchange of commodities on a rational, cooperative basis. As usual, his illustrations of broad political ideas were vivid and calculated to relate to the immediate experience of his listeners. Speaking to workers of the nitrate mines in northern Chile, he explained how, because of the trade sanctions imposed against Cuba, Chile had been forced to invest large sums of money to produce beet sugar while Cuba had had to invest tens of millions of dollars in order to buy and produce nitrogen fertiliser, the end-product of the mineral the miners dug out of the mountain. From examples such as these, Castro drew an alluring picture of a Latin American common market, 'a union of sister nations that may become a large and powerful community in the world of tomorrow'.[9]

The renewal of hemispheric nationalism in many parts of Latin America and the Caribbean in the wake of the 1973 oil embargo by OPEC nations against the West seemed to corroborate Castro's words. The Cuban regime's moderation towards Latin America was in part a reflection of this new reality. The new policy also opened many diplomatic doors. Cuba began to be accepted once more into the community of Latin American nations after its isolation in the previous decade. From 1972, Cuba re-established contacts with Latin American and Caribbean countries and shortly afterwards joined several regional development organisations. In 1975 the Latin American Economic System (SELA) was set up by 25 countries including Cuba in an attempt to coordinate economic policy and reduce their dependence on the United States. Three months previously, the Caribbean Committee of Development and Co-operation had been established in Havana after reciprocal state visits between Castro and the prime ministers of Jamaica, Guyana and Trinidad-Tobago. In the same year, the Organisation of American States (OAS) voted to lift its sanctions against Cuba, though Castro had made clear that the island would never join the US-dominated organisation.

As the most decided opponent of US hegemony in Latin America, Castro welcomed the new initiatives. In the new multilateral organisations, Cuba could help to wean its fellow nations from the influence of the United States, as well as provide a bridge between Latin America and the Soviet bloc. In fact, the advantages for Cuba of membership in these hemispheric bodies were more political than economic. Castro's hopes for the emergence of a new economic bloc in Latin America underestimated the fact that the markets for Cuban products and the advanced technology necessary for the island's development were concentrated in the West, and in particular in Cuba's arch-enemy, the United States. Moreover, Latin American countries shared on the whole a similar pattern of economic activity centred on the production and processing of raw materials and the manufacture of consumer goods, with the result that their economies were more competitive than complementary.[10] For the time being, Cuba continued to depend on the Soviet Union for energy supplies and technology. If the island were to realise its economic potential a fundamental transformation of US–Cuban relations would have to take place. The United States held the key to Cuba's development; it could provide the goods, the credits, the technology and the tourist trade that Cuba so badly needed.

Yet Washington continued to regard the Cuban regime as a risk to US security and foreign policy goals, out of all proportion to Castro's real capacity to influence international events. US policy towards Cuba was still shaped partly by a gut reaction to the traumatic events of 1959–62. But it was also based on the belief that Castroism represented a threat to its major objective of encouraging the spread of Western capital to the Third World. Though there was some pressure within business circles in the United States to normalise relations with Cuba, Washington continued to insist on major concessions in internal and external policy on the part of the Cuban government as a price of détente between the two countries.

The necessity for a rapprochement with the United States was a bitter pill for Castro but one he had always been prepared to swallow. It may well have been urged on him at this time by the Soviet Union as part of its search for East–West détente. Pressure may also have been exerted by the more pragmatic tendencies within the economic agencies of the Cuban government.

Moreover, the US embargo represented a continuous source of anxiety for Cubans. There were numerous flash-points such as the air and maritime hijackings on both sides and the occasional seizure of Cuban fishing vessels by US gunboats. The thaw in US–Cuban relations began indeed with an anti-hijacking agreement signed in 1973 with the Ford administration and continued with secret talks in the following year initiated by Kissinger under the Carter government, while the US government finally relaxed trade restrictions, under pressure from American business interests.[11] In 1975, the United States joined with the majority of the OAS states in voting to end sanctions against Cuba.

However, Castro was not prepared to allow détente with the United States to detract from his objective of alliance-building in the Third World. When the Popular Movement for the Liberation of Angola (MPLA) appealed to Cuba for military aid in 1975 the Cuban leaders responded immediately. The MPLA's assumption of power had been threatened by a South African military incursion in support of right-wing guerrillas. The Cuban government reacted by airlifting 1,000 troops to help defend the capital, Luanda. It was not a move calculated to appeal to the United States. Contrary to what Kissinger maintained, the US was well informed about South Africa's covert invasion plans and CIA agents had collaborated in the operation.[12] When, in addition, Cuba sponsored a conference in Havana in support of Puerto Rican independence, the rapprochement with the United States ground to a halt.

The gains that flowed from Cuba's intervention in the Angolan civil war far outweighed the losses following the breakdown of talks with the United States. The conflict in Angola had arisen on the eve of the country's independence from Portugal. The three guerrilla movements that had fought against the Portuguese had signed an agreement in Alvor in January 1975 calling for a provisional tripartite government and the holding of elections in the same year. It was generally recognised that the MPLA, a left-wing nationalist movement loosely aligned with the Soviet Union and by far the most popular of the three organisations in Angola, would win a large majority of the votes. Its rivals, however, backed by covert CIA aid and South African, Zaïrean and mercenary troops, broke the agreement and launched a two-pronged military offensive against the MPLA, who controlled the capital. In August, South African troops crossed into Angola and in October, on the eve of independence day, launched an all-out drive on Luanda. The rapid Cuban air- and sea-lift that followed the MPLA's direct request to Castro helped to hold the capital. More than 20,000 Cuban troops crossed the Atlantic during the crisis; the flow of arms and soldiers was so great that

Cuba itself was left exposed. By the end of November, the South African troops and the two rival guerrilla organisations were on the retreat, and four months later the MPLA was in control of most of the newly independent Angola.

Most accounts agree that the Cuban decision to send troops to Angola was taken without consulting the Soviet Union.[13] The Cubans had had close contact with the MPLA ever since Che Guevara had trained Congolese guerrillas in 1965. After MPLA leaders had attended the Tricontinental Conference in Havana in the following year, some of their guerrillas had received military training in Cuba. Castro and the Cuban leadership strongly identified with the struggle in Angola on several other accounts. Cuba had deep cultural and ethnic roots in Africa through the Cuban descendants of African slaves. The military expedition to Angola was in keeping with the official Afro-Cuban discourse of the Revolution.[14] The MPLA was a movement in the mould of the Cuban regime, favouring state control of the economy and political centralisation. Cuba's military aid to the MPLA, moreover, increased its prestige among non-aligned nations, raising the hope that it could exert an even greater influence in the Third World. It was no coincidence that, less than four years later, Havana would be the venue of the Sixth Conference of the Non-Aligned Movement and Castro its new chairman.

The rewards of Cuban intervention were even greater on a domestic level. Though the intervention caused inevitable strains as the human cost of military involvement rose, the victory in Angola was a reaffirmation of the strength of the Revolution for many Cubans and a welcome source of national pride after the reverses of the late 1960s and early 1970s. Though he did not control military operations, Castro played a prominent role in the war as a military adviser and overall Commander-in-Chief of the Armed Forces. According to his friend, the Colombian writer Gabriel García Márquez, Castro

*saw off all the ships, and before each departure he gave a pep talk to the soldiers. He personally had picked up the commanders of the battalion of special forces that left in the first flight and had driven them himself in his Soviet jeep to the foot of the plane ramp. There was no spot on the map of Angola that he couldn't identify or a physical feature that he hadn't memorised. His concentration on the war was so intense and meticulous that he could quote any figure on Angola as if it were Cuba, and he spoke of Angolan cities, customs, and people as if he had lived there his entire life.*

In the early part of the operation, García Márquez recalls,

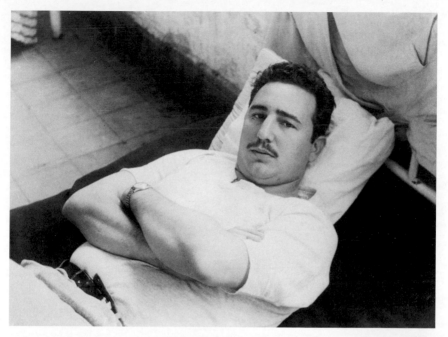

1. Castro rests on a cot during his detention in Mexico in July 1956. © Bettmann/Corbis

2. In the Sierra Maestra in 1959. Behind the bespectacled Castro, Celia Sánchez, and on his left Camilo Cienfuegos. © Alejandro Ernesto/EFE/Corbis

3. Castro with Che Guevara, then President of the Cuban National Bank, and Soviet First Deputy Premier Anastas Mikoyan during his visit to Havana in 1960. © Bettmann/Corbis

4. The bear hug. Castro and Khrushchev at the General Assembly of the UN in 1960. Corbis

5. Castro launches the 1965 Baseball Championship in Havana's Latin American Stadium.
© Hulton-Deutsch Collection/Corbis

6. Castro and Gorbachev embrace during the Soviet Premier's state visit to Cuba in 1989.
© Sygma/Corbis

7. Synchronising secular and sacred time. Castro and John Paul II during the Pope's visit to Cuba in 1998. © Reuters/Corbis

8. The Elián road show. Castro and Elián González during a graduation ceremony in 2004. © Claudia Daut/Reuters/Corbis

9. Castro with the Venezuelan President Hugo Chávez and Evo Morales, later President of Bolivia, at a meeting on the Bolivarian Alternative for the People of Our America (ALBA) in Havana in April 2005. © Claudia Daut/Reuters/Corbis

10. A rare glimpse in 2005 of Castro's wife, Dalia Soto del Valle, mother of five of his sons.
© Jose Goitia/Corbis

11. Chávez with the convalescent Castro on his 80th birthday in 2006.
© Cuba Debate/epa/Corbis

12. Cuba without Fidel. Raúl Castro, acting President of Cuba in 2006, looks at the empty chair of Fidel Castro during a session of Cuba's parliament in December. © epa/Corbis

*Castro remained up to fourteen hours straight in the operations room of the*
*general staff, at times without eating or sleeping, as if he were in the battlefield*
*himself. He followed the details of every battle with coloured pins on the detailed*
*maps which covered the walls, and remained in constant communication with*
*the top commands of the MPLA in a battlefield with a six-hour difference.*[15]

Cuba's military intervention in Angola must also have raised the value of
Havana in the Kremlin's calculations because Moscow could claim not to be
involved. After the 'adventurism' of the Khrushchev years, the Soviet Union
had been carrying out a cautious process of détente with the United States
under the Brezhnev leadership. Its pursuit of rapprochement with the West,
however, was at cross-purposes with Castro's long-term policy of reshaping
relations between the North and South. For the Soviets, Third World politics
were important only to the extent that they affected the balance of power
between the United States and the socialist bloc. For Castro, though he
intoned the ritual of Soviet doctrine, the key issue of world politics was the
problem of underdevelopment and imperialism. Underlying their difference
in strategy lay a deeper, unspoken division about the nature of revolutionary
change.

Soviet orthodoxy continued to maintain that the worldwide triumph of
socialism was inevitable because the internal contradictions of capitalism
would lead to its collapse. The strategy of peaceful coexistence was seen not
as a disavowal of the struggle between the two systems but as a prerequisite
of the eventual victory of socialism. Castro, on the contrary, continually
laid stress on the importance of subjective conditions in the creation of a
revolutionary situation. The Cuban Revolution could only be explained in
these terms; hence the strategy in the 1960s of exporting the Cuban model
to Latin America. Moreover, détente between East and West threatened to
leave the South out in the cold. It is hard not to suspect that Castro's accommodation in the 1970s to the Soviet doctrine of peaceful coexistence was
against his better judgement. His words to Brezhnev in July 1972 had a
hollow ring to them: 'We fully agree with you, Comrade Brezhnev, when you
say that the principle of peaceful co-existence and the successes obtained in
this field can by no means lead to a weakening of the ideological struggle,
which will increase and become more acute in the confrontation of the two
systems.'[16]

Nevertheless, events in Africa from the mid-1970s encouraged the Soviet
leaders to become more involved in that continent even at the risk of
provoking the United States. In this renewal of intervention abroad, the
interests of Cuba and the Soviet Union converged. Cuba's credentials as an

anti-imperialist Third World country were useful to the Soviet Union, while the Cuban leaders, by their material support for Soviet policies in Africa, were able to gain leverage over Moscow. Far from acting as the Kremlin's surrogate abroad, however, the Cuban leaders were able to pursue an independent foreign policy so long as it did not clash with that of the Soviet Union. The Angolan connection, for example, was not a high priority for the Kremlin, and the evidence suggests that it was Cuba, and Castro in particular, who took the initiative and encouraged greater Soviet involvement.[17]

Cuba's participation in the 1977–8 war between Ethiopia and Somalia, on the other hand, responded more to Soviet than Cuban interests. The Horn of Africa represented an area of great geo-strategic value for the USSR. As an ally of the Somali military regime for several years, the Soviet Union had had a naval base at Berbera on the Gulf of Aden. Events in the Horn of Africa in the mid-1970s precipitated a dramatic turn-about of international alliances in the area. In 1974 the US-backed regime of the Emperor Haile Selassie in neighbouring Ethiopia was overthrown by a military coup. The new junta that replaced the old regime, the Dergue, was itself taken over by radical officers three years later. The United States responded by cutting off its aid to Ethiopia, to which the Dergue replied by turning to the Soviet Union for arms. In its turn, the Somali regime, which had a long-standing dispute with Ethiopia over Somali claims to the Ogaden desert in the south, switched its allegiance to the United States. The change in partners also affected the civil war in Ethiopia between the government and the Eritrean Liberation Front. Having previously supported the territorial integrity of Ethiopia, the United States now backed the Eritrean independence movement.

The Soviet Union had sought to reconcile both sides in an effort to maintain its new influence in the region. In March 1977, acting almost certainly with the blessing of Moscow, Castro visited both the Ethiopian and the Somali leaders to seek a settlement.[18] In June, however, the Somali forces, newly armed by the United States, invaded the Ogaden desert. In a move to legitimise its growing military support for Ethiopia, the Kremlin asked for Cuban troops to be involved in the campaign to push the Somali army out of the Ogaden. Strengthened by 15,000 Cuban soldiers and massive Soviet arms shipments, the Ethiopian forces launched a counter-offensive and by February 1978 had driven the Somali army back across the frontier.

Castro had originally supported Somali claims against Ethiopia. The radical shift in the Ethiopian regime in 1977, which brought to power a socialist-aligned junta, presented him with a dilemma. The subsequent about-turn in his policy towards the Horn of Africa could be justified on the grounds that Somalia had transgressed international law by invading the

Ogaden. However, it was more difficult to explain away Cuba's alignment with a regime that was conducting a war of attrition against an oppressed national minority in Ethiopia, the Eritreans, who should have and indeed had once commanded Castro's support. Whereas the Soviet Union had an obvious interest in maintaining the territorial integrity of Ethiopia against secessionist claims because Eritrea commanded a strategic stretch of the Red Sea coast, Cuba had only Soviet goodwill to gain from its military involvement in Ethiopia. Castro attempted to resolve the contradiction by ensuring that Cuban troops were not engaged in the war against the Eritrean Liberation Front and by calling for a semi-autonomous status for Eritrea within Ethiopia. Nevertheless, his support for the Ethiopian military junta could not fail to mar his reputation among some Third World nations.

The price that Cuba was forced to pay for its international alignment with the Soviet Union was at its highest when the Soviets intervened in Afghanistan in December 1979. The invasion could not have come at a worse moment for Castro. The year 1979 had represented a climax in his career as a world statesman. In March, a coup in the neighbouring island of Grenada had brought to power a close ally of his, the popular Maurice Bishop, and in July the old dictator of Nicaragua, Anastasio Somoza, had been overthrown by an insurrection led by the Havana-aligned liberation movement, the Sandinistas. In September, Castro had risen before the representatives of 94 countries and liberation movements that formed the Non-Aligned Movement to make the keynote speech as chairman and host of its sixth conference in Havana. In all these events, Castro was able to demonstrate the new moderation of Cuba's foreign policy. As a kind of elder revolutionary statesman to the new Nicaraguan regime, he enjoined the Sandinistas to be realistic in their policies. They needed to reconstruct the war-devastated economy of Nicaragua with the cooperation of all sectors of society, which meant, Castro implied, maintaining a mixed economy and a pluralist political system. In addition, he urged them to keep up good relations with the United States.[19]

Castro's speech at the conference of the Non-Aligned Movement had also been notable for the tone of conciliation it had adopted towards member countries with which Cuba had differences. Since the 1973 conference in Algiers, he had been the main spokesman of the thesis that the Soviet bloc was the natural ally of the Third World against Western imperialism, as against the argument put forward by China, among others, that the Soviet Union and the United States were both imperialist powers. Conscious that he could not carry many of the member countries with him at the conference, Castro had no longer insisted on Soviet alignment but instead had gone out of his way to reassure the assembly that Cuba would respect the different views represented there.[20]

Cuba's official support for Soviet intervention in Afghanistan, barely three months after the conference, deeply undermined Castro's claim to the moral leadership of the Third World. He was faced by a dilemma. Afghanistan had been a founder member of the Non-Aligned Movement and for Cuba to sanction the massive intervention of Soviet troops in what was clearly a civil war was to make a nonsense of its non-aligned status, especially when it had the role of head of the Movement. At the same time, Cuba could not oppose the Soviet action without endangering its relationship with Moscow. When the Non-Aligned Movement came to vote on a UN resolution condemning the intervention, Cuba was among the nine nations that backed the Soviet Union against 56 that supported the resolution. Despite Cuban efforts to tone down support for the invasion, Castro's standing in the Third World was shaken.[21]

For Castro the Afghan events of 1979 must have evoked the ghost of the 1968 invasion of Czechoslovakia. But now, as then, Cuban support for the Soviet action was not simply the result of Moscow's dictates. Like several military regimes in the Third World, including the Ethiopian Dergue and for a time the Somali junta, the Afghan government was seen by Castro as a progressive force, not merely because it was aligned with Moscow but because it was carrying out a programme of social reforms in an immensely poor and backward society. The collapse of the regime, he argued, would destroy this on-going revolution and hand the country over to pro-Western fundamentalists. As with Czechoslovakia, the cause of instability in Afghanistan was blamed on the machinations of the CIA rather than on its internal contradictions. The Soviet invasion of Afghanistan, as of Czechoslovakia, was therefore justified, in Castro's eyes, on more important grounds than sovereignty. As he put it, 'I think Afghanistan can be a non-aligned country, but one where the revolutionary regime is maintained. If a solution is sought that is based on the idea that Afghanistan should go back to the old regime and sacrifice the revolution, then, unfortunately, I don't think there will be peace there for a long time.'[22] For all his genuine belief that the Kabul regime had to be defended at all costs, Castro must have been well aware that his support for the Soviet action undid much of his effort to become a Third World leader. It was enough to deprive him of a seat on the UN Security Council that would have gone to him in all likelihood as Chairman of the Non-Aligned Movement.

The setback coincided with renewed tensions with the United States. Castro had continued to seek a rapprochement with Washington that would not cripple his efforts to build alliances in the Third World. In the first two years of the Carter administration the Cuban leaders had made strenuous attempts to improve relations with the United States. The upshot was an agreement to set up interest sections in Havana and Washington and a series of accords over fishing rights. Secret negotiations were held over 18 months behind the Soviet back between Castro and Carter's emissaries, led by the Cuban exile businessman Bernardo Benes. They resulted in Castro's offer to allow Cuban exiles to visit relatives on the island and to begin the release of political prisoners. Even as the Cubans began to implement their offer, the Carter administration was sending out confused signals. The hawkish National Security Advisor Zbigniew Brzezinski was unwilling to engage in talks because he was particularly concerned about the Cuban presence in Africa, while his colleague Secretary of State Cyrus Vance was showing some interest in the negotiations with Cuba.[23] Thus the Carter administration showed itself willing to improve relations with Havana but was insisting on concessions on Cuba's part, such as the withdrawal of its troops from Angola, that the Cuban leaders could hardly be expected to make unilaterally. The US demand for Cuban disengagement from Africa provoked Castro into one of his defiant bursts of moral righteousness. Speaking to the National Assembly of People's Power in December 1977, he reminded delegates of the double standards of the United States:

*What moral basis can the United States have to speak about Cuban troops in*
*Africa? What moral basis can a country have whose troops are on every continent*
*. . . ? What moral basis can the United States have to speak about our troops*
*in Africa when their own troops are stationed right here on our own national*
*territory, at the Guantánamo naval base? . . . It would be ridiculous for us to tell*
*the United States government that, in order for relations between Cuba and the*
*United States to be resumed or improved, it would have to withdraw its troops*
*from the Philippines, or Turkey, or Greece, or Okinawa, or South Korea.*[24]

Between 1979 and 1981, when Reagan assumed the presidency, tensions between Cuba and the United States rose to their highest pitch since the missile crisis of 1962. The main trouble centred on attempts by disaffected Cubans to leave the island. A spate of maritime hijackings had taken place against which the US authorities acted faint-heartedly. In April 1980, a small group of Cubans crashed a truck through the gates of the Peruvian Embassy in Havana with the aim of asking for asylum, and a Cuban policeman was killed in the crossfire. Irked by the failure of the Peruvians to hand over the gatecrashers, the authorities withdrew all their guards and a few days later almost 10,000 would-be refugees entered the Embassy. Carter exacerbated the situation by stating that the United States would welcome these 'freedom-loving' Cubans with open arms. The Cuban leaders retaliated by authorising the mass exodus of citizens seeking to emigrate. In a sea-lift operation organised by Miami-based exiles with the agreement of the Cuban authorities, thousands of small boats sailed across to the port of Mariel to pick up the crowds of Cubans who had applied to leave the country. There were violent clashes between the would-be refugees and militants of the Committees for the Defence of the Revolution, who showered them with insults, calling them *gusanos* or worms. More than four months passed and over 100,000 Cubans emigrated before the sea-lift was suspended after Cuba and the United States agreed to resume negotiations.

The Mariel episode, the second such crisis since the Camarioca incident of October 1965 when the government allowed 300,000 people to be boatlifted to Florida, was a traumatic event for Castro. He was clearly taken by surprise at the scale of disaffection that it revealed. Moreover, it coincided with a period of deep private mourning. His constant companion and aide for the previous 23 years, Celia Sánchez, one of several remarkable women who had rallied to Castro's side in the mid-1950s, had died of lung cancer three months previously. She had proved particularly effective in the Sierra Maestra campaign and since then had worked with him as he moved from one abode to another for security reasons and out of a restless habit he had acquired even before the guerrilla campaign. It is not clear whether she had been Castro's lover. He had had several love affairs and in the early 1960s had met Dalia del Soto Valle during the literacy campaigns when she was a teacher in Trinidad. Del Soto had lived with him since then and together they had had five sons. But by all accounts, Sánchez had also furnished some sort of domestic framework for the eccentric and irregular life Castro chose to lead, and quite possibly had provided, along with Del Soto, an emotional stability that helped to ground his volatile nature. There was no obvious sign, however, that the personal loss of Sánchez had affected his political judgement, as has been suggested.[25]

Indeed, Castro was able to turn the potentially damaging incident of the Mariel boatlift to some advantage. The extensive coverage given to the Peruvian Embassy episode and the so-called *marielitos* by the international media and the tales of woe told to US journalists by the newly arrived emigrants were very bad publicity for the Revolution. Yet Castro called the US bluff by mobilising on to the streets the sort of mass support for the regime that appeared to give the lie to claims that there was widespread disaffection among the Cuban population. The exodus also created serious problems for the US government, not only because of the difficulty of integrating so many immigrants but also because many people with minor criminal records and others released by Cuba from prison and psychiatric institutions had joined the evacuation. Castro had dismissed the self-appointed refugees as the dregs of society or the 'lumpen' elements of Cuba, but the motives of the majority of the emigrants were no different from those of others who left the Caribbean islands and Central America to seek a more prosperous life in the United States.[26] Yet the US authorities could not tolerate admitting criminals and mentally ill patients even though the US had offered automatic asylum to all Cubans under the 1966 Cuban Adjustment Act. Thus the Mariel incident left them with several thousand Cubans to whom they could not offer immigrant status nor send back for lack of any protocol with Cuba. Instead they kept them in jail without charge. Finally, some four years later in December 1984, the Reagan administration reached an accord with Cuba, the first immigration agreement between the US and Cuba, whereby the US offered 20,000 visas a year to would-be Cuban emigrants and Cuba agreed to receive those whom the US had refused to accept.[27]

Castro's language in the public forum in this period revealed how much he had been rattled by the Mariel affair. There was no lack of motives for exasperation at the behaviour of the US government which had first failed to respond to Cuban overtures about the emigration problem and then happily turned the whole episode against the Cuban government. In a speech in June, Castro denied that anyone convicted of a violent crime had been allowed to leave but accused the United States of sheltering the real criminals, those Batista henchmen responsible for murder and torture. Angrily he declared, 'Well, let them receive the lumpen now, the thieves of chickens and sheep and pigs and a few other things. Why the former and not the latter? Where is the morality in all this? . . . It's pure hypocrisy.'[28] The whole incident, however, did suggest that the Cuban leaders were out of touch with the feelings of many of their fellow citizens. The subsequent lifting of rationing on many food items and the introduction of free farmers' markets were the most visible by-product of this traumatic episode.

The advent of the Reagan administration in 1981 had brought about a new low in US–Cuban relations. Cuba was seen by the new US government as a Soviet surrogate, and any re-opening of negotiations between the two countries was made dependent on the impossible demand that Cuba abandon its Soviet connection. Reagan further refused to renew the fishing agreement of 1977 and tightened the trade embargo on Cuba. In spite of the new burst of Cold War rhetoric emanating from the White House, Castro and the Cuban leaders continued quietly to seek talks with the United States without making any preconditions. Partly in order to further this process, Cuba drastically cut down on its military aid to Nicaragua and the Salvadorean rebels and began calling for a political solution in El Salvador after the 1981 offensive of the Farabundi Martí Liberation Movement had failed to dislodge the US-backed government army. Bernardo Benes once again would lead informal negotiations with Castro and his aides in 1985. He brought with him an apparent offer on the part of Reagan to lift the embargo and approve a new sugar quota as long as Cuba ceased its efforts to export the Revolution. Castro's response was positive but before it could be conveyed to the US administration, the first broadcast of the anti-Castro exile radio station Radio Martí began, with American collusion. Reagan was surely aware of the effect this would have on the delicate process of negotiations with Cuba.[29]

In fact, the Cuban leaders' fear of the bellicose intentions of the Reagan administration had already been borne out when US marines invaded Grenada in 1983. The pretext for the invasion was the breakdown in law and order after a palace coup had deposed and murdered Castro's friend and ally Maurice Bishop. Cuban military advisers and construction workers were given orders to resist the marines and, indeed, fighting took place for the first time between regular troops on both sides. The outnumbered Cubans, in particular the building workers, inflicted substantial casualties on the marines, suggesting that American troops would have no smooth passage should they attempt to invade Cuba.[30] The events in Grenada renewed fears of a US invasion of Cuba under the militantly anti-Cuban administration of Reagan and prompted the creation of civilian militias to share the defence of the island with the regular armed forces. The Grenada events were a new blow to Castro's hopes for an anti-imperialist alliance in the Caribbean basin. His other ally in the area, the Jamaican Michael Manley, had been defeated in the 1980 elections by the pro-Western conservative Edward Seaga. Most of the English-speaking countries in the Caribbean, for their part, had either actively supported or passively accepted the US action.

Cuba's loss of influence in the Caribbean in the mid-1980s was counter-balanced by renewed opportunities for political and trading links with Latin America. The Falklands or Malvinas War of 1982 had revived an old anti-colonial spirit in the continent that could not fail to be in Cuba's favour. Castro had sent a message of support to the junta in Argentina offering military aid. The collapse of the military dictatorships in Argentina and then in Brazil, combined with new perceptions about the need for regional cooperation among many Latin American governments, helped to end Cuba's isolation. By 1987, Cuba had restored diplomatic relations with most of the continent and trade and credits were flowing between the island and the big economic powers of the region such as Brazil, Mexico, Venezuela and Argentina. Further afield, Cuba had established trading links with several Western European countries, notably Spain, whose socialist government extended substantial guaranteed credit to the island. The new openings, especially to industrialised countries with access to high technology, were a vital component of Cuba's foreign policy strategy in the 1980s. If the United States under Reagan and later Bush Senior were not prepared to lift the economic blockade, Cuba would search for sources of capital goods elsewhere, in particular in the EEC and Japan.[31]

Encouraged by the signs of regional cooperation on the Latin American continent, Castro turned his flair for public relations to the dire problem of Third World debt. During the 1970s, the West had lent millions of dollars indiscriminately to the Third World and in particular to Latin America in an attempt to avoid an international recession by recycling the surpluses generated by oil price rises. The debt that had accumulated by the early 1980s began to outstrip the capacity of many countries even to make the interest payments. In the first six years of the decade, the Third World transferred to the West about $321 billion in repayments of principal and $325 billion in interest repayments, the two together amounting to about 5 per cent of their annual GNP.[32] The strain on their economies, exacerbated by the stringent conditions imposed on many governments by the IMF in exchange for further loans, was borne above all by the millions of destitute people in the Third World. The first outward sign of the looming crisis was the announcement by Mexico in 1982 that it could no longer maintain its interest payments.

Castro's new war-cry was not a mere piece of opportunism. The problem of Third World debt went to the heart of his long-standing campaign to restructure the relations between North and South. Furthermore, he was convinced that the growing debt crisis would create the conditions for the fulfilment of his old dream of Latin American unity. It was also an opportunity, now that his term of office as Chairman of the Non-Aligned Movement had come to an end, to restore his claim to the ethical leadership of the Third World after the Afghanistan setback. In a series of impassioned and closely argued speeches and interviews, Castro became the most articulate advocate of the cancellation of Third World debt. He defended his case on both moral and practical grounds. The survival of Latin America, he argued, hinged on finding a solution to the debt crisis, which was 'the key problem of our time'. He maintained that the debt was so high that it was no longer payable.[33] Any attempt to impose greater sacrifices on the people of the

Third World in order to continue the repayments was also politically unsafe and would result in widespread revolt. In any case, he argued, it was morally unacceptable that underdeveloped countries should be financing the industrialised economies; he calculated that in 1984, largely because of debt repayments, Latin America made a net transfer of $26,700 million to the developed West.

The solution he proposed attempted to bridge two of the major problems facing the world, poverty and the arms race. If the creditor states were to reduce their military expenditure by as little as 12 per cent, the Third World debt could be cancelled by the simple expedient, for instance, of using the savings to issue long-term government bonds to bail out the banks responsible for the loans. A more drastic cut in arms spending, on the other hand, would not only eliminate the debt problem but also pay for a new international economic order that would be to the benefit of all. Castro repeatedly stressed the growing inequality of trade relations between the developed and less developed world. The Third World, he argued, was being impoverished by the widening gap between the price of manufactured goods it was forced to import from the developed economies and the price of its own exports to those economies. He calculated that between 1980 and 1984 alone, the Third World's purchasing power fell by almost 22 per cent. If to this were added the high rates of US interest, the consequent flight of capital from the Third World, the overvaluation of the dollar, the practice of dumping and the rise of the protectionist policies in the West, then Latin America, for one, was being despoiled of thousands of millions of dollars year after year. The cancellation of the debt and the establishment of fair trade relations, Castro added somewhat disingenuously, would also favour the developed nations by providing them with a huge new market in the Third World.[34]

Castro's strategy on Third World debt, therefore, envisaged the formation of a cartel of several debtor nations that would use the threat of non-payment or a moratorium on debt repayments as a bargaining tool to reduce arms spending and to negotiate new terms of trade between North and South. It was a long way from the strategy of the 1960s of spreading Cuba's revolutionary model to the continent. Indeed, Castro seemed to show some disillusionment about the possibility of revolution or socialism in one country. The strain of 25 years of efforts to develop the Cuban economy in virtual isolation and the desperate conditions imposed on the Sandinista government may perhaps have been in his mind when he declared to the Latin American Federation of journalists in 1985, 'I believe that the cancellation of the debt and the establishment of the New International Economic

Order is much more important than two, three or four isolated revolutions. . . . A revolution in poverty is better than the system of exploitation, but you can't meet the enormous needs that have accumulated in all our countries . . . with social changes alone.'[35]

Castro's eloquence on the theme of world debt bore little relation to his ability to influence the process. In the first half of the 1980s Cuba needed to raise few loans from the West and could afford the repayments. Indeed, the Cuban authorities were renowned for the seriousness with which they dealt with their contractual obligations. Moreover, the Cuban economy was cushioned from the worst effects of the Western market by its special relationship with Comecon, though this created problems of a different kind. Nor did Castro carry much weight among the governments of the big Latin American countries which continued in their attempts to renegotiate their loan debts independently of one another, encouraged or leant on by the United States. Only Peru in 1985, under the government of Alan García, made a stand against the terms of its debt repayments, refusing to pay back more than 10 per cent of its annual exports. In the wake of Black Monday, 19 October 1987, when the world's stock markets crashed, the rhetoric of resistance against the debt-service burden among the top Latin American countries rose a few decibels, but their governments failed once again to agree on a debtors' cartel.

It would be wrong, however, to underestimate Castro's influence in Latin America. His proposals for the solution of the debt problem may have had only the force of a moral appeal but it was difficult to avoid the conclusion that, as the debt crisis deepened, some form of united action by the Latin American countries was likely. Castro also had a wide audience among many sections of the Latin American population. He not only enjoyed prestige as the most determined opponent of American hegemony on the continent but was also gaining popularity in the fast-growing movement for social justice within the Latin American Church. During his visit to Chile in 1971, and later in Jamaica and in Nicaragua, Castro had supported the call for a strategic alliance between Christians and Marxists.

The Catholic Church in Cuba, unlike that in many other parts of Latin America had not grown deep roots among the poor in Cuba, in particular in the rural areas. Castro claimed that in pre-revolutionary times there was not a single church in the countryside, where 70 per cent of Cubans were living.[36] His own experience of the Christian Brothers' and Jesuit education had not endeared him to Christianity and as a self-proclaimed Marxist-Leninist he was of course an atheist. Nevertheless, relations between the Revolutionary regime and the Church had improved considerably since the clash of 1960–1. The lowest point in Church–state relations had occurred after the Bay of Pigs invasion in 1961, when the government had banned religious education in public schools, closed down religious schools and expelled dozens of priests in response to the covert support given by members of the clergy to the invasion attempt. The Second Vatican Council of 1962–5, with its stress on social reform, had paved the way for a new dialogue and the Cuban Church had become increasingly reconciled to the Revolution, despite its almost total loss of power and privilege.

In Latin America, however, the Church was the most influential institution among ordinary people, and from the mid-1960s many of its sections had begun to espouse demands for political reform and justice for the poor and oppressed. No revolutionary movement could therefore afford to reject or ignore it. The Sandinista revolution in Nicaragua, for example, was based on a close alliance between socialism and Christianity. Castro now claimed to find not only an identical spirit of austerity and self-sacrifice between the two movements but a common political objective. 'From a strictly political point of view', he said in an interview with the Brazilian priest Frei Betto in 1985,

*. . . I believe that it is possible for Christians to be Marxists as well, and to work together with the Marxist Communists to transform the world. The important thing is that, in both cases, they be honest revolutionaries who want to end the exploitation of man by man and to struggle for a fair distribution of social wealth, equality, fraternity and the dignity of all human beings.*[37]

It was significant that Frei Betto's interview became a best-seller in Latin America.

Indeed, Castro's call for unity between Christians and Communists and his campaign over Third World debt had a deep moral resonance in Latin America. His much-publicised words on poverty, exploitation, repression and nationalism touched many chords beyond the small circles of the Left. Unlike most other Latin American statesmen he was free to voice the widespread aversion to the United States. In fact, he consciously sought the role of the anti-colonial conscience of Latin America and the Third World. Cuba's commitment to the cause of the Third World was evident in its relatively massive aid to nations in many parts of the world. Castro's popularity was due not only to what he said but also to the way in which he said it. His power of rhetoric and flamboyant style captured the imagination of the world's mass media and ensured that Cuba received an attention out of all proportion to its international importance.

Castro's influence abroad, however, was severely curtailed by a widespread perception that Cuba was a Soviet surrogate. Although it is true that the Cuban leaders enjoyed a relative degree of autonomy in domestic decision-making, foreign policy was tied closely to that of Moscow. Furthermore, Cuba's own internal problems suggested that the Cuban Revolution was not a model to be followed elsewhere. Indeed, in the mid-1980s, Castro once again felt obliged to turn his attention to domestic politics and bend his efforts to resolve the growing internal contradictions of the Revolution.

## Notes

1  For an overview of these issues, see J.I. Domínguez, 'Cuba in the international arena', *Latin American Research Review*, XXIII(1) (1988).

2  F. Castro, *Conversaciones con periodistas norteamericanos y franceses* (Política, Havana, 1983).

3  For example, J.M. Elliott and M.M. Dymally, *Fidel Castro: Nothing Can Stop the Course of History* (Pathfinder, New York, 1986), pp. 108 20; F. Betto, *Fidel and Religion* (Weidenfeld & Nicolson, London, 1987), p. 299.

4  For Noriega, see Castro's interview with NBC's Maria Shriver in *Granma Weekly Review* (*GWR*), 13 March 1988, and for the Malvinas, *Granma*, 3 May 1982.

5  C. Blasier and C. Mesa-Lago (eds), *Cuba in the World* (University of Pittsburgh Press, 1979), *passim*.

6  Betto, *Fidel and Religion*, pp. 244–5, 233 5.

7  F. Castro Ruz, *Fidel in Chile* (International Publishers, New York, 1972), p. 119.

8  M. Taber (ed ), *Fidel Castro's Speeches* (Pathfinder, New York, 1983), vol. 2, pp. 13–14.

9  Castro Ruz, *Fidel in Chile*, pp. 136 and 220.

10  S.L. Reed, 'Participation in multinational organizations and programs in the hemisphere', in Blasier and Mesa-Lago (eds), *Cuba in the World*, pp. 297–312.

11  W.S. Smith, *The Closest of Enemies* (Norton, New York, 1987), p. 93. For further discussion of US policy towards Cuba in the 1970s, see M.H. Morley, *Imperial State and Revolution: the United States and Cuba, 1952–1986* (Cambridge University Press, Cambridge, 1987).

12  For an overview of Cuban and US policies towards Africa, see P. Gleisejes, *Conflicting Missions: Havana, Washington and Africa 1959–1976* (University of North Carolina Press, Chapel Hill, NC, 2002).

13  Ibid., for a relatively recent account.

14  A. Kapcia, 'Cuba's African involvement: a new perspective', *Survey. A Journal of East and West Studies*, 24(2) (Spring 1979), pp. 142–59.

15  G. García Márquez, 'Cuba in Angola: Operation Carlotta', in M. Taber (ed.), *Fidel Castro's Speeches: Cuba's International Foreign Policy 1975–80* (Pathfinder, New York, 1981), p. 353.

**16** *GWR*, 9 July 1972.

**17** For example, F. Castro, *Fidel Castro habla con Barbara Walters* (Carlos Valencia, Colombia, 1977), p. 53 and A. Shevchenko, *Breaking with Moscow* (Alfred A. Knopf, New York, 1985), p. 272.

**18** Smith, *Closest of Enemies*, p. 130.

**19** Castro's speech on 26 July 1979, in Taber, *Castro's Speeches* (1981), pp. 293–309.

**20** Taber, *Castro's Speeches* (1981), p. 167.

**21** M.H. Erisman, *Cuba's International Relations: the Anatomy of a Nationalistic Foreign Policy* (Westview, Boulder, Col., 1985), pp. 128–9.

**22** Elliott and Dymally, *Castro*, pp. 18 and 183.

**23** R.M. Levine, *Secret Missions to Cuba: Fidel Castro, Bernardo Benes and Cuban Miami* (Palgrave, New York and Basingstoke, 2001), pp. 85–148.

**24** Fidel Castro, in speech to the National Assembly of People's Power, 24 Dec. 1977, in 'Discursos de Fidel', *Granma*.

**25** For example, P. Bourne, *Castro* (Macmillan, London, 1987), p. 295.

**26** R.L. Bach, 'Socialist construction and Cuban emigration: explorations into Mariel', *Cuban Studies*, 15(2) (Summer 1985).

**27** According to Castro, in I. Ramonet, *Fidel Castro. Biografía a dos voces* (Random House Mondadori, Mexico and Barcelona, 2006), p. 302. For further details about the experience of these people in Florida, see http://www.globalsecurity.org/military/ops/mariel-boatlift.htm (last accessed 2 June 2008).

**28** *Granma*, 16 June 1980.

**29** Levine, *Secret Missions*, pp. 166–7.

**30** Erisman, *Cuba's International Relations*, pp. 146 and 156, n. 41.

**31** J. Stubbs, *Cuba: the Test of Time* (Latin America Bureau, London, 1989), pp. 131–6.

**32** J. Roddick, *The Dance of the Millions: Latin America and the Debt Crisis* (Latin America Bureau, London, 1988), p. 3.

**33** Betto, *Fidel and Religion*, pp. 301 and 297.

**34** F. Castro, *La Cancelación de la deuda externa y el nuevo orden económico internacional como única alternativa verdadera. Otros asuntos de interés político e histórico* (Editora Política, Havana, 1985), pp. 101, 122–5, 156–7; Betto, *Fidel and Religion*, pp. 299–300.

**35** Speech to Fourth Congress of FELAP, 7 July 1985, quoted in P. O'Brien, 'The debt cannot be paid: Castro and the Latin American debt', *Bulletin of Latin American Research*, 5(1) (1986), p. 56.

**36** Betto, *Fidel and Religion*, p. 181.

**37** Ibid., p. 276.

# CHAPTER 8

# Straightening the Rudder

In February 1986, Castro rose before the delegates of the Third Congress of the Cuban Communist Party to launch a new offensive on the domestic front, ponderously entitled the 'Rectification of errors and negative trends'. It marked his return to the centre of the political stage in Cuba after a decade or so during which his presence had loomed less on the domestic scene. His speech vilified talk of liberalising the economy and attacked corruption, corporatism, materialism and selfishness in Cuban society. It pressed for higher productivity and lower consumption and appealed for a return to egalitarian moral values. In short, Castro was calling for yet more sacrifices on the part of the Cuban people.

The immediate background to the new campaign was the worsening economic situation in Cuba in the mid-1980s. It is true that the economy had recovered in the 1970s after the disappointing growth rates of the previous decade. On the basis of the macroeconomic indicators employed by socialist countries, the global social product (or GSP) in Cuba had risen in the first half of the 1970s by an average of 14.8 per cent, to slow down to an annual rate of 4.6 per cent between 1976 and 1979. Yet by the mid-1980s a sharp decline was evident, exacerbated by unfavourable weather conditions, low productivity, inadequate planning and the tightening of the US economic embargo by the Reagan administration. By 1986, Cuba had a record deficit of over $199 million and a foreign debt of $3.87 billion, 6.9 per cent higher than in 1985, while GSP grew by only 1.4 per cent over the previous year. Furthermore, credit from the West fell because unusually Cuba had been unable to service its accumulated debt of over $6 billion.[1]

The ups and downs of Cuba's economic performance had not affected the state's considerable investment in social reform, foreign aid and military involvement abroad. Underpinned by long-term credit and trade agreements with the Soviet Union, the Cubans had achieved standards of health and literacy rivalling those of developed countries. The infant mortality rate, a common yardstick of development, had dropped from 60 per thousand live births in 1958 to 13.3 in the mid-1980s. On the eve of the Revolution there had been only one doctor for every 5,000 Cubans. Thirty years later there was one per 400. Average life expectancy had risen to 74 from 57 and only 2 per cent of the population was illiterate compared to 24 per cent in 1958. All children of primary-school age now attended school whereas only 56 per cent had done so before the Revolution.[2]

The bare figures conceal the extent of social and economic change in Cuba. The countryside in particular enjoyed the benefits of the massive injection of state funds. Not only had the traditional pattern of class relations been swept aside by expropriation and nationalisation, but the old blight of unemployment and underemployment had also been virtually eliminated. Small rural towns of between 500 and 2,000 inhabitants, endowed with running water, electricity, clinics and schools, now dotted the countryside where once much of the peasant population had been scattered about in jerry-built huts surrounded by tiny plots of land. Latifundia had given way to state farms, state-assisted cooperatives and small but productive private holdings, though the reorganisation of the agrarian sector had not taken place without trauma. There was no poverty or disease of the kind that ravaged much of Latin America, including the most developed of its economies. The Cubans had access to an unrivalled breadth of social and recreational services and educational opportunities. At the same time, Cuban medical personnel, engineers, teachers and military advisers were working in dozens of poor countries as part of the government's generous foreign aid programme.

The most conspicuous shortfall in Cuban society was the lack of consumer goods. But Castro was adamant that the success of the Revolution had to be judged in part at least on the basis of health, housing and education and not in terms of the availability of consumer goods. The very phrase 'living standards' drew his scorn as he railed against the 'terrible national egoism' that he felt it implied. To the customary applause, he declared, 'To tell the truth, we would like ten or twenty metres more of cloth per capita, but that is not our problem at the moment; our problem is development, our problem is the future. We can't mortgage the future for ten metres of cloth!'[3] None the less, despite widespread disgruntlement, the supply and range of basic consumer goods had improved considerably since the lean years of the late 1960s. This was the result mainly of economic growth but it was helped also by the new policy of allowing goods to be sold at a higher price in state-run 'parallel markets', and by the institution in 1980 of the 'free farmers' markets' where private smallholders could sell off their surplus at unpegged prices. These liberalising measures were part of an attempt in the mid-1970s to introduce a number of market mechanisms into the economy. After the disastrous sugar campaign of 1970, Cuba's war-type economy of the late 1960s had been modified; a new framework called the System of Direction and Planning of the Economy (SDPE) had been brought in, allowing a certain decentralisation of planning and management and a new range of material incentives. The aim had been to improve efficiency and stimulate production.[4]

Although Castro was careful not to criticise the new system directly, he was clearly uncomfortable with it. It was no coincidence that measures of economic liberalisation in the past had been introduced during the two occasions when Castro's model of a centralised and 'moral' economy had been under particular pressure: in 1964 after the failure of the industrialisation drive, and after the 1970 crisis. His latent mistrust of market mechanisms was strengthened in the mid-1980s when it appeared that the economy was beginning to suffer severe strains. Matters came to a head over the 1985 plan drawn up by the Central Planning Board (*Juceplan*) under its head Humberto Pérez, a Moscow-trained economist. On Castro's personal intervention, the plan was overridden on the grounds that it provided for an excessively swollen budget without taking into account the economic situation in Cuba. One of the most important problems, Castro implied, had been that the decentralisation of economic decision-making had given rise to corporatist tendencies in the bureaucracy. Justifying his action, he told the National Assembly,

*during all these years, since we began our first efforts of planning and development, a sectorial spirit has reigned in all the organizations, in all the Ministries . . . a battle by each institution for the limited resources available. This criterion, this style . . . has been declared abolished and it has been established that the plan should be everyone's plan and that the economy was the economy of everyone.*[5]

Bypassing the *Juceplan*, Castro set up a new committee to draw up a revised plan for 1985 that drastically pared down state expenditure, gave priority to exports over imports and instituted measures to save resources. Shortly afterwards, Humberto Pérez, the technocrat most associated with the SDPE, was removed from his post and in 1986 dropped from the Politburo.

With the so-called Rectification campaign, Castro broadened the target of his criticism. In a series of congresses between 1986 and 1987, he launched into an attack on the 'errors and negative trends' that had arisen during the previous years. At the same time he called on the Cubans to raise productivity, lower consumption and renew voluntary labour, in particular the voluntary construction teams, the Microbrigadas. His handling of these lengthy meetings was quintessentially Castro. He engaged delegates in a running dialogue, enquiring about the smallest details of their work and using the information provided to illustrate his broader themes. Few institutions escaped the lash of his tongue. He denounced the low productivity of Cuban industry, blaming management for allowing resources to be wasted, the technocrats for failing to carry out proper job evaluation and workers for taking advantage of low work norms to earn excessive bonuses. He denounced the rise of a new crust of small entrepreneurs who had seized the opportunities offered by the introduction of market mechanisms, such as the free farmers' markets, to enrich themselves. He noted that as a result of these trends income differentials were growing and consumerism was creeping in, while voluntary labour had become devalued. In general, over the past few years, he went on, discipline had declined as well as respect for the law.[6]

As in 1970, the new campaign responded in part to mass pressure from below. By the mid-1980s a generalised feeling of disaffection had spread, in particular among the urban population, and was beginning to be reflected somewhat cautiously in sections of the press. Havana, as the political, administrative and industrial hub of the island and the most populated city in Cuba, appeared to be the hotbed of these criticisms. The source of discontent was not merely the continuing problem of the poor supply of subsidised goods, the high price of produce sold on the parallel market or the quality of services such as public transport. It was also that the sacrifices being demanded by the leaders were unequally spread. It was well known that there were people who were taking advantage of the shortages to make a handsome profit out of the new more liberal system. There were others in the administration, the military or the state enterprises who were felt to be abusing their privileges. Stories abounded about old boy networks, rake-offs, high expense-accounts and the use of state cars for private purposes. In a speech to the Third Party Congress, Castro took up some of these complaints, acting characteristically as a sort of self-appointed spokesman of popular discontent against the administration. His reputation as 'the synthesis of the best virtues of the people' was thereby strengthened. As a leading member of the Central Committee and a Castro protégé said at the same Congress, 'In no small number of meetings and assemblies during these past months, I have heard people regret the fact that once again it has been comrade Fidel who has had to confront the deviations and mistaken policies'.[7]

Castro's sharpest invective was directed at his old *bêtes noires*, the bureaucrats and technocrats. Seizing on the example of the Ministry of Construction (MINCONS), whose representatives in the hall must have squirmed in their seats at his remarks, he declared with heavy sarcasm:

*To appeal to the MINCONS and say to them . . . please build a day-care centre in Guanabacoa because there's a new factory . . . that needs a workforce and doesn't have it or has a crisis on its hands because 200 women have to pay 60, 70, or 80 pesos plus food to have their children looked after, MINCONS couldn't build a single day-care centre, not one! Because simply to ask them to build a day-care centre was enough to make them faint. . . . How can you ask such a terrible thing, to build a day-care centre in Gaunabacoa with all the commitments we already have and all the projects that we never finish?*

Castro's example of the day-care centre was not picked out of the air; he meant to drive home the connection between social needs and economic development that was the essence of his 'moral economy'.

Indeed, moral images dominated his speeches about the economy. Conjuring up a rather tasteless image in the heat of his speech, he accused some of Cuba's technocrats and bureaucrats of, 'suffering from and trans-mitting a sort of ideological AIDS . . . that was destroying the Revolution's defences'.[8] This new bureaucratic disease, according to Castro, was no less than the spread of a 'capitalist or petty-bourgeois' spirit among people who appeared well-versed in Marxism but who mistakenly pinned their faith on market mechanisms, forgetting the primacy of revolutionary consciousness.[9] In the past, Castro had repeatedly attacked bureaucratic deviations. His renewed offensive in the Rectification campaign hinted at the rise since the 1970s of a new layer of managers in the administration and the state enter-prises closely associated with the reformist measures of the SDPE. These favoured greater autonomy for management, plant-level profit schemes, material incentives, wage differentials and a greater number of consumer outlets for skilled workers.

Castro's offensive, however, was not against the SDPE itself; he merely argued that it had been applied inefficiently (and in some cases corruptly) and that it had gone too far. The Rectification campaign therefore was neither a return to the 'war economy' of the 1966–70 period nor a rejection of the new system of economic management but an attempt to restore a balance between the two. It was significant that despite his attack on private entrepreneurship within Cuba (the farmers' markets were closed in 1986) Castro did not question the official policy of encouraging joint-venture agreements between Cuban state enterprises and private foreign companies.

Behind Rectification lay the compelling need to respond to the economic crisis in Cuba in the mid-1980s without sacrificing the principles of the Revolution. Castro evidently believed that the price of any further economic liberalisation was too high for Cuba: on one hand, it was demobilising the people and on the other it was undermining the egalitarian basis of the Revolution. In the conditions of persistent underdevelopment and the continuing blockade by the United States, Castro believed the government could not afford to relinquish its control over the economy, nor could the Cuban people relax or 'indulge' in consumerism. The survival of the Revolution depended on generating the highest possible level of surplus for investment in defence, overseas commitments and social welfare. In a declining economy this meant tightening the national belt even further and boosting productivity without raising wages. In his opinion, only a partial return to more centralised controls and a restoration of moral incentives alongside material rewards could ensure the right equilibrium.

Castro's stern words throughout the second half of the 1980s were not those of a revolutionary puritan or an ageing Stalinist clinging to outworn dogma, as some commentators have suggested.[10] They were based on a perception that the system of economic management introduced in the mid-1970s was not working well and that, while it had to be reformed, the Cuban leaders had also to renew their traditional instruments of decision-making and mobilisation. Castro had always believed that the economy had to be directed centrally; as he put it in 1988, 'There is a key principle of socialism which is especially valid for a developing country: the centralisation of decisions on the use of resources in the economic field.'[11] But he had had to give way when his own model had come under strain. In fact, there was nothing new about Rectification. It was a means of 'straightening the rudder' to 'correct' the course of the Revolution that Castro had employed ever since he had come to power, first after the failure of the industrialisation campaign in the early 1960s, then during the radical phase between 1966 and 1970, and more recently following the crisis of 1970. All four policy shifts were cyclical responses to internal and external pressures, of which the most important was the pressure of the world market.

Similar strains, though of an altogether different magnitude, affected the Soviet bloc in the mid-1980s, prompting a section of the Soviet leadership headed by Gorbachev to launch a programme of economic reforms or *perestroika* (restructuring). The Rectification campaign in Cuba could be said to have begun before *perestroika* in that Castro launched his first broadside against inefficiency in 1984. Both Castro and Gorbachev were pursuing the same objective, to increase productivity and economic efficiency in a declining economy, but the means they used diverged because the obstacles they faced were different. Castro later claimed he had welcomed Gorbachev's first statements about restructuring the Soviet economy but had rapidly formed a very negative opinion of the measures applied by the Soviet leader.[12] For Castro *perestroika* weakened the state's control over the economy and introduced a radical set of market mechanisms to stimulate rationalisation and productivity. Rectification, on the other hand, strengthened state control and centralised planning of the economy. The accompanying policy of *glasnost* or openness in the Soviet Union was above all a campaign to break up the entrenched interests in the Party and the bureaucracy that were blocking reform. In a small and centralised society like Cuba, no section of the Party or the bureaucracy had formed an autonomous power base such as those found in the Soviet Union.

It is true that Castro used a similar method to bring to heel what he saw as vested bureaucratic interests. Like Gorbachev, he encouraged criticism from below in order to shake up the intermediate layers of the Cuban state. Like the Soviet leader, he orchestrated these voices of censure, conducting affairs from the speaker's rostrum, as a sort of chairman and devil's advocate rolled into one. Often, as in the congress of the Young Communists (UJC) in the spring of 1987, Castro insisted that his ministers attend meetings in which they were subjected to forceful criticism from rank-and-file delegates. This had always been Castro's way of dealing with internal conflicts within the Party and society at large. In an interview with NBC in 1988, he claimed, 'we have *glasnost* here, we have always had it. No party in the world has been more self-critical than the Communist Party of Cuba. None. Examine our history and you will see *glasnost* on a large scale.'[13]

Yet there was an essential difference between the two processes. Whereas Soviet *glasnost* had opened up a Pandora's box of demands that threatened to undermine the fragile stability of the USSR, the Cuban version, if it could be called by the same name, was a decidedly controlled and limited affair. It appeared that dissent was tolerated to the extent that it suited the leadership. At a time when Castro was anxious to root out inefficiency and petty corruption among officials at all levels, criticism was allowed to flourish as long as it was directed against malpractice or bureaucratic immobility. But criticism that questioned the principles of the Revolution itself was hardly permissible. Cubans who had been jailed under a law that made oppositional activities treasonable were now being released, but there was still a long way to go before open dissent against official policy could freely emerge outside the institutions of the state. The oblique complaints in the bolder columns of the press could hardly compare with the critical dialogue that was taking place in the Soviet Union.

Indeed, it could be said that the only truly investigative reporter in Cuba was Castro. He still went round the island, though less often than in the 1960s, his keen eye picking out evidence of abuses and inefficiencies. Where he approved criticism, it poured forth. During his walkabouts, people mobbed him for solutions to small local problems, knowing that his word was the administration's command. Castro had surrounded himself with a small group of about 20 bright young technicians and administrators who acted as his personal assistants and troubleshooters. This Co-ordinating and Support Group had become the training ground for future government leaders, and several cabinet ministers had been drawn from its ranks. It suggested once again that though he did not ignore official channels, Castro's instincts had always been towards central control and direct action. 'In my office', he said in an interview with the *Washington Post* in 1985, 'I have 20 comrades who are on the road constantly visiting factories, hospitals, schools, co-ordinating, helping everyone and they are not inspectors, they are people who go round, see how the situation is, co-ordinate one organism with another.'[14] Moreover, he was the only consistent source of statistics about the economy and the society. It was mainly Castro who, from the rostrum and the television screen, informed the people what was going on in Cuba.

Nevertheless, it would be wrong to assume from this that once again, as in the 1960s, he exercised almost unlimited power. An intense debate took place within the party and the leadership before and during the Rectification campaign and spread downwards through the institutions and the local assemblies to the street. The new programme was almost certainly the result of a consensus arising in part from divergencies among the leadership and pressures from below. The discussions were often heated, leading to open disagreements between top officials and once between Castro and one of his ministers in the National Assembly itself.[15] If heterodox political views were still considered beyond the pale in the late 1980s, there was a much more critical debate over policy-making within the boundaries of the Revolution than there had been in the two previous decades.

Nor did Castro's return to prominence on the domestic stage signal a power shift within the regime. Instead, it was a renewal of the populist style of the 1960s in the service of a new social mobilisation. The modest range of decentralised management and material incentives set in place in the 1970s did not require the same sort of charismatic leadership that accompanied campaigns for patriotic exertion. As the supreme commander and the most effective communicator among the leadership, it inevitably fell to Castro to lead the offensive that he had almost certainly initiated in the first place. While there was a dramatic turnover of middle-ranking party members and of managers and officials in the economic ministries in the wake of the Rectification campaign, the changes of personnel among the top leadership did not suggest that there had been any serious divisions. Rather, they indicated a shift in emphasis similar to the practice of cabinet reshuffles; the ministers who were replaced were those most closely associated with the policy failures. In the 1986 elections to the Politburo, of the 27 members of the 1980–5 Politburo nine lost their seats but retained their position in the Central Committee, one died, one was transferred to the Secretariat and one retired because of old age.

The picture of Castro made popular by some of the Western press as an eccentric holding out against the inevitable forces of modernisation epitomised by Gorbachev was thus a distorted one. The campaigns for *perestroika* and Rectification arose from different political needs and traditions, as Castro pointed out in his speech to the National Assembly on the occasion of Gorbachev's visit in 1989.[16] In contrast to the Soviet Union, Cuba was a small and relatively homogeneous society whose members could still be mobilised to perform feats of collective endeavour when called on by the state. Whereas the Soviet reformers saw liberalisation as a means of releasing energies blocked by the dead weight of bureaucracy, the Cuban leadership believed on the contrary that they needed to strengthen their grip on the economy and on society in order to motivate their citizens to work harder and to defend the Revolution against the threat of American aggression. Rectification was their response to the three-way vice of economic decline, popular dissatisfaction and the enduring need for the state to cream off a substantial portion of the national surplus.

For all their dissimilarities, *perestroika* and Rectification were closely bound together. Castro may have dismissed the idea of a Cuban *perestroika* on the grounds that it was inappropriate, but he could not escape the effects of Gorbachev's reforms. *Glasnost* and *perestroika* were trendy; the call for a greater effort that was at the heart of the Rectification campaign was not. One of the new slogans associated with the campaign, *Ahora sí podemos construir el socialismo* (translated in the official Cuban daily *Granma* as 'Now we are really going to build socialism'), sounded a rather jaded note, as if all the sacrifices in the past had been in vain, and it became the target of much popular criticism. Among a few sections of the Party, such as some of the old pre-Revolutionary Communists and some of the Young Communists, there was considerable, albeit muted, admiration for Gorbachev. For once, a Soviet leader appeared to have upstaged Castro. More importantly, the restructuring of Soviet economic management had serious implications for the special relationship between the two countries. Gorbachev intended to introduce more cost-effective principles in the Soviet Union's international trading links. Already since his accession to power in 1985, the price the Soviet Union was paying for Cuban sugar had fallen from eleven times the world market price to three. And as far as international relations were concerned, any improvement in Soviet–US relations would bring about a decline in the geo-strategic importance of Cuba for the Soviet Union.

Castro and his ministers had made only veiled criticism of *perestroika* in the concern not to upset relations with the Soviet Union.[17] The differences between the Soviet and Cuban leadership became explicit during Gorbachev's visit to Cuba in April 1989. The Soviet leader gave an unequivocal warning of the new approach: 'As life moves ahead, new demands are being made on the quality of our interaction. This applies particularly to economic contacts – they should be more dynamic and effective and bring greater returns for both our countries, both our peoples.'[18] Henceforth, Cuban economic agencies would have to deal less with the Soviet bureaucracy than directly with buyers and suppliers acting on new criteria of profitability. The Soviet Union would seek to restore a greater balance of trade between the two countries and reduce the concealed price subsidies built into Cuban–Soviet trade. For his part, Castro insisted that Cuba would not stray from the Cuban socialist model. These hidden agendas lay beneath the much fanfared 25-year treaty of cooperation signed jointly by Gorbachev and Castro during the former's visit to Cuba and the one-year protocol agreed between the two countries shortly afterwards.

Another serious effect for Cuba of Gorbachev's 'new political thinking' was his tacit withdrawal from Third World politics. In the late 1960s, Castro had criticised the Soviet Union for its lukewarm support for national liberation struggles, such as that waged in Vietnam. Nevertheless, under Brezhnev in the 1970s, the Kremlin had been heavily involved in military and commercial aid to Soviet-aligned countries, viewing the Third World as an arena of East–West confrontation. Gorbachev explicitly rejected this conception of international relations. He argued that the problems of poverty and conflict in the underdeveloped world could only be solved by concerted action between the superpowers and they therefore had to be subordinated to the primary objective of détente between East and West. Though he claimed there was an important role for Latin America in the process of détente, it was clear that the Third World was to be a more or less passive spectator of superpower negotiations. Moreover, Gorbachev hinted that he was more interested in the trading potential of Latin American countries than in their political colour.[19]

The growing convergence between Moscow and Washington in the late 1980s was welcomed by Castro only to the extent that it led to international détente. A substantial cut in arms expenditure would release money that could be made available for development aid or to underwrite Third World debt. US–Soviet détente would also pave the way for a renewal of US–Cuban relations and the dismantling of the economic embargo of the island. However, Castro did not believe that the United States had changed its spots. A strategic retreat of the Soviet Union from the Third World would leave Cuba and other countries such as Nicaragua dangerously exposed to American harassment. Four months before Gorbachev arrived in Cuba, Castro had declared in a speech commemorating the thirty-second anniversary of the *Granma* landing,

*The question of the survival of humanity is a problem that affects us all; peace is a problem that affects us all . . . we sincerely support the peace policy of the Soviet Union . . . but still, survival and peace have a different meaning for some countries and for others; there are two kinds of survival and two kinds of peace: the survival of the rich and the survival of the poor, the peace of the rich and the peace of the poor . . . it's almost certain that the way the empire [the United States] conceives peace is among the powerful, peace with the Soviet Union and war with the small, socialist, revolutionary, progressive or simply independent countries of the Third World.*[20]

He made his disquiet evident during Gorbachev's visit. Contrasting the revolutionary process in Cuba and Russia, he indulged in a sardonic and somewhat incautious gibe at the Soviet Union, declaring that there had been no Stalinism in Cuba, 'unless I am considered . . . a sort of Stalin, and in that case I would say that all my victims in our country are in excellent health'. He went on to make an implicit criticism of Gorbachev's policies: 'We know what the expression of new international political thinking means, a new mentality in handling problems. But we don't have any assurances, we still don't have them. We don't have any indication that the imperialists have adopted this new international thinking. On the contrary, we have many reasons to distrust their conduct.'[21]

The problem for Castro was not just that Moscow was pulling out of its military commitments to the Third World but that it was redefining its trading links and foreign aid programme to bring it more in line with capitalist practices. Despite his reassuring words to the contrary, Gorbachev's reforms contained a hidden menace that eventually both the security and the economic viability of Cuba might be undermined by Soviet withdrawal. Castro's ability to play off Moscow and Washington against each other would be considerably reduced now that the Soviet Union no longer saw Cuba as a lever against the United States. Gorbachev's new international policy, by downgrading the Third World as an agency for change, also threatened to erode Castro's ability to play an active role in world affairs. Cuban military missions abroad, though they were not always established at Moscow's bidding, had fitted in with Soviet strategy and had relied on its military and diplomatic support.

The most spectacular of these had been the Cuban operation in Angola. For 13 years Cuban troops, backed by Soviet arms, had held together the fragile independence of Angola against the incursions of South Africa and the harassing operations of its client guerrilla organisation, Unita. The military victory of Cuban and Angolan troops over the South African army at Cuito Cuanavale in May 1988 had helped to force Pretoria into negotiations to end the conflict in Southern Africa and to recognise the independence of Namibia. Although the resulting Brazzaville Accords stemmed in large measure from the convergence of policy towards that area between Reagan and Gorbachev, the Cuban involvement had been decisive in convincing Pretoria that the cost of further military action was too high. The US was forced to accept the participation of Cuba in the negotiations, even though it sought later to downplay Cuba's role in the liberation of Southern Africa.[22] On the other hand, Cuba's standing among many Third World countries, in particular among the Front Line states, was as high as it had ever been. Such prestigious operations, however, were far less likely now that the Soviet Union was drawing back from any overt political involvement in the Third World.

Indeed, at the end of the 1980s, Castro's options were narrowing both at home and abroad. He was faced by increasing economic strains and growing dissatisfaction among many sections of the population, exacerbated by the return of thousands of veterans of the Angolan war. The crackdown on speculators profiting from the shortage of goods was not simply an ethical gesture but was intended to reassure a restless population that the government would be fair in its treatment of all citizens. Hence the infuriated reaction of the leadership to the discovery in June 1989 that top officials had been smuggling millions of dollars worth of Colombian cocaine into the United States. The case against them gives a fascinating glimpse into the different cultures that grew around Cuban efforts to bypass the embargo. But it also says something about the relations of power in the top echelons of the regime.

As Castro later acknowledged, both military and civilian government agencies had set up clandestine networks to trade Cuban products for dollars with which to buy vital supplies and spare parts that were subject to the embargo.[23] It seemed that the government turned a blind eye to these activities while they officially prohibited them. A veteran of the Sierra Maestra campaign and a much lauded military commander in the Angolan and Ethiopian wars, General Arnaldo Ochoa Sánchez, appeared to have gone way beyond these tacit arrangements. It was one thing to buy arms on the black market for the Nicaraguan Sandinistas, as he had done, but quite another thing to trade in drugs. Ochoa appears to have made contact through his military aides with Colombian left-wing guerrillas and to have been buying drugs from them to sell clandestinely to US dealers. He had apparently raised huge sums of money that he stashed away in his collaborators' houses on the island. This trade, it was presumed, was for the purpose of buying goods vital to his operations in military administration. The operation had enjoyed the tacit approval of the Minister of the Interior, another veteran of the Revolution, José Abrantes.

Castro later claimed that they were acting for patriotic reasons not for self-enrichment, although it also seems they were siphoning off a small proportion of the money for their own consumption and displaying it somewhat ostentatiously. But they had not represented any political threat. 'The worst thing', Castro said, 'is that those who got involved in this [business] did so on the assumption that they were helping the Republic' But for Castro, they had broken an ethical code fundamental to the Cuban Revolution.[24] In the trials that followed, the four officers were sentenced to death for high treason while Abrantes was condemned to a 20-year prison term. That the whole affair was more than just a case of individual waywardness on the part of a handful of officials is suggested by the wide-ranging purge of the Interior Ministry that followed the trials. The fact that it was Fidel Castro who had had to order the investigation in the first place, perhaps because the accused were too high up in the echelons of the government, emphasised once again how much the health of the regime continued to depend on his authority.[25]

The trial, broadcast at length on Cuban television in an edited version, appeared to lend weight to the growing complaints among many sections of the Cuban population about the abuse of power by some officials. Popular criticism was directed not only at the paucity and poor quality of consumer goods and the inadequacy of certain public services but also at corruption among officials, epitomised by the growth of an 'old boys' network' nicknamed *sociolismo* from the Spanish word for partner, *socio*. The Cuban leadership was also criticised from within the party structure for its reluctance to share power. The strongest challenge on this account came from the new generation of Communists. 'We are living in a period of healthy insurgency', its daily paper declared in August 1988. 'The scant regard paid to it gives rise often to palpable nonconformity. . . . The just desire for a more comfortable existence raises the need for the greater participation of everyone in the search for solutions to the problems of the country.'[26] The impatience of the young militants for more democracy, expressed notably in the 1987 Congress of the Young Communists, was creating tension between the two generations.[27] Indeed, the new generation betrayed little reverence towards the sacred cows of the Revolution.

Castro alone continued to command enormous admiration but there were also many ordinary people who were saying that it was time he should retire. Characteristically, he was able to disarm potential criticism by assuming the mantle of devil's advocate. In a meeting with an official youth cultural organisation, for example, Castro was reputedly shaken by the discontent expressed by young writers and artists with the policies and behaviour of the government's cultural officials. One of the youthful critics was interrupted by the powerful head of the Department of Revolutionary Orientation and Propaganda, Carlos Aldana, who complained about the rancorous atmosphere in the hall, but Castro, in his turn, interrupted him and told him to listen to the criticism.[28]

While Cuba was no longer so useful to the Soviet Union, it remained a prime target of American hostility under the new administration of George Bush Senior. The campaign of Rectification could at best eradicate some of the corruption and inefficiency that had beset the administration of the economy and society. It might encourage further patriotic efforts on the part of many Cubans. But it could not pull off a miracle of development. It would be no exaggeration to say that the dilemmas confronting Castro and the Cuban leadership at the end of the decade, though different in kind, were as great as any they had had to face during the previous 30 years.

## Notes

1  M. Azicri, *Cuba: Politics, Economics and Society* (Pinter, London, 1988), pp. 140–1 and 144–9.

2  J. Stubbs, *Cuba: the Test of Time* (Latin America Bureau, London, 1989), p. v.

3  *Granma*, 1 Dec. 1986; *Bohemia*, 14 Dec. 1984.

4  H. Pérez, *Sobre las dificultades objetivas de la revolución. Lo que el pueblo debe saber* (Política, Havana, 1979).

5  *Granma*, 5 Jan. 1985.

6  *Granma*, 1 Dec. 1986.

7  Carlos Aldana, quoted in *Granma*, 1 Dec. 1986; the quote on Castro's reputation was extracted from *Juventud Rebelde*, 18 Sept. 1988.

8  *Granma Weekly Review (GWR)*, 13 Dec. 1987.

9  *Granma*, 9 June 1986.

10  For example, T. Szulc, *Fidel: a Critical Portrait* (Hutchinson, London, 1987).

11  *GWR*, July 24 1988.

12  I. Ramonet, *Fidel Castro. Biografía a dos voces* (Random House Mondadori, Mexico and Barcelona, 2006), p. 325.

13  *GWR*, 13 March 1988.

14  *Granma*, 12 Feb. 1985.

15  Author's interview with José Ramón Vidal, editor of *Juventud Rebelde*, Sept. 1988.

16  *GWR*, 16 April 1989.

17  M.J. Bain, 'Cuba–Soviet relations in the Gorbachev era', *Journal of Latin American Studies*, 37(4) (2005), pp. 769–91.

18  Speech to the National Assembly, in *Visit of Mikhail Gorbachev to Cuba* (Novosti Press, Moscow, 1989), p. 10.

19  Ibid., pp. 17 and 22.

20  Speech on 5 December 1988, available at http://www.cuba.cu/gobierno/discursos/1988/esp/f051288e.html (last accessed 3 June 2008) or *GWR*, 18 Dec. 1988

21  *GWR*, 16 April 1989.

22  Castro, in Ramonet, *Castro*, pp. 296–7.

23  Ibid., pp. 331–8.

24  Ibid., pp. 332, 338–9.

25  *GWR*, 22 June and 10 July 1989; *Juventud Rebelde*, 26 June 1989. For a speculative analysis of the trials, see J. Preston, 'The trial that shook Cuba', *New York Review of Books*, 7 December 1989. On the other hand, Franko Mora in 'Cuba's Ministry of Interior: the FAR's fifth army', *Bulletin of Latin American Research*, 26(2) (2007), pp. 222–37 suggests that the trial was part of a strategy by the military to take over the Ministry of the Interior. For another very different version of the episode, see the book by one of Ochoa's close collaborators, the journalist Norberto Fuentes (*Dulces Guerreros Cubanos* (Seix Barral, Barcelona, 1999)), who managed to survive the purges and went into exile. Fuentes claims Ochoa was the nucleus of an alternative revolutionary leadership.

26  S. Cruz, 'Sí, hay arreglo', *Juventud Rebelde*, 30 Aug. to 5 Sept. 1988, p. 2.

27  Author's interview with José Ramón Vidal, Sept. 1988.

28  Author's interview with Ramón Fernández-Larrea, Sept. 1988.

# CHAPTER 9

# A Special Period

The collapse of the Communist regimes in Eastern Europe from 1989 onwards and of the Soviet Union itself at the end of 1991 appeared to deal a mortal blow to the Cuban state. The economy had remained afloat largely through their support. Almost all of Cuba's trade had been with the Comecon countries, which had provided credits to cover its increasing trade deficit as well as developmental loans and massive price subsidies. By 1991, the Soviet bloc's support of Cuba was equivalent to some 37 per cent of the total debt of developing nations towards donor countries.[1] The last Cuban–Soviet Trade Pact had been signed in 1991 and had envisaged a transition over a period of one year towards a new system of trade, conducted in hard currency and at world market prices. As long as the regime retained friends in high places within the Soviet state, however, some continued support could be expected. In the aftermath of the failure of the internal pro-Soviet coup of December 1991 and with the subsequent dissolution of the Soviet Union, all the Cuban backers in Russia were swept from power.

The news of the attempted coup was relayed to Castro at the end of the Pan-American Games, as the Cuban leaders were celebrating the triumph of their athletes over those of the United States. Their initial euphoria quickly gave way to concern as the coup turned into a rout, and to alarm as the Soviet Communist Party and the Soviet Union itself disintegrated.[2] Boris Yeltsin was known to be hostile towards the Cuban regime. A military leader close to the Russian leader had stated, 'Perhaps the best favour we could do to the Cuban people would be to cut off all collaboration with the Castro regime so that the island may return to the path of world civilization.'[3]

The new governments in Russia and the Commonwealth of Independent States rapidly dismantled their links with Cuba. By 1992, most Soviet personnel had left the island and in June 1993, the last of the Soviet troops, 500 Russian soldiers and families of the Motorized Infantry Brigade, which had been there since 1962, set sail for Russia. During an international conference on the Missile Crisis in 1992, Castro declared that the disintegration of the Soviet Union was 'worse for us than the October Crisis', and in a speech to the National Assembly a year later he described the resulting loss of preferential trade and aid as a 'treacherous, devastating blow'.[4]

The sudden decline in Comecon and Soviet trade and aid had a dramatic effect on the Cuban economy. Bereft of its generous and lenient godfather, the economy went into free fall. Between 1989 and 1993, GDP sank by 35 per cent while the export of Cuban goods fell by 79 per cent. Despite a modest recovery from the middle of the decade, the value of these exports at the beginning of the new millennium was still 70 per cent below that of the 1980s. Similarly, the import of goods shrank to 43 per cent of that of their pre-1989 days. The Cuban government was forced into the international finance market for high-interest bearing loans to fund its galloping trade deficit.[5] A range of other economic indicators was equally negative. Manufacturing and agricultural output fell and in the sugar sector, the traditional mainstay of the Cuba economy, production halved. Only in the high-value technologically intense sectors, such as oil, nickel and natural gas, was there any solace, the result of an earlier shift in economic policy. A surge of exports in these sectors enabled the Cuban economy in the post-Soviet period to fund vital imports.[6]

Faced with a rapidly deteriorating economy, the Cuban leadership responded with a series of piecemeal initiatives designed to fill the gap left by the collapse of Soviet and East European trade and to re-orient the economy towards new trading partners. At the beginning of 1990, Castro declared a new policy called the Special Period in Time of Peace, an adaptation of wartime emergency plans drawn up when it was feared that President Reagan might institute a total naval blockade of Cuba. The measures it entailed, the reduction of food subsidies and cuts in public expenditure, were similar to those measures of adjustment common to other Third World countries at the time, except that the basic welfare of Cubans was protected to a greater extent than the poor elsewhere, as Castro was keen to point out.[7] Production was partially militarised, fuel and electricity were cut, farmers were encouraged to use oxen ('the noble ox', as Castro now described it, trying to make a virtue out of necessity) and a whole range of projects and social programmes was suspended.[8]

A Food Programme was also launched in an attempt to overcome the problems in the production and supply of foodstuffs created by the phased withdrawal of Soviet trade. It involved a huge investment of money and labour, requiring yet again the mass mobilisation of volunteers, such as students, from outside the agrarian sector. Like many such initiatives in the past, it was blighted by shortages and the inadequacies of central management (the students, for example, abandoned the fields to sit their summer exams and many of the crops rotted where they stood).[9] Should the Special Period fail or should the embargo tighten, Castro warned, Cubans would face Zero Option, total isolation from the rest of the world.

Despite the expectations it had aroused, however, the twice-postponed Fourth Congress of the Cuban Communist Party of October 1991 failed to make any far-reaching economic reforms. The 'free farmers' markets' of the early 1980s were not re-established and only a very limited range of private businesses of an individual and artisanal nature were sanctioned. But as the crisis deepened, the regime was forced to announce further reform measures. Production was reorganised on state-owned sugar plantations, creating smaller workforces and awarding material incentives and small plots of land to the labourers. In July 1993, the internal use of the dollar was finally legalised, after years of frenzied exchange on the black market. Yet it was a measure designed more to control the booming submerged economy, and to bring in much needed hard currency from Cubans in exile, than to stimulate production.[10] Individual businesses in a hundred further occupations already flourishing underground were sanctioned and state farms were turned into cooperatives. And at the beginning of 1994, Castro announced a monetary reform package that eliminated state subsidies on a whole range of goods and services, introduced progressive taxation and set in place a convertible currency.

After the collapse of the special relationship with the Soviet Union, the economic strategy of the Cuban leadership was to achieve a reinsertion of Cuban trade into the world market. This was to be accomplished, without any fundamental reform of the domestic command economy, by finding new outlets for Cuba's traditional exports such as sugar, nickel, citrus fruit and tobacco, by expanding tourism and by marketing the much prized biotechnological products developed in Cuba's laboratories. All these activities were beset by problems: the continued US embargo made it difficult to find new trading partners, neighbouring economies produced a similar range of traditional exports, the production of sugar and nickel depended on the import of fuel, spare parts and technology which Cuba could ill afford, and Cuba's infant pharmaceutical industry could hardly compete on the international market in which multinational firms enjoyed far greater resources for research and development.

The export sector, in particular, needed to attract foreign capital and know-how in order to compete in the world market. To this end, the regime encouraged the growth of joint ventures with foreign capital. By the mid-1990s over a hundred major joint ventures of various forms were in operation, mostly in the tourist sector, with Cuba providing the personnel and the infrastructure and foreign firms the technology and the market.[11] Castro, always at the centre of economic decision-making, participated in the negotiations, which often had to take place in secret because it was feared that pressure from Washington might discourage foreign investors.[12] The growing presence of foreign firms meant that, increasingly, Cuba had four different economies, a thriving black economy providing some 60 per cent of the population's basic food needs, an independent, enclave export sector, a hard currency consumer market open to those with dollars and a nationalised economy marked by low productivity and severe rationing and reliant to a great extent on voluntary work.[13]

The contradictions generated by this kind of mixed economy did not help ordinary Cubans accept the worsening of their living conditions. As prices rose and supplies of basic commodities dwindled, living standards plummeted. Average calorie intake fell to 900 a day (compared to a norm of 2,500) and diseases associated with malnutrition and vitamin deficiency, banished from Cuba by the Revolution in 1959, began to re-appear. A new disease, optical neuritis, also spread and was only brought under control in September 1993. Ordinary Cubans had to suffer increasing power cuts and reductions in public services, while for most, Chinese-made bicycles became the only means of private transport after drastic rationing of fuel (even the army had to parade on bikes in traditional patriotic celebrations).

The different opportunities offered by the mixed economy (some Cubans, for example, had easy access to dollars) served to erode the egalitarian basis of the Revolution and this in turn increasingly undermined the legitimacy of the state itself. Even the privileged position enjoyed by the party and military elites was subverted by cuts; unlike the black marketeers and Cubans with generous relatives in exile in Miami, they had little access to dollars.[14] Cuba's continued achievements in health and education – with one of the best ratios of doctors per capita and one of the lowest rates of infant mortality in the world – must have seemed to many Cubans poor compensation for the inadequacy of their diet and the absence of consumer goods. The historical role which Castro had assigned Cubans of standing up to the US ('Our people know that on their shoulders rests a great historical responsibility'[15]) was difficult to sustain when they were going hungry.

Besides, an appeal to the 'heroism' of the 1960s must have meant little to a new generation of Cubans. The growing disenchantment among young Cubans was probably intensified by the sense of alienation from the largely ageing political elite, despite the exaltation of the myth of youth in official ideology.[16] The swell of discontent over conditions in Cuba led in August 1994 to a new exodus, the third since 1965, when tens of thousands of mainly economic refugees, many of whom were in their twenties, left for the Florida coast in rudimentary craft including home-made rafts and rubber tyres. Some perished on the way, adding to the death toll already swollen by the sinking of a tug stolen in July by would-be immigrants.[17] In the same month, riots broke out in Havana over the worsening of conditions of daily life. As with the Reagan administration a decade earlier, the new immigrant crisis led the Clinton government to negotiate a new quota of entry visas with Cuba under the Cuban Adjustment Act 1966, setting off a huge wave of applications.

While they created fissures in Cuban society, the new reforms did not challenge the basic model of the command economy. They were seen as piecemeal reforms arising out of the emergency created by the loss of the Soviet connection; as in time of war, economic decisions had to be improvised since no long-term planning was possible during the transition to new economic relationships. Though noticeably less energetic than before, Castro was once again in his element; emergencies had been the stuff of his career. Surrounded by his special group of advisors, he roamed the island, initiating inspired and sometimes less than inspired improvisations to problems of production and supply. Always susceptible to technological elixirs, he was prone to launch programmes that had been insufficiently tested, some of which appeared to fail or generated costs they were meant to avoid.[18]

Economic reform, therefore, was the product not so much of new thinking about the economic system but of the regime's sheer need for survival. Aware of the contradictions of dollarisation, Castro introduced the measure on television (thereby breaking with the precedent of closed National Assembly deliberations) by stating, 'It hurts but we must be intelligent . . . and we have the right to invent things to survive in these conditions without ever ceasing to be revolutionaries.'[19] On the contrary, Castro continued to assert the regime's orthodoxy in the midst of a worldwide collapse of Soviet-style socialism. The slogan 'Socialism or Death', first coined at the beginning of 1989 on the thirtieth anniversary of the Revolution, became the rallying cry of all his speeches. And Castro never ceased to berate capitalism. Announcing the monetary reform measures package of January

1994, he declared, 'Authorising private commerce would be a political and ideological turnaround; it would be like starting along the path towards capitalism. . . . I find capitalism repugnant. It is filthy [una porquería], it is gross, it is alienating . . . because it causes war, hypocrisy and competition.'[20]

Like the Chinese leadership's attempt to balance modernisation with authoritarian rule, Castro was trying to carry out a partial re-integration of the economy into the world market without significantly altering the internal order.[21] Far from encouraging reform, the collapse of Soviet and East European socialism reinforced his belief that any tinkering with the political system would have disastrous consequences. Though he felt Gorbachev had wanted to 'perfect' socialism, the Soviet leader's policies of *glasnost* and *perestroika* had undermined the legitimacy of the Communist Party. 'A process was unleashed', Castro said, referring to Gorbachev's reforms, 'which led to the destruction of the party's authority, and destroying the authority of the party meant destroying one of the pillars . . . of socialism.' The disintegration of the Soviet Union was thus seen as a result of errors rather than of any systemic flaws.[22]

In a speech to the National Assembly in March 1993, Castro lamented the consequences of the collapse of the Soviet Union,

*What we are seeing is whole nations dying from disillusionment because of mediocre political illusions that were put into their heads. . . . Some of these former socialist countries don't know what they are or what they're going to do. . . . There is no plan, no order, no programme, there is nothing and what can come of nothing . . . but chaos?*

Indeed, much was made in the state-controlled mass media of the problems facing the people of the Commonwealth of Independent States as a result of the adoption of market reform and pluralism.[23]

The experience of the Sandinistas in Nicaragua, who had embraced social democracy and ended up losing the elections in February 1990, also suggested that any uncontrolled political *apertura* was too dangerous an experiment. While the US offensive against Cuba continued, any substantial political reform would be seen as weakness, encouraging Washington to escalate its demands. Castro hinted that if the embargo were lifted and US–Cuban relations were normalised, 'another form of political leadership' might become possible, though he insisted that this would not be a bourgeois democracy.[24]

Yet in the wake of the corruption trials of 1989, when the leadership had launched a campaign of mass assemblies to shore up the legitimacy of the regime, it became clear that there was a groundswell of support for political reform and a partial liberalisation of the economy.[25] A reformist tendency emerged within the Party, one of whose more cautious exponents was the head of ideology and international relations Carlos Aldana. Backed by some intellectuals and top administrators, the reformists advocated a number of significant reforms: limited political pluralism, including permission for opposition figures to stand in elections, partial economic reform, an independent media, a lay as opposed to an atheist state and a return in the regime's propaganda to a stress on the national origins of the Revolution as opposed to its 'international socialist' credentials.[26] This was no programme of *perestroika* but it was enough to challenge the position of the more conservative sections of the Party and the rest of the leadership, who viewed any reform with suspicion in the light of events in Eastern Europe and the Soviet Union. Thus it was no surprise that Aldana was sacked in September 1992 and replaced by a more conservative man, an ex-ambassador to the Soviet Union, though part of the official explanation for Aldana's removal was the sadly familiar one that he had been involved in a financial scandal.[27]

The Fourth Party Congress, however, voted in favour of elements of the reformists' programme. The article in the Party's constitution committing it to atheism was removed, while the Party itself was partially redefined to include its 'national character'. The Congress also approved the direct election of deputies to the National Assembly. These were not significant changes; while candidates for the Assembly could now be elected directly in a secret ballot, they had to be chosen as candidates by selection committees of the grass-roots organisations at municipal level and while they need not be party members, no non-party organisation could put up candidates. Thus in the general elections of February 1993, 70 per cent of candidates were party members and all candidates, including two Protestant ministers who were eventually elected, were listed in the so-called 'united ballot' proposed by the government. The choice offered voters, therefore, was to vote for the official slate, abstain or spoil the ballot. In the event, with a turnout of 98.8 per cent, 88.4 per cent voted for the united ballot, 7.2 per cent spoilt the ballot and a further 4 per cent partially abstained by voting for only one candidate on the list.[28]

The purge of the reformists, therefore, did not signal a total rejection of reform. Sacking their leading proponents while appropriating some of their proposals was a way of acknowledging their ideas without allowing them to challenge the regime. Conversely, it satisfied conservative opponents of change within the Party and the military without abandoning the possibility of limited reform. The action of the leadership suggested once again that Castro was not free to dictate policy but had constantly to balance conflicting interests within and outside the Party.

Despite his rhetorical defence of socialist orthodoxy, however, Castro's speeches and interviews increasingly stressed a theme that had been constant throughout his political career: that the primary contradiction in the contemporary world was not between social classes but between North and South, between developed and developing nations. Cuban socialism, a mix of centralism, austerity and social justice, was presented as a model not for industrialised economies, as in orthodox Marxist texts, but for Third World countries. In an interview in a Spanish magazine, he stated, 'Marx thought that socialism was the natural outcome of a developed capitalist society. But life has taught us that socialism is the ideal instrument of development in countries that have been left behind.' In a similar interview with a Mexican reporter in 1991, he said, 'They talk about the failure of socialism but where is the success of capitalism in Africa, Asia and Latin America?'[29] After the collapse of Soviet socialism, Castro set himself up even more emphatically as the champion of the world's poor against the post-Communist triumphalism of liberal capitalism. At the Fourth Congress, he declared messianically, 'Now we have a universal responsibility . . . we are struggling not only for ourselves and our ideas, but for the ideas of all the exploited, subjugated, pillaged and hungry people in the world.'[30]

Nevertheless, the potential for solidarity among Third World countries had perhaps never been lower than in the mid-1990s. Cuba's erstwhile allies in Latin America and Africa had either lost power or had embraced the neo-liberal Washington Consensus. It was symptomatic that Castro's friend and the former socialist Prime Minister of Jamaica Michael Manley had been hired by Cable and Wireless to try to persuade the Cuban government to award the British firm a contract to modernise Cuba's telephone network.[31] Nevertheless, Castro still commanded widespread popular support in Latin America, as was evident in his visit to Bolivia and Colombia in the summer of 1993 during which he was besieged by crowds of well-wishers. He remained for many a symbol of defiance against the continued economic and cultural imperialism of the United States. But his old Bolivarian vision of a Latin America united against the predatory North behind tariff and debt barriers no longer held any charm for Latin American leaders who had renegotiated their debt problems and were keen to gain new credits and benefit from closer trading links with the United States.[32]

Cuba might have become once again an acceptable political partner in Latin America, having abandoned its continental guerrilla strategy long ago. Castro was welcomed by the Mexican President Carlos Salinas at the summit meeting of Latin American heads of state in Guadalajara (to which for the first time, the US was not invited) and the Caribbean common market (CARICOM) was discussing trade with the Cuban government. But Cuba's policies and those of most Latin American leaders were moving in opposite directions, as Castro himself recognised.[33] For its own part, the Latin American Left had abandoned the democratic centralist and state socialist model still espoused by Cuba, while the Pan-American anti-imperialist traditions of Lázaro Cárdenas and Perón were being radically redefined by their heirs, Carlos Salinas and the President of Argentina Carlos Menem. For the time being, Castro's attempt to invoke a radical, nationalist Latin American heritage could win him neither a new following in the continent nor a renewed legitimacy in Cuba.[34]

Similarly, since Rectification and in particular after the collapse of the Soviet Union, the Cuban leadership tended to play down analogies with the October Revolution in favour of the autochthonous origins of the Cuban Revolution and its Latin American connections.[35] The previous flow of articles about fraternal links with Eastern Europe and the Soviets gave way to columns about contemporary Latin America and the heroes of Latin American and Cuban independence. Socialism became a synonym for the peculiar nature of Cuban experience, though Cuban leaders continued to use the rhetoric of Marxism-Leninism. The works of Che Guevara, a fierce critic of Soviet revisionism, were once again promoted by Castro. 'My admiration and my sympathy for Che have grown', said Castro in an interview in 1992, 'as I have seen everything that has occurred in the socialist camp, because he was firmly opposed to the methods of building socialism using the categories of capitalism.'[36] In the February 1993 elections to the National Assembly, Castro himself stood as a candidate in a constituency at the foot of the Sierra Maestra which included some of the suburbs of Santiago; it was a symbolic gesture, helping to evoke the early days of the Revolution. Alongside the ponderous dogma of Soviet socialism, Castro renewed the Guevarist appeal to justice and egalitarianism as the essential categories of the Revolution. Thus in his last years as leader, Castro reached back to the early values of the Revolution before his adoption of Marxism-Leninism.

Castro's continued legitimacy among Cubans rested above all on his appeal to beleaguered nationalism. The victory of the Democrats in the 1992 US elections did not lessen the American offensive against Cuba, despite Castro's optimism about Bill Clinton's intentions.[37] The Cuban Democracy Act (otherwise known as the Torricelli Amendment) of November 1992, giving the US President powers to ban all US subsidiaries based in third countries from trading with Cuba, had been promoted by a Democrat and supported by Clinton himself, though twice the United Nations voted by an overwhelming majority against the US embargo of Cuban trade. Castro's demands for ever greater sacrifices by the Cuban people could be justified by the 'blockade' of Cuba and political centralisation legitimised by the sense of siege. The same feelings of insecurity had led to the creation of vigilante groups or Rapid Response Brigades of volunteers in 1991 to counter a potential fifth column; more often than not they were employed to harass representatives of Cuban human rights organisations or individuals demanding political reform.

The US trade embargo against Cuba was ratcheted up following the shooting down by the Cuban air force in early 1996 of two civilian aircraft belonging to the Cuban exile organization Hermanos al Rescate (Brothers to the Rescue). The organization had begun to violate Cuban air space and in two audacious raids in January dropped anti-Castroist leaflets over Havana. On 24 February two of three of their aircraft attempting the same sortie were shot down without warning by Cuban fighter planes. In retaliation, President Clinton signed one of the most controversial bills in the history of the US. The Cuban Liberty and Democratic Solidarity (Libertad) Act (otherwise known as the Helms-Burton Bill) had been passed by the Senate in 1995 but kept on ice. The Act entailed a highly contentious escalation of the embargo by threatening to sanction all countries, institutions and firms outside the US that either extended loans to Cuba (such as the World Bank) or traded with Cuba. US firms were also threatened with sanctions if they imported from other countries any products containing material originating in Cuba. According to the Act, the new, intensified embargo could only be lifted once a transition government was in place in Cuba and property confiscated by the Cuban government in the 1960s had been returned to its original owners if they were US nationals, accompanied by appropriate compensation.

The scope of the Act was a breathtaking expression of the US's brief tenure as sole world hegemon in that it extended US law to the rest of the world. It was this crucial element of extraterritoriality that stirred countries trading with Cuba into fierce opposition to the Act. Cuba was Britain's seventh largest trade partner and the UK government under the Conservatives immediately lodged a strongly worded diplomatic note in protest and urged the EU to take action.[38] In October, the EU Council declared that the Act violated freedom of trade and instructed firms in the Union to ignore the legislation, while it sought to force the US to repeal the Act. After a series of EU–US negotiations, the US government agreed to exempt the EU from the extraterritorial clauses of the Act. From then on,

at six-monthly intervals, first Clinton then George W. Bush signed successive waivers of those clauses to all third parties yet continued to threaten its
implementation in the hope that it might serve as a deterrent. The Act failed
to prevent Cuba expanding its foreign trade yet it remained a continual
threat to this trade and a source of anger and resentment on all sides.

The clauses concerning Cuba envisaged a tightening of the embargo
(for example by strengthening regulations on remittances to Cuba and
licences for US citizens to travel to the island) and an escalation of anti-
Castro propaganda. The lifting of the embargo was made conditional on the
realisation of a transition to democracy in Cuba defined in terms so stringent they hardly conformed to any realistic scenario for negotiated political
change beyond the collapse of the regime. Castro's response to the Act was
as usual combative. The divisions the Act created between the US and its
allies as well as the international trade organisations were a new means
for Castro of rallying nationalist sentiment but also reassuring Cubans that
they were not isolated. In two speeches on 31 March and 30 April 1996 he
described it as 'that brutal and genocidal Helms Burton law' that was also
'harming the sovereignty of the rest of the world'. Yet, he went on, 'we see
the number of those in the world disgusted [with the US] spreading like
wildfire, and people inventing formulas to make investments in Cuba and
do business in Cuba, in one way or another'.[39]

The polarising effects of the intensified US embargo no doubt deepened
the anxiety of the more conservative of the Cuban elites, especially in the
Party. The limited economic liberalisation of the Special Period had already
raised some alarm because its effects threatened to weaken the command
economy as well as undermine egalitarian principles of the Revolution.
Their insecurity extended to some of the new ideas coming out of research
centres that the Party had created in the mid-1970s, ideas that appeared to
question party orthodoxy. A new cycle of investigation into Cuban party
intellectuals reminiscent of the actions against *Lunes de Revolución* in 1961
and *Pensamiento Crítico* in 1969 began just weeks after the signing of the
Cuban Liberty and Democratic Solidarity (Libertad) Act. Two of these centres
were the subject of intervention by the Central Committee and the Politburo.
Unusually, the documents and the minutes of the internal investigation
into one of them, the internationally respected Centre for the Study of
America (Centro de Estudios sobre América or CEA), were smuggled out of
Cuba and published, despite the state's directive that they should be destroyed.[40]
They provide an interesting glimpse into the minds of Party hardliners.

The CEA had originally been assigned the task of studying Cuba's relations with Latin America. It had been classified as an NGO in 1988 although

most of its staff were Party militants. By the 1990s, the research publications of the CEA were focusing increasingly on Cuba's internal politics and were discreetly exploring reforms of the economic and political system. The case against the staff in March 1996 was that they had deviated not only from their original mission but also from the official line. The chair of the Party commission investigating the centre, the veteran leader José Balaguer, made clear what this orthodoxy consisted of. According to the minutes, he stated, 'The official language is the language of Fidel Castro and to this is added the language of the minister of the economy, Carlos Lage' (and presumably the other top officials of the regime). The report of the commission was presented to the Central Committee by Raúl Castro, accusing the researchers of 'falling into the spider's web spun by foreign Cubanologists, in reality the servants of the United States in its policy of fomenting the fifth column'.[41] The commission's demand for self-criticism and confession of errors on the part of the centre had the unmistakable whiff of a Stalinist purge and was countered by a spirited defence by its staff. A letter of appeal they sent to the Castro brothers asking for support was left unanswered.

Although none of the academics involved lost their state contracts, they were removed from the centre and dispersed to other institutions, from where several abandoned Cuba and continued their critical activities abroad. What the case exemplified was a continuing sense of paranoia among Party hardliners towards ideological and political heterodoxy, a fear intensified by the consequences of *perestroika* in the Soviet Union. They rationalised this insecurity as the need, generated by the US siege, for a unipolarity of approach and thinking. The outcome made clear that the limits of internal debate were set by Castro and they were narrow indeed. Further measures to constrict the activities of intellectuals and journalists were taken three years later with a new law, the Law number 88 for the Protection of National Independence and the Economy of Cuba, nicknamed the 'gag law' (or *ley mordaza*) by opponents, which gave the authorities scope to interpret any independent media activity or intellectual pursuit as support for the Helms-Burton Act.[42]

The flushing out of reformist intellectuals coincided with the first moves against the Special Period measures. Raúl Castro, acting no doubt with the full support of his brother, proceeded to criticise the effects of the market reforms he had supported three years earlier. The first restrictions were imposed on the small private sector that had emerged in the spaces opened up by the Special Period. Thus some self-employment licences were suspended or had their fees raised, taxes on the takings of licensed private enterprises such as the family-run restaurants, the *paladares*, were increased and raids were made on those suspected of 'trafficking' with the opportunities created by the Special Period.

The Cuban state's treatment of its internal critics was progressively under scrutiny by foreign governments. The EU applied its policy of conditionality whereby cooperation with Cuba was tied to progress on human rights and political liberalisation on the island. Under the new conservative government of José María Aznar, Spain brought its economic assistance to Cuba to an end, provoking a break in diplomatic relations between the two countries. The feeling of encirclement can only have been deepened by the sequence of terrorist bombings of Havana hotels, restaurants and discotheques between April and September 1997, in one of which an Italian tourist was killed. The alleged main instigator of the atrocities was the notorious ex-CIA agent Luis Posada Carriles, who had been held responsible for the 1976 bombing of a Cuban airliner and the death of all its passengers, and was supported by the right-wing exile organization the Cuban American National Foundation.[43]

In these circumstances, Castro's successful effort to engineer a visit to Cuba by Pope John Paul II in 1998 was something of a coup because it brought a much-needed international legitimacy at a time of isolation. The visit was a long time in the making. The slow rapprochement between the Cuban Catholic Church and the state had been accelerated in the mid-1980s, helped by the condemnation of the US embargo by the Vatican and the Cuban and US Churches. Other growing common ground was solidarity with the Third World against capitalist exploitation, a campaign originally launched by Pope John XXIII in the Second Vatican Council of 1962–5, and criticism of consumerist society in the developed world. For his part, John Paul II had made a particular target of the neo-liberal consensus of the 1980s onwards. Despite diametrically opposed beliefs, the rapprochement was facilitated not just by the opportunities it offered but by a common ethical stance over key issues such as poverty and equality. It was a marriage of convenience between political and religious faith.

Castro, who had increasingly been stressing the links between religion and socialism,[44] had initiated meetings with Cuban and American Catholic bishops from the mid-1980s onwards, while the Vatican began to build bridges with the Cuban state. A constitutional amendment was passed in July 1992 eliminating religious discrimination, while membership of the Cuban Communist Party was opened to Catholics in the Fourth Congress of the same year. In 1996, Castro went to Rome for an audience with the Pope in which no doubt the project of a papal visit to Cuba was discussed. In preparation for this visit the government declared Christmas Day a national holiday in 1997 and allowed the Cuban Cardinal Ortega to broadcast a Christmas sermon on national television.

John Paul II's visit to Cuba in January 1998 was thus the result of careful calculation on both his and Castro's part of the advantages and risks it entailed. For the Pope, it represented an opportunity to mobilise the faithful and press for democratic reform in Cuba. No doubt he had in mind his first papal visit to Poland in 1979, which had played such an important role in creating the conditions for the Polish transition to democracy 10 years later. At the same time, Cuba was a useful platform for the Pope, not just to demonstrate his opposition to the US embargo but beyond that to denounce the excesses of neo-liberal capitalism. His speeches were shrewdly modulated to ensure a balance between support and criticism of the Cuban Revolution.[45] For Castro, the risks of the visit were much greater than for the Pope. As we have seen, the state was deeply apprehensive about the development of civil society outside its control. Of the informal networks that had to be monitored vigilantly, faith-based communities were among the most important.

The impact of the Pope's visit on Cubans was judged very differently by the state and the oppositionists. For Castro, the mass gatherings for the Pope's four masses in different parts of the island did not resonate strongly among Cubans. On the contrary, those who assembled to hear the Pope's words, according to Castro, demonstrated respect for them because that is what the state had asked them to do, and when the accompanying speeches were hard on the regime, as in Santiago, he claimed that much of the audience left. Others have argued that the Pope successfully appealed over the head of the state to embedded religiosity and Christian morality among Cubans that had not been allowed expression.[46] In the event, the visit proved a success for both the Pope and for Castro. John Paul II undoubtedly mobilised Cuba's Catholics and extracted from the regime the release of around 300 prisoners and greater leeway for the activities of the Church. For Castro, the papal visit afforded some degree of global legitimacy at a time of crisis but also appeared to confirm his claim that Christianity and socialism shared some basic assumptions, an important component of his effort to build a new post-Soviet identity that would appeal to Latin America.

After the collapse of the Soviet Union most non-Cuban commentators were confidently predicting the imminent downfall of Castro's regime. But his continued survival in 1990s should not have come as a surprise. There was no organised opposition to the state in Cuba because it was not allowed and any attempt to muster collective criticism of its policies was severely repressed. The absence of opposition did not mean there was no social and political dissatisfaction. On the contrary, there were diffuse resentments above all over social and consumer issues, such as inadequate diet, unemployment, inequalities, shortages in the supply of goods and so on. The living conditions of Cubans had only marginally improved in the late 1990s after the hardships of the early years of the decade. Yet the political situation was stable and generic support for Castro was still strong. The army remained the most powerful institution in Cuba and the loyalty of the top echelon of officers to Castro was unquestionable. The price of discordance with the leadership was high; among the accusations against General Ochoa in his trial in 1989 was that he had shown signs of 'populism' though there was no evidence that he had had any popular support. And Castro had always been careful to maintain equilibrium between the different 'families' of the regime to ensure unity and to forestall any challenge to the state. Nevertheless, while the economy continued to be brittle and the US harassment of Cuba unrelenting, Castro's Revolution remained precarious.

## Notes

1  C. Mesa-Lago (ed.), *Cuba after the Cold War* (University of Pittsburgh Press, 1993), p. 151.

2  R.E. Quirk, *Fidel Castro* (Norton, New York, 1994), p. 832.

3  *Latin American Weekly Report*, 12 Sept. 1991.

4  *The Guardian*, 22 Feb. 1992; *Granma International*, 28 March 1993.

5  C. Mesa-Lago and J.F. Pérez-López, *Cuba's Aborted Reform: Socioeconomic Effects, Internacional Comparisons, and Transition Politics* (University Press of Florida, Gainesville, 2005), pp. 27–70.

6  C. Mesa-Lago, 'The Cuban economy in 2006–7', Paper to the Annual Meeting of the Association for the Study of the Cuban Economy (ASCE), 2007, Table 2.

7  In an interview with Tomás Borge, *Un grano de maíz, conversación con Fidel Castro* (Fondo de Cultura Económica, Mexico, 1992), pp. 178–9.

8  Mesa-Lago, *Cuba after the Cold War*, pp. 165–7.

9  Ibid., pp. 227–44.

10  'Keeping the faith', *The Economist*, 9 Oct. 1993.

11  L. Larifla, 'Fin du CAEM et sous-développement dévoilé à Cuba', *Problèmes d'Amérique Latine*, 10 (July–Sept. 1993), pp. 40–1; *Latinamerica Press*, 30 Sept. 1993.

12  Mesa-Lago, *Cuba after the Cold War*, p. 202.

**13** *Latin American News Service*, week ending 18 Feb. 1994; Larifla, 'Fin du CAM', p. 50; J.I. Domínguez, 'Cuba's switch from state economy', *Financial Times*, 26 Jan. 1994.

**14** *The Economist*, 9 Oct. 1993. A CIA spokesman, appearing before the US Senate's Intelligence Committee in July 1993, argued that the legalisation of the dollar would 'aggravate social tensions and distinctions in Cuba because only a small proportion of the population will receive hard currency from overseas' (*Caribbean and Central America Report*, 26 Aug. 1993).

**15** Borge, *Un grano de maíz*, p. 194.

**16** A. Kapcia, *Cuba: Island of Dreams* (Berg, Oxford, 2000), p. 209.

**17** According to an official Cuban report as recounted by Castro to Ignacio Ramonet, the stolen tug had not been sunk by a Cuban patrol boat but by one of two other tugs that had chased it when it left port (I. Ramonet, *Fidel Castro. Biografía a dos voces* (Random House Mondadori, Mexico and Barcelona, 2006), pp. 307–9).

**18** Mesa-Lago, *Cuba after the Cold War*, pp. 234–8 refers to several recent examples among which are the substitution of liquid fodder for imported grain for feeding pigs and the mass production of a locally invented 'multiplow'.

**19** *Latin American Weekly Report*, 15 July 1993.

**20** *Latin American Weekly Report*, 13 Jan. 1994.

**21** A number of top officials were sent to China to study the effect of economic reforms there (*Caribbean and Central America Report*, 27 Jan. 1994).

**22** Borge, *Un grano de maíz*, p. 48; *Granma International*, 5 May 1991.

**23** Castro quote from speech to National Assembly on 15 March, available at http:/www.cuba.cu/gobierno/discursos/1993/esp/f150393e.html (last accessed 3 June 2008); *New York Times*, 13 Jan. 1993.

**24** Borge, *Un grano de maíz*, p. 120.

**25** M. Pérez-Stable, 'Charismatic authority, vanguard party politics and popular mobilizations: revolution and socialism in Cuba', *Cuban Studies*, 22 (1992), p. 19.

**26** *Latin American Weekly Report*,13 Jan. 1994.

**27** *New York Times*, 12 Oct. 1992; *Financial Times*, 26–27 Sept. 1992. The official explanation stated also that Aldana had been guilty of 'deficiencies in his work and serious errors of a personal nature in the fulfillment of his duties'. For further details see *Granma International*, 18 Oct. 1992.

**28** *Economist*, 6 March 1993; official figures gave a 99.62 per cent turnout and only 3.05 per cent blank votes and 3.9 per cent spoilt ballots.

**29** *Cambio 16*, 25 June 1990; *Siempre*, 30 May 1991.

**30** G. Reed, *Island in the Storm: the Cuban Communist Party's Fourth Congress* (Ocean Press, Melbourne, Victoria, 1992), p. 32.

**31** *Financial Times*, 25 Nov. 1993; *Caribbean and Central America Report*, 27 Jan. 1994. In the event, the deal fell through, perhaps as a result of US pressure.

**32** *Reuter*, 9 Aug. 1993. Castro had also attempted to appeal to the Presidents of Mexico, Colombia and Venezuela in 1991 in an unscheduled visit to Cozumel where they were meeting. He had come back empty-handed, having been told that Cuba could not be admitted to regional trade pacts until it carried out substantive political and economic reforms.

**33** Borge, *Un grano de maíz*, p. 160.

**34** R. Rabkin, 'Cuban socialism: ideological responses to the era of socialist crisis' *Cuban Studies*, 22 (1992), p. 29.

**35** A typical example is A. Hart's article 'A battle for the identity of Our America', *Granma International*, 18 April 1993.

**36** Borge, *Un grano de maíz*, pp. 80–1.

**37** During the July 1993 summit of Latin American leaders in Brazil, Castro declared 'It seems to me that Clinton belongs to another generation of Americans. . . . I have the impression he's a decent person and a peaceful one' (*Associated Press*, 5 Aug. 1993).

**38** House of Commons Research Paper, 'Cuba and the Helms Burton Act', 14 December 1998.

**39** http://www.cuba.cu/gobierno/discursos/1996/esp/f310396e.html (last accessed 10 June 2008); http://www.cuba.cu/gobierno/discursos/1996/esp/f300496e.html (last accessed 10 June 2008).

**40** They are published in the annexes of M. Giuliani's *El caso CEA: intelectuales e inquisidores en Cuba:¿Perestroika en la isla?* (Ediciones Universal, Miami, 1998).

**41** Ibid., p. 50; Balaguer comment on p. 203.

**42** For the text of the law, see http://www.cubanet.org/ref/dis/021699.html (last accessed 10 June 2008).

**43** Posada Carriles was reputed to be responsible also for attempts on Castro's life and enjoyed a certain benevolent inaction on the part of the FBI until his arrest in 2005. For further details, see A.L. Bardach, *Cuba Confidential: Love and Vengeance in Miami and Havana* (Random House, New York, 2002) and declassified national security archives available at http://www.gwu.edu/ ~nsarchiv/NSAEBB/NSAEBB153 (last accessed 9 June 2008).

**44** For example, in his interviews with F. Betto, in Betto, *Fidel and Religion* (Weidenfeld & Nicolson, London, 1987), p. 276.

**45** For example, his sermon in Havana on 25 January, 'Homilía pronunciada en la Celebración Eucarística en el Arquidiócesis de la Habana', available at http://www.nacub.org (last accessed 10 June 2008).

**46** For Castro, see Ramonet, *Castro*, p. 381; for opposing views, see S. Pedraza, 'Impact of Pope John Paul's visit to Cuba', in *Papers and Proceedings of the Eighth Annual Meeting of the Association for the Study of the Cuban Economy (ASCE)*, 8 (1998), pp. 482–5 and K.S. Zagacki, 'Pope John Paul II and the crusade against Communism: a case study in secular and sacred time', *Rhetoric and Public Affairs*, 4(4) (2001), pp. 689–710.

# CHAPTER 10

# Autumn of the Revolutionary Patriarch

The 1990s had been the bleakest decade of the Cuban Revolution. Yet by the beginning of the new millennium the ageing leader and his regime received a new boost of economic and political oxygen through the changing configuration of international geopolitics. With the collapse of Communism in Europe, the bipolar world of the Cold War had given way briefly to the unipolar world of US hegemony, only to make way for a new multipolar world of competing states in which old powers such as Russia and newly emerging economies such as China, India and Brazil increasingly challenged the economic supremacy of the US. In Latin America, a new cycle of social democratic and populist governments emerged, largely in response to the failure of the neo-liberal measures essayed under pressure from the US and the IMF by the governments of the 1990s. This was marked by a new phenomenon that promised more than the cyclical left–right patterns of previous decades in that non-traditional groups such as women and people from poor and ethnic backgrounds were penetrating the preserve of the hitherto white, male and middle-class political elites and acceding to positions of power, often with the backing of new, popular movements.

Fortuitously, Cuba benefited from the new spaces opened up in this changing geometry of world power. The advantages it derived were both political and economic and it was able to trade on its relatively high level of development in areas such as medicine and biotechnology. Relations between Cuba and the CARICOM countries in the Caribbean, which had already snubbed the United States by establishing diplomatic relations with the island in 1972, were strengthened in 2000 by a new trade and economic cooperation agreement.[1] Castro's friend Lula da Silva won the elections in

Brazil in 2002 and brought to power a centre-left government sympathetic to Cuba. This was followed three years later by the election of another close ally, Evo Morales, in the Bolivian elections.

Leading the rescue of Cuba from international ostracism and economic crisis was Hugo Chávez' Venezuela. Castro had first met Chávez in Cuba in the mid-1990s, after the latter had served a two-year jail term for orchestrating a left-wing civilian and military coup against the corrupt Venezuelan partiarchy. Chávez was a great admirer of Castro and the Cuban Revolution in its almost 50-year struggle against US imperialism. Chávez had cast himself in the Bolivarian mould ('un auténtico bolivariano', Castro claimed[2]) or rather, in that of the Bolívar of 1826, by when the anti-imperialist Liberator had moved away from his earlier liberalism to demand lifelong presidency, censorship and circumscribed democracy. Chávez saw himself alongside Castro as the leader of a new anti-capitalist movement in Latin America. Like Castro, Chávez was both populist and paternalist, using the media and in particular his weekly TV programme *Aló Presidente* to transmit a unilateral vision of a Venezuelan and Pan-American revolution. His version of socialism was as unorthodox as Castro's, combining statism, economic nationalism and egalitarianism. Politically shrewd though he was, his rhetoric was at times a vaudeville adaptation of that of the Cuban leader, rough-hewn, fanciful and swaggeringly populist.[3]

When Chávez was elected President in 1998, he began to reshape trade relations with Cuba on conditions that were highly beneficial to the island. Venezuela's huge oil reserves allowed Chávez to extend patronage across Latin America and the Caribbean, striking mutually advantageous deals with governments, such as that of Argentina under Néstor Kirchner, behind the back of the IMF and the US. But no country benefited as much as Cuba. Indeed, Chávez' Venezuela had taken over from the Soviet Union as the economic mainstay of the Cuban Revolution. From the first Cuba–Venezuela agreement of 2000, Cuba began to receive considerable quantities of oil. By 2006 these had risen to 100,000 barrels a day at a preferential price of $27 per barrel, far below average world prices, amounting to a subsidy of about $1.8 billion and providing at least half of Cuba's national consumption. Venezuela also invested heavily in the Cuban economy, in particular in its valuable nickel mining industry. By 2007 this investment had reached $4 billion. In exchange, Cuba provided Venezuela with technical support and personnel in education, sports and above all health. At one point, anything between 22,000 to 26,000 Cuban medical staff were in Venezuela, among which were more than 50 per cent of Cuba's primary care doctors, whose salaries were paid by Venezuela.[4]

This was an unprecedented barter of merchandise trade for human capital and in this sense Cuba was providing invaluable aid to a less socially developed country at the expense of its own people. The Cuban government had identified medical diplomacy as a useful tool of international trade and solidarity since the early 1990s. Offering health services as part of its foreign policy generated status and influence abroad. Cuba's medical outreach went way beyond Latin America. It provided disaster relief as well as treatment in those fields in which it specialised. For example, over 18,000 mainly child victims of the Chernobyl disaster were brought to Cuba to be treated for radiation free of cost.[5] The Cuban government established medical schools abroad and trained foreign medical students in Cuba also at no cost. This health diplomacy extended even to countries that were internationally aligned against Cuba. Yet its main focus was Latin America because Castro saw the continent as a community of purpose with a shared history.

Indeed, Castro's long-standing ambition to create a Latin American front against the US took shape in 2004 when the Bolivarian Alternative for the People of Our America or ALBA was set up with Chávez, in opposition to the neo-liberal US-sponsored Free Trade Area of the Americas (or ALCA in its Spanish version). By 2007, Nicaragua, Bolivia, Ecuador and several English-speaking islands of the Caribbean such as the CARICOM group had signed up to this new regional solidarity front. At last, Castro's ambition to fulfil Martí's Our America appeared to be bearing fruit. Yet it was a largely political project for regional and social development relying on the continued munificence of oil-rich Venezuela under Chávez. Those countries in Latin America with more powerful economies such as Brazil, Mexico, Argentina and Chile were wary of distancing themselves too much from the neo-liberal Washington Consensus, for all their social-democratic rhetoric. Nevertheless, ALBA helped to pull Cuba out of its relative international isolation and give it a new voice in Pan-American relations. In September 2006, Cuba was elected for the second time to lead the Non-Aligned Movement of 118 countries, and by 2007 Cuba had diplomatic or consular relations with 182 countries, and Havana hosted seemingly endless international conferences.

Cuba's standing on the international stage was also boosted by China. An increasingly powerful voice in international relations, China had defended Cuba against the US embargo in the UN and in other international bodies, and had started to build close relations with Cuba since the collapse of the Soviets in 1991. In the new millennium China's economic support for Cuba was stepped up through a series of agreements signed by Castro and the two Chinese Presidents Jian Zenin and Hu Jintao between 2001 and

2006 in Havana and Beijing. There could be no greater cultural contrast than that between the dour Chinese leaders and the flamboyant Castro (even when confined to a wheelchair in 2006 after breaking his knee in a fall). China offered interest-free credits, grants, loans and massive investments (above all in Cuba's mining industry). Many joint ventures were set up in both Cuba and China. By the middle of the decade, China had become Cuba's second most important trading partner after Venezuela, accounting for some 15 per cent of its trade.[6]

A balance sheet of Cuba's trading partners in the new millennium would need to include the rather paradoxical fact that the US, notwithstanding its embargo, continued to export to the island. The ban on trading with Cuba had allowed competitors such as Canada to move into the island's market. In 2000, the Bush administration gave into pressure from American agricultural interests and their Congressional allies and relaxed the embargo on US–Cuban trade under the Trade Sanctions Reform and Export Enhancement Act on the grounds that food could be classified as humanitarian aid. But Cuban purchases came at a high price because they had to be upfront and dollar-only transactions. Thus between 2001 and 2006, Cuba bought $2.2 billion worth of these American products, making it the 25th largest agricultural export market for the US and the US the island's seventh largest trade partner.[7] Southern states of the US such as Louisiana, Mississippi and Alabama benefited in particular from this covert relaxation of the embargo.

The considerable benefits that Venezuela and China brought to the Cuban economy, however, did not compensate for the loss of the Soviet connection. It is true that relations with Russia had improved considerably since the first years of post-Communism. In the new millennium, Russia was absorbing as much as 25 per cent of Cuban exports and in December 2000 Putin had paid a state visit to Cuba.[8] However, economic indicators for 2006–7 betrayed a considerable shortfall in comparison to 1989 when Cuba was benefiting from full trade with the Comecon countries. Manufacturing and agricultural output, for example, was still comparatively low, in particular in sugar production, which was 820 per cent below its 1989 figure. Exports in general had fallen 48 per cent while imports had risen 16 per cent leaving a deteriorating trade balance and a growing external debt. The positive factors included the rise of output in natural gas (3,091 per cent over 1989), oil (a 303 per cent rise) and nickel, and a considerable increase in the number of tourists from 270,000 in 1989 to 2.2 million in 2006, generating gross revenue of some $2.1 billion.[9] In contrast to the austere years of the early 1990s, the Cuban economy was showing substantial growth by the middle of the first decade of the new millennium, thanks in great measure to the new trading partners. Thus the economic contributions of Venezuela and China (as well as substantial investments from multinationals such as the Canadian-based mining and oil company Sherritt International and the Spanish oil company Repsol) helped the Cuban economy to survive by the seat of its pants rather than to overcome its structural deficits.

The government's response to the easing of the crisis of the 1990s was to launch a new cycle of anti-market recentralisation in 2003. The Special Period measures had been brought to a halt in 1996; now they were reversed. Under the new legislation, the dollar no longer became legal tender and all hard currency held by individuals and state enterprises had to be exchanged for convertible pesos for a 10 per cent fee. The Ministry of Foreign Trade re-established control of all exports and imports previously handled by the different state enterprises, permits and licences for small businesses were revoked and self-employment was restricted to the military and to state employees. The relatively small and officially sanctioned parallel market that had emerged in the spaces opened up by the Special Period was effectively closed down.

Castro's own rationalisation for renewed state control over the economy was that the Special Period had multiplied opportunities for corruption and created 'profound inequalities'.[10] Real wages in the state sector, which embraced some 77 per cent of the workforce, had suffered a sharp decline whereas those of private sector workers with access to the tourist industry or to foreign-operated production or joint ventures had risen spectacularly. A waiter in a restaurant could earn many times more than a doctor. Private sector workers were not the only ones to benefit. Those with access to dollars through the remittances of relatives in the US had enjoyed rising living standards. That is, the growing inequalities were articulated largely in terms of a dual economy: the Cuban peso economy and the dollar or convertible peso economy.

The Special Period had thus undermined the rise in living standards made by poorer sections of Cuban society during the first two decades or so of the Revolution. Among these were above all the blacks, who accounted for some 34 per cent of the Cuban population. Since around 84 per cent of Cuban émigrés were white, black families had relatively little access to dollar remittances and moreover had limited opportunities to work in the tourist industry, either as employees or in self-employment.[11] The result, according to official calculations, was that the lower fifth of the population received 7 per cent of total national income while the upper fifth obtained 58 per cent. Thus at the end of the 1990s Cuban society may have still been the most egalitarian society in Latin America because of its health care and education but it was increasingly unequal in terms of individual income and consumption, even possibly approaching levels to be found in some developed and developing capitalist economies.[12]

However, Castro seemed more concerned to justify the new measures as a means of combating corruption, inefficiency and abuse of power. He launched a new campaign to root out these 'illegalities' on 17 November 2005 in a speech at the University of Havana. 'As you know', he said to the students, 'we are engaged in a battle against vices, against the diversion of resources, against theft . . . Do not think that the theft of materials and resources originated today, or in the special period; the special period deepened [the problem], because the special period created much inequality and allowed certain people to have too much money.' Extensive coverage in the newspaper of the young Communists, *Juventud Rebelde*, exposed cases of corruption across the island. Official prices and weights and measures were being circumvented in numerous shops, petrol was being siphoned off at petrol stations, goods were diverted at the ports, all for private sale, black markets sprang up near building sites to sell some of the material and resources of the state were being used for private use or profit. Moreover, limited decentralisation among the ministries and in local government had led to wasteful practices and the unnecessary multiplication of scarce resources such as petrol.[13]

The problem with Castro's focus on corruption is that it glossed over the difficulty many Cubans had in making ends meet and the predicament facing many state enterprises and institutions as a result of deficits over which they had no control. There were of course individuals involved in minor robbery as well as networks of more or less organised crime but there was also a widespread 'banal' corruption, the purpose of which was to compensate for low living standards. Unemployment, low salaries, poor housing and the frequent unavailability of basic foodstuffs at subsidised prices had led many poorer Cubans to resort to pilfering, trafficking, evasion of state controls and so on simply in order to survive. For their part, state organisations resorted to the ever-growing black market to make up for the lack of resources, bureaucratic logjams and shortages of supplies. Some service enterprises like medical centres may indeed have begun surreptitiously to charge their better-off clients. The result was a creeping and covert privatisation of goods and services that continued despite the new offensive.[14] In other words, the source of inequality and corruption was not simply market reform but more importantly the Cuban command economy itself.

Rather than the Chinese model of authoritarian market socialism, or its Vietnamese equivalent, the Doi Moi, Castro and the Cuban leadership had reverted once again to their own model of a moral economy managed on behalf of citizens by the elites at the head of the state. As in the previous anti-market cycle of the mid-1980s, Castro attributed the deep-lying structural problems faced by the Cuban economy mainly to decentralisation, waste, inefficiency and selfishness. By centralising economic decision-making into the hands of those committed to the values of the Revolution, a new means could be found to balance sustained economic growth with the development of human and social capital. That this value-based approach to economic management was a return to the idealism of the early days of the Revolution had been acknowledged by the slogan given to the campaign launched in 2000, 'The Battle of Ideas'.

Greater centralisation meant not just the macro-management of the economy by the core of the political elites led by Castro but its micro-management. It meant also intensifying state patronage and paternalism. The allocation of consumer goods and social services would henceforth be determined from above on largely political criteria. So, for example, Castro promised in his ground-breaking speech to distribute 2.5 million Chinese electric pressure cookers to the poorer sections of the population to encourage them to save energy but also, it can be assumed, to assure them that the state was looking after them.[15] The dilemma was that such state initiatives often papered over deeper socio-economic problems. For example, unemployment among young people had become disproportionately high since the Special Period. In an effort to tackle this problem, the state organised courses to retrain either unskilled workers or people with skills no longer in demand in a changing economy. Unemployed people without work were expected to enrol in these courses to develop more appropriate skills. The problem was that many simply did not show up (and were therefore classified as 'desvinculados' or 'detached') or rarely attended. Official figures in 2006 indicated that there were 146,000 'desvinculados' but the number was probably much higher, according to the newspaper of Communist Youth, *Juventud Rebelde*.[16]

This 'remoralisation' of economic life in Cuba needed the support of a new social movement. Once again, as he had with the Microbrigadas in the 1980s, Castro turned to the youth movement of the Communist Party and also to the thousands of young social workers, many of them young women and many from the less cosmopolitan eastern part of Cuba, who had been mobilised by the campaign three years earlier to improve education throughout the island. This new 'army' of political workers was given its own housing and transport and enjoyed the status of a special relationship with Castro and his inner circle.[17] As he had done in the second half of the

1980s, Castro also surrounded himself with a team of young communist advisors who acted as an informal parallel government, supervising the work of the state institutions and generating new ideas of governance and policy. It had always been one of his strategies to mobilise new generations of Cubans at all levels to revitalise the Revolution and dislodge or galvanise entrenched bureaucracies.

The campaign was launched as part of a recycled 'grand strategy' for the Cuban economy, made possible by the new links with Venezuela and China. Castro's speech of 17 November 2005 outlined some of the key aspects of this development strategy. It envisaged a massive investment in cleaner and alternative sources of energy, replacing wasteful and polluting technologies such as power stations with smaller generators in a new 'energy revolution' that was launched at the beginning of 2006.[18] Cuba's record on sustainable development was already high by international standards. According to data it submitted to the United Nations, Cuba was the only country in the world during the period 1975 to 2003 to meet the UN's minimum criteria for sustainability, whereby the Human Development Index is matched with the ecological footprint, or measure of demand on the biosphere.[19] Of course, Cuba's relative success in this area derived in part from the economic crisis it had suffered after the collapse of the Soviet Union. Nevertheless, sustainable development became a key part of the state's strategy in the new millennium.

In addition, the plan proposed measures to intensify the shift from reliance on remittances, tourism and cheap primary exports towards the generation of high value-added exports. Cuba's traditional exports such as sugar, tobacco and citrus fruits, as well as the newer ones like nickel and oil, would be rationalised and re-equipped to ensure greater productivity, but a new emphasis would be placed on petroleum derivatives, pharmaceuticals and biotechnology as well as medical and educational services more typical of a 'knowledge economy'.[20] As a result of these, Castro claimed in his speech, 'we'll move from being an idiot country to one leaving all the others behind'.

This radical policy shift logically had needed the consent of the different elites at the apex of the Cuban state. No evidence is available about internal debates in the leadership because of the hermeticism of the state so any attempt at analysis can only be based on surmise and an interpretation of the veiled institutional statements and comments of key individuals, above all of Castro himself. The membership of the Politburo, the Council of State and the Council of Ministers was multiple and overlapping and no individual or group had an independent power base, yet there were competing interests among their representatives in the leadership based on different functional roles in government. The two most important of these institutions were the Party and the military or the Ministry of the Armed Forces (which since 1989 had brought the Ministry of the Interior, responsible for national security, largely under its control).[21]

Unlike most military institutions, the Cuban Armed Forces (FAR) played a central role in the nationalised economy, administering a range of enterprises from mining, tourism, real estate, IT and construction to agriculture and livestock. Many of these activities put the officers in close touch with the multinationals involved in joint ventures in Cuba. Military technocrats had also played an important role in the campaign beginning in the late 1980s to streamline the management of military-run firms, the *Sistema de Perfeccionamiento Empresarial*, through which some decision-making was delegated to officer-managers and material incentives were offered to the workers in order to raise productivity.[22]

The halt of the Special Period measures in 1996 and the shift in 2003 from limited economic liberalisation and subsidiarity towards the centralised, political control of the economy led to a haemorrhage of influence among the technocratic officers and managers of non-military enterprises, giving rise, as in the 1980s, to tensions between the beneficiaries of the shift, the more conservative Party leaders who were wedded to the traditions of Soviet centralisation and sections of the armed forces that favoured the Chinese path. As so often, Castro did not openly take sides and continually sought to maintain an appearance of even-handedness even while he steered the process towards the new paradigm.[23] He could count on Raúl Castro as Minister of the FAR to ensure military discipline. While his brother had been a partisan of greater liberalisation in the 1980s, he had also been the most prominent advocate of the return to orthodoxy in 1996 and 1997.

A new round of sackings and replacements began. The Minister of Economics and Planning and the Minister of Finance and Prices, both closely associated with the reforms of 1993–6, were replaced by hardliners. The main victim of the new strategy was Marcos Portal León, the powerful civilian Minister of Basic Industry in charge of a range of important industries, who was sacked in October 2004 for excessive 'self-sufficiency'. In the discourse of the regime, this was likely to mean that he had not sufficiently toed the new line or that he had created networks of influence that undermined the command hierarchy of Cuban governance.[24] His dismissal was no doubt meant to be exemplary and it was all the more significant in that he was married to one of Castro's nieces.

The new policies coincided with a fresh cycle of repression against dissidence and human rights activities. Castro argued that this crackdown was the result of the changing dynamic of US–Cuban relations after the election of George W. Bush in 2000, rather than the shift in internal policies.[25] At the turn of the new millennium, the fractured relations with the US had turned into something of a competitive road show over the Elián González incident. This 5-year-old boy had been rescued by two men in a cabin cruiser off the coast of Florida after the boat he had been travelling in with his mother and several others capsized in late November 1999 as they tried to gain illegal access to the US, and all were drowned except the boy and a young couple. Relatives of Elián in Miami attempted to keep the boy against the wishes of his father, who had remained in Cuba. The case aroused anti-regime demonstrations among exiles in Florida and massive pro-Castro demonstrations in Cuba until the American courts ruled six months later that he should be returned to the island to be with his father. Castro seized this fortuitous and immensely photogenic opportunity to mobilise popular nationalist feelings at a time of internal social and economic tensions.

The election of George W. Bush a few months later led to a renewed US policy of interference in internal politics in Cuba, seen as a muscular promotion of liberal democracy (or, in the words of the new head of the US Interests Section James Cason, as 'unswerving support for Cuba's struggling, valiant civil society') while it was condemned by its critics as a blatant policy of destabilisation (and by Castro as 'provocation').[26] The hardening of the Bush administration's policy towards Cuba had been signalled in the post-9/11 rhetoric by the inclusion of Cuba in the new 'axis of evil', arousing fears in Cuba that the US was planning a military invasion, directly or by proxy as in 1961. Cason began contacting human rights activists throughout Cuba as soon as he arrived in September 2002 and issued press statements criticising the Cuban state for its human rights record.

As part of the so-called Varela Project, activists had been collecting signatures in the belief that the Cuban constitution allowed them to propose a law of democratic reform once they had secured 10,000. While they reached the figure and beyond it, the government had organised a counter proposal stating the irrevocably 'socialist' nature of the Cuban Constitution and had collected 8 million signatures, almost 99 per cent of the electorate. Cuban security subjected these activists to repeated harassment yet the organiser of the Project, Osvaldo Payá, was allowed to go to Strasburg in 2002 to receive the European Parliament's annual Sakharov prize for Freedom of Thought. The activists were only arrested when Cason began to organise meetings with them and invited other diplomats to join him. Castro claimed later that he had not realised immediately how serious the threat of US intervention was because he was too engaged in state activities and had had to rest because of an infection, the implication being that his constant supervision of events in Cuba was crucial for its security.[27]

The issue came to a head on 15 March 2003 when the government arrested 75 of the human rights activists, sentencing them to long terms in prison. Both these arrests and the execution of three Cubans who had tried to hijack a ferry at the beginning of April provoked protests across the international community. The EU imposed sanctions and closed down its new mission in Havana only a week after it had been inaugurated. Castro led popular demonstrations against foreign embassies that had protested over the abuse of human rights in Cuba. Then in 2004 the UN Human Rights Commission passed a resolution criticising the arrests. Thus the downward spiral of US–Cuba relations now dragged in other powers. The EU only suspended its sanctions at the beginning of 2005 but several of its member embassies continued to invite activists to their functions, provoking a boycott of official receptions by the Cuban government in what was nicknamed the *canapé* war and a new round of arrests in July.

Castro later argued that Cason's 'provocations' were part of a US strategy to trigger arrests in Cuba in order to undermine the pro-Cuban support of Western liberals and left-wingers and put them on the defensive in advance of the Anglo-American invasion of Iraq.[28] Whether there was a connection between the two or not, the arrest or the intimidation of dissidents, trade unionists and human rights activists in Cuba was a long-established practice and moved in cycles defined by the intensity of their initiatives and by the degree of internal and external vulnerability felt by the state. But it was not just activists of one kind or another who suffered harassment but also librarians and independent journalists who published articles outside Cuba (such as Óscar Espinosa Chepe). Not all those arrested were charged and when trials were held they often fell short of international standards of fairness, according to Amnesty International. A common charge was the crime of 'social danger', a term embracing a range of behaviour from drunkenness to 'anti-social' activities, such as human rights protests.[29]

Immensely damaging though it was for its international reputation, the Cuban government's response to agitation over human rights was prompted by more than just a renewed fear of US interventionism under George W. Bush. The rationale of cold war and siege had shaped its national defence and security doctrine and appeared to dominate every aspect of economic, political, social and cultural life in Cuba.[30] Numerous organisations existed at every level to ensure internal security, from the military and security forces to the Committees for the Defence of the Revolution and the Rapid Response Brigades, whose task was to curb social disturbance and collective dissidence. Civil society was tightly circumscribed, and the limited mechanisms of consensus were controlled by the state. No criticism was tolerated outside the narrow constraints of self-criticism regulated by the state. Instead the government sought to manage society through vertical controls. Access to global information was limited, not just as a result of the technological problems of internet coverage but through state intervention. The effect was a sort of cultural autarky. This suggested a deep-lying insecurity among the leadership about ideological contamination of Cubans; thus the protection of the core values of the Revolution could only be entrusted to the revolutionary elites, who themselves were subject to constant scrutiny by their *compañeros* to ensure they followed the straight and narrow path.

Castro himself repeatedly argued that human rights were above all social rights, that is, health, literacy, education and the absence of poverty. He had little sympathy, on the contrary, for political rights such as the freedom of expression, which for him was equivalent to the right to private property. Moreover, he saw it as a meaningless construct if it was not accompanied by social rights and conditions free of the political constraints that had been necessary to survive the 'blockade' of Cuba by the US. In this, at least, he had the imprimatur of Amnesty International, which called for the end of the US embargo on the grounds that it undermined Cuban economic, social and cultural rights. Thus when Castro insisted, as he often had, on the necessity of a critical spirit within the Revolution he did not envisage this as a questioning of any of its values or strategies but as a means of 'perfecting' the system.[31]

Castro's 'management' of Cuban society came to an abrupt halt at the end of July 2006. He suffered an intestinal crisis, diagnosed as diverticulitis, during his visit to Argentina for a meeting of Latin American heads of government. On his return, he underwent a lengthy operation on 27 July and four days later, for the first time ever but only provisionally, devolved his responsibilities to the second in command, his brother Raúl. The carefully timed announcement of his illness aroused brief euphoria among sections of the Cuban exile community in Florida, dissipated by the news of his slow recovery. The list of functions he delegated is a reminder of how central he was to the state. He was First Secretary of the Central Committee of the Communist Party, Commander in Chief of the Armed Forces, and President of the Council of State and of the Government, and as such head of state. He was also Impulsor Principal (or Principal Promoter) of the National and International Programmes for Public Health, Education and the Energy

Revolution, each of which functions he delegated to specific members of the Politburo on his illness.

On his birthday on 14 August he appeared on TV in his sickbed with Chávez at his bedside cracking jokes. News of his progress were carefully rationed over the following months, probably to reassure Cubans and the world's media that he was still alive without alarming them with images of his frailty. But it was only 17 months later, in January 2008, that a new video clip was broadcast showing him in an informal meeting with the Brazilian President Lula da Silva. Castro continued from his place of convalescence to issue patriarchal messages to the Cubans in a sort of stately blog, 'Las Reflexiones de Fidel Castro', about international events and revolutionary principles, which appeared at irregular intervals of anything between a few days and a month.[32] As his strength returned, he appeared to have quickly reassembled his group of young advisors (playfully nicknamed the Talibanes by Cubans), whose role was no doubt to monitor events and processes taking place throughout Cuba and more importantly to relay messages from him to the different levels of leadership. Indeed, there can be little doubt that Castro continued to pull government strings from a distance, even from his sickbed.

However, his formal role as head of state finally came to an end on 18 February 2008 when he declared unequivocally that he was giving up all his positions of leadership in the Cuban government. The timing of his announcement was not fortuitous. He had been elected as deputy for Santiago in the general elections of 21 January, provoking speculation that he wished to return to power. The new National Assembly was about to elect the Council of Ministers on 24 February. His withdrawal a few days before this election indeed suggested that rather than wishing to relinquish power he had finally decided he was too weak to resume it. His replacement by Raúl Castro together with another old veteran, José Machado Ventura, as one of the Vice-Presidents was a clear message that any policy reform of the Cuban government was going to be a highly controlled affair. It could be surmised also that Fidel Castro wished to continue pulling government strings. He had not formally given up his position as one of the deputies for Santiago in the National Assembly nor that of First Secretary of the Political Bureau of the Party.

Indeed, it would not be fanciful to imagine that he might continue to pull strings beyond the grave. The strength of the legacy he bequeathed to Cuba after almost half a century in power was such that, as long as the Castroist state remained in power, any reforms would probably have to be undertaken in his name, whether they conformed to his principles or not.

# Notes

1 For details, see http://www.crnm.org/caricom_cuba.htm (last accessed 3 June 2008).

2 Castro, in I. Ramonet, *Fidel Castro. Biografía a dos voces* (Random House Mondadori, Mexico and Barcelona, 2006), p. 473.

3 In a summer 2007 broadcast of *Aló Presidente*, Chávez backed his unsuccessful campaign to change the Constitution to allow him to stand indefinitely as President by arguing that Venezuela's socialist revolution was like an unfinished painting and he was the artist (*The Guardian*, 26 August 2007). The close collaboration between Castro and Chávez was evident from an early stage. Castro claimed to have played an important part in foiling the attempted coup against Chávez in 2002 by coordinating information and persuading top-ranking officers loyal to Chávez to mobilise their troops and to send an elite force to rescue him from the island where he had been abducted (Castro, in Ramonet, *Castro*, pp 473–6).

4 C. Mesa-Lago, 'The Cuban economy in 2006–7', Paper to the Annual Meeting of the Association for the Study of the Cuban Economy (ASCE), 2007; H. Dilla Alfonso, 'Hugo Chávez y Cuba: subsidiando posposiciones fatales', *Nueva Sociedad*, 205 (Sept./Oct. 2006), pp. 144–5.

5 *Planet Ark*, 30 March 2005.

6 Daniel Erikson, 'Cuba, China, Venezuela: new developments', in 'Cuba in transition', *Papers and Proceedings of the Fifteenth Annual Meeting of the Association for the Study of the Cuban Economy (ASCE)*, 15 (2005), pp. 410–18.

7 C. Mesa-Lago and J. Pérez López, *Cuba's Aborted Reform: Socioeconomic Effects, International Comparisons, and Transition Politics* (University Press of Florida, Gainesville, 2005), p. 38; Mesa-Lago, 'Cuban economy', p. 18.

8 C. Foss, *Fidel Castro* (Sutton, Stroud, 2006). On the other hand, the Russians closed down the Lourdes intelligence centre without consulting the Cubans (L. Coltman, *The Real Fidel Castro* (Yale University Press, New Haven, 2003), p. 321).

9 Mesa-Lago, 'Cuban economy', *passim*. Mesa-Lago discounts the new methodology introduced in 2003 by the Cuban state in which the value of social services and price subsidies is added to the conventional methods for calculating economic growth.

10 Quoted in Ramonet, *Castro*, pp. 541–2.

11 Mesa-Lago and Pérez López, *Cuba's Aborted Reform*, p. 98.

12 H. Dilla Alfonso, 'Cuba: the changing scenarios of governability', *Boundary 2*, 29(3) (2002), p. 67.

13 Text available at http://www.cuba.cu/gobierno/discursos/2005 (last accessed 3 June 2008); Castro, in Ramonet, *Castro*, pp. 540–6. *Juventud Rebelde* kept up its campaign against corruption over the next two years, publishing a sequence of investigative articles in October 2007.

**14**  Ó. Espinosa Chepe, 'Privatización a la cubana', *El País*, 9 Nov. 2006.

**15**  A.R.M. Ritter, 'Cuba's strategic economic reorientation', in 'Cuba in transition', *Papers and Proceedings of the Sixteenth Annual Meeting of the Association for the Study of the Cuban Economy (ASCE)*, 16 (2006), p. 146; Castro speech of 17 November 2005, available at http://www.cuba.cu/gobierno/discursos/2005 (last accessed 3 June 2008).

**16**  *Juventud Rebelde*, 25 Nov. 2007.

**17**  Ibid.; Ritter, 'Cuba's strategic economic reorientation', p. 146.

**18**  See, for example, *Granma International*, 18 Feb. 2006.

**19**  Living Planet Report 2006, p. 19, available at http://www.panda.org/news_facts/publications/living_planet_report/lp_2006/ (last accessed 3 June 2008).

**20**  Ritter, 'Cuba's strategic economic reorientation', p. 141.

**21**  F. Mora, 'Cuba's Ministry of Interior: the FAR's fifth army', *Bulletin of Latin American Research*, 26(2) (2007), pp. 222–37.

**22**  D. Amuchástegui, 'FAR – new generations in power: understanding scenarios of continuity', in 'Cuba in Transition', *ASCE*, 16, pp. 366–70; J. Espinosa., 'Vanguard of the state: the Cuban armed forces in transition', *Problems of Post-Communism*, 48(6) (2001), pp. 19–30.

**23**  Dilla Alfonso, 'Hugo Chávez y Cuba', pp. 141–58.

**24**  'Nota Oficial', *Granma International*, 14 Oct. 2004. Other reasons for the dismissal are given in the official note, such as the recent spate of power cuts for which he had ultimate responsibility. But these were not stated as the primary motive.

**25**  Castro, in Ramonet, *Castro*, pp. 397–412.

**26**  James Cason, Chief of US Interests Section, Havana, at http://www.state.gov/p/wha/rls/rm/39815.htm (last accessed 3 June 2008); J. Sweig, 'Fidel's final victory', *Foreign Affairs* (Jan./Feb. 2007); Castro, in Ramonet, *Castro*, p. 402.

**27**  Ibid., pp. 398–9.

**28**  Ibid., pp. 406–7.

**29**  Amnesty International media briefing AMR 25/003/2007 29 January 2007; Annual Report 2006, available at http://web.amnesty.org/report2006/cub-summary-eng (last accessed 3 June 2008).

**30**  J.A. Blanco, 'The mother of all reforms', *Focal Point*, 6(5) (June 2007), pp. 1–2, available at http://www.focal.ca. (last accessed 3 June 2008).

**31**  Castro, in Ramonet, *Castro*, p. 491; Amnesty International, AMR 25/003/2007 29 January 2007.

**32**  See http://www.jornada.unam.mx/reflexiones (last accessed 3 June 2008).

# Castro's Legacy

Any historical retrospect of Castro's political career and legacy is likely to be provisional for some time. The main reason for this is that his most ambitious objectives have not yet been realised. For almost half a century, Castro's Cuba sought to achieve goals that have escaped most other small ex-colonial nations in a globalising world, that is, socio-economic modernity, social justice and Third World solidarity. The international impact of this struggle has been out of all proportion to the size and potential importance of the island. Cuba under Castro became a model for national liberation struggles and progressive anti-systemic movements in the Third World. The moral capital it accumulated over the years derived from its defiance of the US and its international support for Third World struggles for national liberation and development. Castro's words about injustice, violence, poverty, neo-imperialism, capitalism, international debt, globalisation and so on have resonated across the developing world. Despite the unswerving hostility of the most powerful country in the world situated less than 90 miles away (or 90 millimetres, as Castro once suggested), the Cuban state under Fidel Castro survived nine hostile US administrations and implemented policies that continually flouted not just Washington but the supposed global triumph of liberal capitalism. It achieved a degree of development in health, education, ecological sustainability and social infrastructure in general that surpassed that of most countries in the developing world and even that of some developed countries. These successes were due in great measure to Castro's ability to tap the creative energies of millions of Cubans in defence of a 140-year-old aspiration for national emancipation.

Yet the Revolution has still failed to achieve the most important utopian goal that its leader had set in the Moncada programme and in the heady days of revolutionary triumph. Cuba has been unable to break out of economic dependence and has suffered a trade deficit for most of the time, requiring one form or another of external patronage, such as the current support of the government of Chávez and the credits extended by China. Cuba's economy is still precarious, and the socio-economic gains that its citizens have won are continually under threat, as Raúl Castro recognized in his first speech as acting head of state on 26 July 2007.[1] Wages barely cover the basic necessities of life for many Cubans, prices are high, public transport is creaking, affordable food is in short supply and daily life is surrounded by prohibitions of one sort or the other. Even the showcases of the Revolution, medicine, housing and education, suffer from deficiencies and shortages. The Cuban state cannot rely forever on the heroic discourse of siege and *patria* without rewarding its citizens with a better standard of living and greater levels of popular democracy.

The Revolution has also left a heartbreaking legacy. A small number of Cubans have been imprisoned at different times merely for political dissidence, whatever justification the Cuban state has given for their sentence. Many more Cubans abandoned the island because they were opposed to the new state. The first who left were those closely linked to the Batista dictatorship and to the oligarchy. They were followed soon by those who objected to the radicalisation of the Revolution. Since then, probably the majority of Cubans who have left the island did so above all because they were seeking the greater opportunities for economic self-advancement offered by the United States. The Revolution and the US governments' obsessive opposition to it created a fault-line that has divided thousands of families living on either side of the Straits of Florida. Policies by successive US administrations deepened the gulf separating them by making contact difficult, in particular by preventing travel or blocking or limiting financial assistance from the exiles to their poorer relatives in Cuba. Equally, Cubans found it difficult to contact or visit their relatives in Florida. To much acclaim on 26 December 2007 in the Teatro Mella in Havana, the Cuban singer Pablo Milanés sang movingly about this separation:

> My brother Jacinto
> Who lives in La Habana
> Doesn't know if his daughter
> Who had a grandaughter
> Whom he doesn't yet know
> Knows that his mother
> Died suddenly.
> The authorities won't let him go . . .[2]

That fault-line runs through families of all classes. We need look no further than Castro's own family. His former father-in-law was public prosecutor during the Batista dictatorship as well as legal counsel for the greatest exploiter of labour in pre-revolutionary Cuba, the United Fruit Company. His brother-in-law served as deputy to the Interior Minister and was made Senator under Batista. Later one of his nephews-in-law, Lincoln Díaz-Balart, played an important role in drawing up the Helms-Burton Act as a Republican Congressman in Florida. One of Castro's sisters, Juana, left Cuba in 1964 and in a press declaration in Mexico denounced her brother and his Revolution. Castro's daughter by his relationship with Natalia Revuelta in the 1950s, Alina Fernández Ferrer, abandoned the island in 1993 and published her memoirs in 1997 in which she was bitterly critical of both her father and the Cuban Revolution.[3]

Despite the family links or even because of them, the politicised exiles see Castro and his supporters as the Other, the 'internal' enemy that has betrayed the true Cubans. Many in the anti-Castro community in Miami have been involved in repeated efforts to subvert the Revolution and some of its more violent members have been engaged in sabotage and murder.[4] Conversely, for many Cubans on the island, the anti-Castroist exile community functions as the Other, the false Cubans who collaborated with the Batista dictatorship and the exploitation of the island by US imperialism, blocking its path towards emancipation.

The Cuban Revolution that Castro crafted and led (and remained, in a sense, its intellectual proprietor) was an authentic response to underdevelopment and neocolonial dependency of a nationalist elite drawn mainly from the middle classes and backed by the vast majority of Cubans. Despite the labels it has attached to itself, the Revolution was essentially part of the wave of anti-colonial struggles in the Third World during the post-war period led by disaffected or disenfranchised members of the educated urban middle class such as Nasser, Nkrumah, Nyerere and Ben Bella. As in Cuba, the driving force of the latter movements was the need to achieve economic as well as national independence through modernisation. Because many of its leaders came from a class closely bound up with the state (military officers or lawyers for example) the new regime tended to see the state as the fundamental instrument for the transformation of society. In order to overthrow the colonial or neocolonial regimes, the new elites had to mobilise different strata of the population around a programme of social reform and national self-assertion.

In these new nations in the Third World, political and economic centralisation in one degree or another was in many cases unavoidable because of internal contradictions or external pressures, for example from the ex-colonial powers. Such pressures often led to a political alignment with the Soviet bloc. Thus a centralised state, a more or less nationalised economy and a populist base became the hallmarks of many post-colonial govern-ments in Africa, for example. Because of this formal resemblance to socialism, the doctrines on which they were based were called socialist when in fact their main inspiration was nationalist in the sense that they were nation-building projects in culturally or ethnically heterogeneous societies; hence the emergence of Islamic or African 'socialism'.

Cuban socialism was also in part a strategy for modernization as well as a nationalist project. But its roots were Pan-American as well as Cuban. An important source from which Castro drew inspiration was the Latin American struggles for emancipation against the Spanish empire led by Simón Bolívar, and the anti-imperialist movements of the 1930s and 1940s. During the Great Depression, new political movements emerged, as in Mexico, Argentina and Brazil, seeking to break out of the cycle of depend-ence on the export of traditional cash crops or raw materials by mod-ernising the economy. To do so, they mobilised mass movements both to wrest political control from the traditional elites whose rule had rested on command of the export economy and also to destroy the hegemony of US economic interests. Of these movements, the most influential in the Latin American continent was that of Perón in Argentina. As a student, Che Guevara had been a supporter of Perón, and Castro himself took part, as we have seen, in the anti-imperialist student congress in Colombia in 1947 sponsored by Perón. Other populist Latin American leaders who influenced Castro included the immensely popular Colombian politician Jorge Gaitán, whose assassination sparked off the riots that Castro joined in 1947, and Colonel Jacobo Arbenz, whose attempt to carry out land reform as President of Guatemala was cut short by an American-sponsored armed invasion in 1954, witnessed by Che Guevara and no doubt recounted at length to Castro when they met shortly afterwards in Mexico.

The main source of the inspiration and legitimacy of Castro's Revolu-tion, however, was the Cuban nationalist tradition in its more radical ver-sion. Castro saw his own movement as the culmination of a time-honoured struggle for independence and development stretching from the first revolt against colonial rule in 1868 to the student rebellion of the 1930s. His supreme self-confidence, indeed his almost messianic sense of destiny, was based on the conviction that he embodied that struggle. Castro and his tightly knit vanguard saw themselves as custodians of the Cuban national interest as defined by *cubanía*, an imagined collective identity first delineated by white Cuban and Afro-Cuban heroes who fought against colonialism and for Cuban independence in the nineteenth century.[5] *Cubanía* meant modernisation (that is the socio-economic and cultural development of Cuba) on Cuban terms, not on terms set by liberal capitalism, which would limit and distort the nature of this modernisation. Thus revolutionary Cuba sought to overcome the neocolonial status of most Third World societies in the globalised economy by using the state to attempt to achieve sustainable economic growth and a high level of social protection and socio-economic equality.

Yet, unlike its African or Islamic counterparts, Cuba's espousal of socialism was more than just the intellectual scaffolding for this nationalist project; socialism provided the moral and ethical codes expected of the citizen and the state. Beyond this, it offered a progressive vision of a world rid of injustice and exploitation. Within these parameters, Castro and his governing elite allowed limited internal debate, more open at times of economic crisis, shut down when it was deemed to threaten the Revolution. No dissent or public criticism or even human rights campaigning was allowed outside this paradigm. Any such activity was regarded as counter-revolutionary, anti-patriotic. The protocols of democracy and freedom of expression were subordinated to the perceived needs of security and development in the tradition of Lenin's democratic centralism. The Cuban state under Castro was thus progressive and authoritarian, populist and socialist, an equation so apparently contradictory that it disconcerted many of its supporters as well as some of its opponents. For his part, Castro's legitimacy derived from his charismatic authority, his ethics and his incarnation of the heroic myths of Cuban patriotism.

Though Castro claimed to have effected a juncture between Martí and Marx, the values that guided him throughout his political career were drawn more from Cuban traditions. García Márquez wrote that Castro had injected Martí in the bloodstream of the Marxist revolution whereas it could be argued rather that Castro had injected Marxism into the Martí tradition.[6] The vein of millenarian regeneration and voluntarism that ran through his political thought had much more in common with Hispanic and above all Cuban nationalism than with European socialism or Soviet Communism. Castro's claim to have paid consistent attention to the ethical dimension of his policies and actions derived above all from the Martí tradition, as he acknowledged, though this is not to deny the undoubted influence of socialism and indeed religion on that tradition (after all, Castro was educated by Jesuits). A striking manifestation of Castro's concern to locate the Cuban Revolution within the progressive traditions of European political thought were his arguments about the connection between ethics, morality, power and violence. His frequent attempts to justify anti-systemic violence as a variant of the just war theory, in particular in anti-colonial struggles, represent an innovative contribution to a long-standing polemic.[7] The genealogy of Castro's thinking could be traced back to the Enlightenment, in particular to Rousseau's notions of social contract and moral authority and to Voltaire's enlightened despotism.

The Cuban state's official adoption of Marxism-Leninism was motivated not merely by expediency but by the belief held by Castro and other leaders of the Revolution that Communism offered the only possible model of economic growth and the only international movement with which they could identify. Fundamental to this alignment with the Soviet Union was its anti-Americanism. The pragmatic side of this identification became clear in 1992 when the reference to the Dictatorship of the Proletariat was deleted from the Cuban constitution after the collapse of the Soviet Union and Martí became more prominent than Marxism-Leninism in public discourse. But there were elements of Marxism that merged with ideas transmitted through the Cuban radical tradition. The two most important of these were the notion of proletarian international solidarity, translated in the Cuban version into solidarity with the 'poor and oppressed peoples' of the world, and a teleological faith in the inevitability of progress or, in its Marxist version, of socialism. In its journey to Cuba, just as in its other Third World appearances, the content of Marxism was transformed. Indigenous populist traditions became absorbed by Marxist-Leninist terminology and translated into new categories: people became proletariat, nation became class and nationalism became socialism.

Yet the experience of the Cuban Revolution hardly conformed to the classical Marxist axiom that it was modernisation and class struggle that created the conditions for socialism. On the contrary, the Revolution took place in a semi-developed economy and was led largely by a middle-class elite claiming to act on behalf of the people. The labour and student agitation under the Batista dictatorship did much to foster political change. Yet the mythologisation of the Cuban Revolution laid emphasis on the armed struggle as a people's struggle or *pueblo en armas* based above all in the Sierra, from where the guerrillas emerged to liberate the city or *llano* (the plain) and beyond that the oppressed Third World. The myth of the guerrilla, as heroic, self-reliant, untainted by the city, outnumbered yet victorious, became embedded in the codes of the Revolution, alongside the iconic images of its bearded heroes, the *barbudos*.[8]

Despite his claim that a 'people's government' came to power in 1959, Castro also repeatedly stressed that the people were not ready to assume government. 'The people', he argued in an interview in 1985, 'had to be led to the road of revolution by stages, step by step, until they achieved full political awareness and confidence in their future.'[9] Workers had been tainted by the experience of capitalism, according to this view, and the revolutionary leadership had to oversee the development of their socialist consciousness. As Castro readily admitted during his tour of Chile in 1971, 'We have been working on building our workers' movement', as if the working class was a construct from above.[10] Similarly, in a speech to the Ministry of the Interior in 1986, he attacked the abuse of material incentives, claiming that it 'corrupts nothing less than those whose consciousness we are obliged to preserve'.[11] Hence labour problems such as absenteeism and low productivity were seen as the result not of any contradiction between workers and the new state claiming to act on their behalf, but of old habits or new forms of corporatism. The Marxist notion of working-class power was absent from Castro's thinking; it meant for him either 'selfishness' or the 'demagogic and criminal' ideas of Yugoslav-style self-management.[12]

Indeed, in Castro's political theory, socialism was not so much a question of power as one of distribution and ethics. As in other Third World countries that hoisted the socialist banner, it was articulated as an egalitarian philosophy whose main component was the welfare state. In this sense, Castro assimilated some of the classical values of European socialism, values that were embedded in any case in Cuba's radical traditions. Societies were defined as socialist also if their states owned the means of production. Castro was thus able to describe China as socialist in an interview in 1977 even though he considered its foreign policy at the time reactionary: 'China is socialist but it is not internationalist . . . I believe China is a socialist country because there are no landlords nor capitalists there.'[13] The apparent contradiction between China's domestic and foreign policies stemmed from a 'deformation' of socialism on the part of its leaders, as if the two practices could be autonomous from one another.

In fact, Castro's definition of China reflected his own conception of state policy as the preserve of a political leadership free to conduct government affairs without control from below and therefore able to change course virtually at will. The structures of popular participation set up in 1976 did not shift power from the leadership to the people so much as create channels through which popular demands could rise to the top and directives from above could flow down to the people. Power still remained in practice in the hands of an enlightened leader or group of leaders, though these had to be responsive to the interests of the different elites within the state and to popular aspirations as far as they could be expressed publicly.

The political dimension of Castro's socialist populism sprang from three main sources: the formative experiences of imprisonment on the Isle of Pines, and of the guerrilla struggle, in which military hierarchy and obedience had been necessary for survival; a corresponding belief that only the loyal and battle-hardened leaders could be trusted to steer the Revolution in the right direction; and the conviction that in the conditions of 'siege' and scarcity there was no room for pluralism in the style of Western liberal democracy. The Bay of Pigs invasion had burned the old fear of the United States on the psyche of the Cuban leaders, so much so that anti-Americanism became almost the raison d'être of the Revolution, just as, with far less justification, 'communist subversion' in Central America and the Caribbean became an obsession of Washington. The notion of siege was an essential part of the mythology of the Revolution, encouraging mobilisation, revolutionary offensives and popular militarisation around the guerrilla model of the Sierra Maestra.[14]

To understand the lure of state control in Cuba, the full extent of America's offensive against Cuba has to be appreciated. The US government devoted large sums of money to undermine the Cuban state, from inside and outside. Every two years the official Commission for Assistance to a Free Cuba, whose chair under the George W. Bush administration was Condoleeza Rice, received an ever higher annual budget ($80 million in July 2006) to fund pro-American NGOs and other groups in Cuba, intensify radio and TV transmissions to the island and entice Cubans to leave the island through grants.[15] According to US Senate reports, the CIA's second largest station in the world was based in Florida. At the height of the under-cover American offensive in the 1960s and 1970s, it was from here, just across the water from Cuba, that the CIA controlled an airline and a flotilla of spy ships operating off the coast of Cuba, and ran up to 120,000 Cuban agents, who dealt in economic sabotage, assassination and terrorism, and economic and biological warfare.[16] Some 500 hours of anti-Castro propaganda were broadcast weekly from radio stations in Florida. Successive US governments, in particular the Reagan and George W. Bush administrations, mobilised their most powerful resources to bring Cuba to its knees. Over 600 plans to assassinate Castro were devised. Nearly 3,500 Cubans have died from terrorist acts, and more than 2,000 are permanently disabled. As an ex-CIA agent has said, 'no country has suffered terrorism as long and consistently as Cuba'.[17]

Political centralisation and state control in Cuba, therefore, were above all a response to a deep sense of national insecurity. But Castro saw them also as a means of transforming Cuba. In his eyes, the life-or-death struggle to defend the new Cuba and build a sustainable socialist economy required discipline and austerity, not political and cultural pluralism. This 'puritanism' was an almost unavoidable feature of poor states in the Third World seeking modernisation in a globalised environment. It coloured Castro's response to events elsewhere. Just as he disapproved of the Prague Spring of 1968, so he condemned the student protest in Tiananmen Square. The Cuban press reported only the official Chinese version of what happened, and the Cuban government sent an undivulged message of support to the Chinese leaders after the massacre.[18]

The concentration of political, social and economic decision-making in the hands of Castro and his vanguard produced mixed results. The most positive were in social infrastructure, especially in the field of health. Cuba claims to have more doctors per head than any other country in the world and its average health expenditure as a percentage of GDP is as high as that of developed countries, according to World Health Organization figures. Castro demonstrated a continual willingness to study health models elsewhere and apply those aspects that were most suitable to the socio-economic and political conditions in Cuba; thus despite its economic problems and consequent low health budget, the island enjoys a holistic and community-based primary health care system rivalling or even surpassing any other in the world.[19]

Centralisation, however, carried considerable penalties in economic performance. The interventionist and improvisatory nature of economic decision-making often led to dislocations in production and supply. The ever-energetic Castro, armed with panaceas from supposedly cutting-edge literature on economic management and technology, would rove across the island, changing priorities, shifting resources, tinkering with organisation. The result was sometimes over-ambitious targets, the most notable of which was the 10 million ton sugar harvest plan of 1970. It also led repeatedly to the overstretching of resources, shortages and mismatches, the dispersal of experience and skills and often the waste of resources.[20]

Political centralisation also created a habit of deference and passivity. The criticism from new generations, when there was any, was directed at bureaucratisation and corruption, not at any of the basic strategies of the Revolution. The Communist Youth newspaper went further, complaining in November 2007 about the absence of debate even over routine matters not affecting principles or strategic objectives.[21] The fact that an official

paper such as *Juventud Rebelde* could voice such criticism indicates some
margin of internal dissent. As the 'proprietor' of the Revolution, Castro
encouraged debate and criticism but it had to be on his terms and within
the limits he set. The pivot of the state was Castro, in whose image it was
created and sustained. The paternalistic or populist relationship between
Castro and Cubans was legitimated repeatedly through El Comandante's
lengthy speeches and his direct interventions in the administration of Cuba,
often in circumvention of the structures of governance. He would take over
the handling of crises and lead offensives against institutions when he considered they had become too independent, such as the restructuring in 1989
of the Ministry of the Interior, which led to numerous dismissals and its
takeover by the Ministry of the Armed Forces. His interventionism was at
times intended to reorient economic and political policies. At other times it
could be interpreted as a means of generating tension and competition to
prevent the development of any power base independent of his authority.[22]

Castro denied that the Cuban government was in any way presidentialist.
'In our country', he asserted, 'decisions are important, fundamental decisions are always analysed, discussed and made collectively . . . I have real
authority, of course, I have influence, for historic reasons, but I don't give
orders nor govern by decree.'[23] Clearly Castro needed to win the consent of
the different elites of the state to carry out policies, and in that procedural
sense, the government was a collective one. But it was unlikely that decisions
could be taken without his support and that individuals would be promoted
in the ranks of the government without his direct or indirect patronage.

It was Castro on the whole who held together the disparate elements of
Cuban society, the people and the elites, the young and the old, the black
and the white, through his own charismatic authority. Castro's socially
cohesive function played a vital role in a society where, in particular
at times of economic crisis, there were still disparities of income and
opportunity, articulated around ethnicity, class, gender, age and region.
Nevertheless, popular images of Castro varied, from the all-Cuban hero, the
daring tough-talking man of the people who faced up to the Americans, to
the solicitous and incorruptible patriarch. Incorruptible he certainly was. No
reliable analysis would dispute his own claim that he lived a spartan life and
had no personal wealth.[24] He was also seen by some Cubans as a ranting old
greybeard and possibly by a small minority within Cuba as a tyrant.

The fact that politics in Cuba was so often refracted through the image
of one man meant that any criticism of its basic values was seen an implicit
attack on Castro himself. The opportunities for democratic debate and
decision-making were diminished by his moral and political hegemony.

On the other hand, there were very few icons of Castro during his long tenure in office. This was in striking contrast to most Third World leaders of his generation. Other historic figures of the Cuban Revolution, especially Guevara, had been sacralised and their images appear everywhere. Castro preferred to play down his historic role, not so much out of modesty but because the greater the stress on collective action the more the Revolution conformed to its socialist label. [25] He disapproved of the iconography of living politicians, probably because he wished them, and himself, to be judged continuously by their political actions.

This may be one of the reasons he kept his private life highly confidential. It was an open secret in Cuba that he had had several lovers and several illegitimate children. Only in the new millennium was the mother of five of these children and his partner of many decades, Dalia Soto, seen in public ceremonies but never alongside him, while his children with Soto were expected to keep a low profile. During his long recuperation from surgery care was taken to shield the pale and shrunken leader from public view. Yet despite this absence of outward symbols of El Comandante or his projection as a man of flesh and blood, Castro was an almost permanent presence on the island. The Castro myth was embedded in Cuban life – in politics, in popular culture and discourse – a sort of banal iconography that needed no statues or monuments. As one commentator has suggested, Castro was the 'unidentified elephant in every room in Cuba'.[26]

The construction of a Castro myth in a post-Castro Cuba has not yet begun. Compared with Che, whose 'heroic' death and 'perpetual' youth are icons that lend themselves to myth construction as well as commercialisation, Castro's mythologisation is more problematic because of the vicissitudes of his leadership as well as his ageing and illness, which rubbed off some of the appeal of the heady days of the Revolution. The image of the old and sometimes interminable patriarch is less likely to appeal to new generations who have not experienced invasion and siege.

In fact, Castro's legacy is immensely difficult to predict. Quite simply, he cannot be replaced. As long as the Cuban Revolution survives in name, and there is no indication that it will not, any departure from the script he wrote will need the imprimatur of Castroism. Yet the internal pressures and the external opportunities for change are so powerful they cannot be ignored. Cuba can still only function in a global capitalist market whose operations work against the social achievements of the Revolution. The market socialism route chosen by China leaves key sectors of the economy in the hands of the state but liberalises a range of economic activities the effects of which would undermine some of the core values of Castroism.

Castro's own preferred option of seeking modernisation through the state by means of a Pan-American regional strategy, in which each participating economy exchanges mutually complementary goods and services, remains something of a gamble. It depends on Chavez' continued munificence and the creation of a network of allies throughout Latin America. Yet Chavez' Venezuela and Morales' Bolivia (and to some extent Correa's Ecuador) may be too fragile a basis for Cuba's future à la Castro. Other much bigger Latin American economies, even those of governments as sympathetic to Cuba as Lula's Brazil (which extended new credits to and signed further agreements for economic collaboration with Cuba in January 2008), prefer to follow the new post-Washington Consensus whereby market liberalism is still the orthodoxy, however tempered by state intervention. For all its trade and credits, China is unwilling to replace the Soviet Union as godfather to the Cuban economy. It goes without saying, in other words, that the lifting of the US embargo remains crucial to Cuba's prospects.

At the same time, the internal demands for change among Cubans are virtually unstoppable. They intensified after Raúl Castro promised 'structural and conceptual transformations' in the economy in his speech at the end of 2007 while he was Acting head of state. Encouraged by the leadership, an unusually open debate about these changes had taken place for many months.[27] The timid reforms announced in spring and summer 2008 did little to quench the demand. The extent of popular disquiet was echoed in the last haunting words of Milanés' song:

> Has it been worthwhile?
> I ask, I don't know
> Has it been worthwhile?
> I answer, I don't know.

So there can be no final conclusion to this book. Surviving American hostility was an extraordinary achievement in itself. Some of Castro's most cherished plans were realised and are a model for the rest of the world, both First and Third. But despite enormous sacrifices on the part of Cubans, his grand vision remains unfulfilled and its continued pursuit is full of risks. The assessment of Castro and his Revolution made three years ago by his friend Gabriel García Márquez is perhaps as appropriate to Castro's legacy now as it was to his rule then: 'I believe he is one of the greatest idealists of our time, and perhaps this may be his greatest virtue, though it has also been his greatest danger.'[28]

# Notes

1  In *Granma International*, 27 July 2007; M.A. Centeno, 'The return of Cuba to Latin America: the end of Cuban exceptionalism?', *Bulletin of Latin American Research*, 23(4) (2004), pp. 403–13.

2  From the song 'Dos preguntas de un día' ('Two questions of one day') quoted in M. Vicent, '2008, el año de la verdad en Cuba', *El País*, 31 Dec. 2007.

3  *Alina. Memorias de la hija rebelde de Fidel Castro* (Plaza y Janés, Barcelona, 2007); J. Castro, 'Yo acuso'. *Juanita Castro denuncia a su hermano Fidel* (n.p, Miami, 1964(?)).

4  For a vivid account of the anti-Castro exile community in Miami, see A.L. Bardach, *Cuba Confidential: Love and Vengeance in Miami and Havana* (Random House, New York, 2002).

5  A. Kapcia, *Cuba: Island of Dreams* (Berg, Oxford, 2000).

6  García Márquez, in D. Shnookal and P. Álvarez Tabío (eds), *Fidel Castro: My Early Years* (Ocean Press, Melbourne, Victoria, 2005), p. 16.

7  D. Jayatilleka, *Fidel's Ethics of Violence: the Moral Dimension of the Political Thought of Fidel Castro* (Pluto Press, London and Ann Arbor, Mich., 2007); on Castro's acknowledgement of ethics, see I. Ramonet, *Fidel Castro. Biografía a dos voces* (Random House Mondadori, Mexico and Barcelona, 2006), pp. 114–15, 236–9; on the link between his ethics and religion, see F. Betto, *Fidel and Religion*, (Weidenfeld and Nicolson, London, 1987), *passim*.

8  Kapcia, *Cuba*, pp. 183–8.

9  Betto, *Fidel and Religion*, p. 149.

10  F. Castro Ruz, *Fidel in Chile* (International Publishers, New York, 1972), p. 131.

11  *Granma*, 8 June 1986.

12  Castro Ruz, *Fidel in Chile*, pp. 15 and 131.

13  F. Castro, *Fidel Castro habla con Barbara Walters* (Carlos Valencia, Colombia, 1977), p. 68.

14  Kapcia, *Cuba*, pp. 183–8.

15  *Voice of America*, 10 July 2006.

16  J. Didion, *Miami* (Weidenfeld and Nicolson, London, 1987), pp. 90–1; W. Hinckle and W.W. Turner, *The Fish is Red: The Story of the Secret War against Castro* (Harper & Row, New York, 1981).

17  P. Agee, *The Guardian*, 10 March 2007.

18  This was confirmed to the author by the Chinese Press Attaché in London in 1993. For the Cuban press response, see *Granma Weekly Review*, 18 June 1989. See also Castro's comments on CNN quoted in Mesa-Lago, *Cuba after the Cold War* (University of Pittsburgh Press, 1993), p. 200.

**19** World Health Organization (WHO), 'Country Profile. Cuba (2008); WHO, *World Statistics* 2006 (2007); S. Boseley, 'First world results on a third world budget', *The Guardian*, 12 September 2007; P. Pieroni, 'Health care in Cuba: from revolution to evolution' (International Institute for the Study of Cuba, London Metropolitan University, n.d.).

**20** See, for example, G.B. Hagelberg and J. Alvarez, 'Command and countermand: Cuba's sugar industry under Fidel Castro', 'Cuba in transition', *Papers and Proceedings of the Sixteenth Annual Meeting of the Association for the Study of the Cuban Economy (ASCE)*, 16 (2006), pp. 123–39.

**21** R. Ronquillo Bello, 'Marañas de la fábula', *Juventud Rebelde*, 25 Nov. 2007.

**22** F. Mora, 'Cuba's Ministry of Interior: the FAR's fifth army', *Bulletin of Latin American Research*, 26(2) (2007), p. 230.

**23** Castro, in Ramonet, *Castro*, p. 515.

**24** Ibid., pp. 551–2; Skierka, *Fidel Castro: a Biography* (Polity Press, Cambridge, 2004), *passim*; P. Bourne, *Castro* (Macmillan, London, 1987), *passim*.

**25** L. Lockwood, *Castro's Cuba, Cuba's Fidel* (Random House, New York, 1969), p. 329.

**26** Bardach, *Cuba Confidential*, p. 227. Details of Castro's sentimental and family life appear in a number of biographies such as those by Quirk, Szulc and Skierka (see the bibliographical essay at the end of this volume); further details can be found in 'Castro's family', *Miami Herald*, 8 October 2000 and http://www.fidelcastroruz.net/familia/dalia.php (last accessed 3 June 2008).

**27** For an anti-Castroist, American assessment of the options facing the Cuban leadership in the absence of Castro, see B. Latell, 'Raul Castro: confronting Fidel's legacy in Cuba', *The Washington Quarterly*, 30(3) (Summer 2007), pp. 53–65.

**28** In Shnookal and Álvarez Tabío, *Castro*, p. 24.

# Bibliographical Essay

Few political figures in history can have divided opinion as much as Fidel Castro. His demonisation or canonisation has left little space for balanced accounts of his life and work, at least outside academia and serious journalism. The harshest judgements have often proceeded from erstwhile supporters. A leading activist of the 26th July Movement, Carlos Franqui, declared in 2006: 'It is an incontrovertible truth that the triumph of the Castroist Revolution has been, and still is, the most tragic event in the history of Cuba.'[1] The bitterness of much anti-Castro diatribe has led to a defensiveness on the part of many who would otherwise voice criticism of aspects of Castro's policies as part of their global support for the Cuban Revolution. Yet even within academia there are deficits in the explanatory frameworks from which the Cuban Revolution is judged. Thus, for example, the liberal school of thinking, such as that in the US-based Association for the Study of the Cuban Economy (ASCE), tends to view economic policy in Cuba from the perspective of the 'end of history', liberal consensus whereby economic liberalisation is the only game in town. This is true of political analyses, which are often framed within terms of reference that make the record of human rights and formal democracy in Cuba the principal test of political legitimacy. Castro was always the first to point out the deficits in liberal democracies, arguing that social and welfare rights are as important as, if not more important than, formal political rights, which are often quite limited. As he said in an interview with Tomas Borge, 'I think there cannot be real democracy in the midst of social inequality, in the midst of social injustice, in the midst of societies divided between rich and poor.'[2]

Yet those who defend the Cuban Revolution are tempted to gloss over the deficits in its own democratic record, in reference not just to human rights but also to popular participation in governance. It is difficult to deny that the Cuban state is centralised, populist and in some measure authoritarian. Equally, the formal structures of democracy are more channels for communicating policies taken by the elites than means of involving citizens in decision-making. Some of the political analyses of the Cuban Revolution also ignore the dominant radical tradition in Cuban history, that is, its historical, cultural roots in a 140-year-old struggle for modernisation and emancipation. Finally, those biographies of Castro are incomplete that do not sufficiently take into account the historical models that inspired him and that he mobilised to establish legitimacy, in particular the radical tradition of *cubanía rebelde* that is so central to Cuban identity.

## Books in English

Many of Castro's own words through his speeches and written work have been published in English. Individual speeches have appeared in translation throughout his period as head of state. Collections of selected articles and speeches are also published but both represent only a tiny proportion of Castro's prolific output as an orator. Although repetitive and verbose at times, these speeches are an important source for understanding his ideas and discourse. Pathfinder Press and Ocean Press have published collections of speeches in recent years, such as *Capitalism in Crisis: Globalization and World Politics Today* (published also by Global, London, 2004). Speeches from the period up to the triumph of the Revolution are published in *Revolutionary Struggle 1947–1958* (Cambridge, Mass., 1972). Three collections are published by Harvester Press: M. Taber, *Fidel Castro Speeches* (1981, 1983) and *In Defence of Socialism* (1989). Selected speeches appear in M. Kenner and J. Petras (eds), *Fidel Castro Speaks* (Allen Lane, London, 1970). His speech at the Moncada trial appears in *History Will Absolve Me* (Jonathan Cape, London, 1968) while selected speeches made during his tour of Chile in 1971 appear in *Fidel in Chile* (International Publishers, New York, 1972). An invaluable collection of letters, documents and recollections of the Sierra and *llano* campaigns is contained in two books by one of the leading members of the 26th July Movement who eventually broke with Castroism, Carlos Franqui: *Diary of the Cuban Revolution* (Viking Press, New York, 1980) and *Family Portrait with Fidel* (Random House, New York, 1984) (a rather truncated English version of a book first published in Spanish). A penetrating essay on Castro by García Márquez can be found in D. Shnookal and P. Álvarez Tabío (eds), *Fidel Castro: My Early Years* (Ocean Press, Melbourne, Victoria, 2005).

Several lengthy interviews with Castro have appeared in English; one of the most interesting is his interview with the Brazilian theologian Frei Betto (*Fidel and Religion*, Simon & Schuster, New York, 1987) during which Castro clearly warmed to his interviewer and spoke at some length about his childhood and youth, as well as giving his views on Christianity and Marxism and the problem of Third World debt. Another interview of considerable interest was conducted soon after the collapse of the Soviet Union by Castro's friend, the Sandinista leader Tomas Borge (*Face to Face with Fidel Castro: a Conversation with Tomas Borge*, Ocean Press, Melbourne, Victoria, 1993). The radical American journalist Lee Lockwood interviewed Castro in the summer of 1965 and produced a fresh, sympathetic but not uncritical portrait of Castro and the Revolution in the mid-1960s with some striking photos in black and white: *Castro's Cuba, Cuba's Fidel* (Random House, New York, 1969). A fourth interview worth consulting was held in 1985 by the black Democratic Congressman Mervyn M. Dymally and his foreign affairs adviser J.M. Elliott: *Fidel Castro: Nothing Can Stop the Course of History* (Pathfinder, New York, 1986).

There has been a proliferation of biographies of Castro, some of which contain useful insights. The authors of relatively early political biographies include Herbert L. Matthews (who first brought Castro to the world's attention after interviewing him for the *New York Times* in 1956 in the Sierra Maestra) and Maurice Halperin. For their part, Charles Mills Wright and Theodore Draper covered more general aspects of Castro's Cuba and Castroism. By far the best informed and most balanced biography is also the most recent. The German journalist, Volker Skierka's *Fidel Castro: A Biography* (Polity Press, Cambridge, 2004) is a well-translated edition of a book published in German in 2000. Worthy of mention also is Peter Bourne's *Castro* (Macmillan, London, 1987), a somewhat maverick portrait by a psychiatrist and former adviser to President Carter, marred slightly by an overemphasis on Castro's allegedly problematic relationship with his father as a driving force of his actions. A more evenhanded account is that by an American journalist, Tad Szulc, who has followed Castro's career for many years and was able to interview him at length (though, according to Castro himself, he was not officially given the wide facilities that he claims). Szulc's *Fidel: a Critical Portrait* (Hutchinson, London, 1987) contains a wealth of personal detail and Castro's own observations but, like Bourne's biography, deals cursorily with the post-1970 period, a period as important and as fascinating as the early years. Both are relatively lightweight in their analysis of the ideological or historical context. A sympathetic and interesting portrait of Castro as a young man appears in Lionel Martin's *The Early Fidel: Roots of Castro's Communism* (Lyle Stuart, Secaucus, NJ, 1978) though he somewhat overstates both the ideological debt the youthful Castro owed to Communist ideas and the working-class base of the 26th July Movement in the early 1950s. Two further biographies can be mentioned: Georgie Anne Geyer, *Guerrilla Prince: The Untold Story of Fidel Castro* (Little, Brown, Toronto, 1991) and Robert E. Quirk, *Fidel Castro* (W.W. Norton, New York, 1993). The first is too deeply informed by Cold War perspectives to offer any new insights and while the second is thoroughly documented, both are so relentlessly hostile towards Castro that they fail to convince. Several interesting accounts sympathetic to Castro in different degrees can be found in Marta Harnecker's *Fidel Castro's Political Strategy: from Moncada to Victory* (Pathfinder, New York, 1987); Dayan Jayatilleka's *Fidel's Ethics of Violence: the Moral Dimension of the Political Thought of Fidel Castro* (Pluto Press, London, 2007), a suggestive analysis of Castro's political ethics, and the British Ambassador to Cuba from 1991–4 Leycester Coltman's *The Real Fidel Castro* (Yale University Press, New Haven, 2003) contains some well-balanced insights. An unreservedly pro-Castro analysis by Sheldon B. Liss (*Fidel! Castro's Political and Social Thought*, Westview Press, Boulder, Col., 1994) examines his political thought but is somewhat starstruck in its assertion of the orthodoxy of Castro's Marxism-Leninism. Clive Foss' *Fidel Castro* (2nd edn, Stroud, Sutton, 2006) is a brief and succinct introduction for those unfamiliar with the subject.

Of books published earlier that deal with Cuba and Castro's role in the Revolution, several are worthy of mention. The ex-editor of the 26th July Movement's newspaper, Carlos Franqui, who was to have been Castro's official biographer until he left Cuba in protest at the turn to Communism, has written an uneven and impressionistic account of the Cuban leader, the effect of which is somewhat spoiled by his visceral opposition to Castro (*Family Portrait with Fidel*, Random House, New York, 1983). The same is true of the book of another 26th July leader, Mario Llerena (*The Unsuspected Revolution: the Birth and Rise of Castroism*, Cornell University Press, Ithaca, NY, 1978) though it contains interesting details and documents concerning the external relations of the Movement. A more balanced though critical account of Castro in the 1960s can be found in K.S. Karol, *Guerrillas in Power: the Course of the Cuban Revolution* (Hill & Wang, New York, 1970) and in the analysis of the French agronomist René Dumont (*Is Cuba Socialist?*, Viking Press, New York, 1974), one of many European intellectuals whose support for the Revolution turned sour in the late 1960s. Hugh Thomas's encyclopaedic work on the history of Cuba, *Cuba: the Pursuit of Freedom* (Harper and Row, New York, 1971), is by far the most complete study of the historical background of the Revolution but is less satisfactory as an examination of Castro's political ideas and strategies and it is very much out of date.

Books dealing with the Revolution itself are legion. Only a few need to be mentioned here for the light they throw on Castro. The most serious accounts are the academic monographs published by American universities specialising in Cuban studies, among which the following stand out: Jorge I. Domínguez, *Cuba: Order and Revolution* (Harvard University Press, Cambridge, Mass., 1978); Carmelo Mesa-Lago, *Cuba in the 1970s: Pragmatism and Institutionalization* (University of New Mexico Press, Albuquerque, 1974) and his more recent book on the Cuban economy with co-author Jorge F. Pérez-López, *Cuba's Aborted Reform: Socioeconomic Effects, International Comparisons, and Transition Policies* (University Press of Florida, Gainesville, 2005); Edward Gonzalez, *Cuba under Castro: the Limits of Charisma* (Houghton Mifflin, Boston, 1974); Andrew Zimbalist (ed.), *Cuban Political Economy: Controversies in Cubanology* (Westview Press, Boulder, Col., 1988). Wayne S. Smith's *The Closest of Enemies* (W.W. Norton, New York, 1987) contains some interesting inside analysis of Cuban–American relations during the Carter administration and the early years of Reagan's presidency. Also worthy of inclusion in this list of more general works are five books: Max Azicri, *Cuba: Politics, Economics and Society* (Pinter Publishers, London, 1988); Peter Marshal, *Cuba Libre: Breaking the Chains* (Victor Gollancz, London, 1987); Louis A. Pérez Jr, *Cuba: Between Reform and Revolution* (Oxford University Press, New York, 1988); Marifeli Pérez-Stable, *The Cuban Revolution* (Oxford University Press, New York, 1988); and Jean Stubbs, *Cuba: the Test of Time* (Latin American Bureau, London, 1989). Finally, Antoni Kapcia's *Cuba: Island of Dreams* (Berg, Oxford, 2000) is an intense study of ideology and myth in the history of Cuba.

## Books in Spanish

Many of Castro's speeches have been published in Cuba and elsewhere. They include Fidel Castro, *Por el Camino Correcto* (Editora Política, Havana, 1988). Of interest also are his interviews with Barbara Walters of NBC: *Fidel Castro habla con Barbara Walters* (Carlos Valencia, Colombia, 1977); with American and French journalists in *Conversaciones con periodistas norteamericanos y franceses* (Editora Política, Havana, 1983); and with the Mexican daily paper *Excelsior*, published in 1985 by Editora Política: *La cancelación de la deuda externa y el nuevo orden económico internacional como única alternativa verdadera*. The Italian TV journalist Gianni Minà has published the transcript of his interview with Castro, *Habla Fidel* (Editorial Sudamericana, Buenos Aires, 1988), which provides some fascinating personal details about the Cuban leader. Tomas Borge's interview with Castro appeared first in Spanish in 1992 as *Un grano de maíz. Conversación con Fidel Castro* (Fondo de Cultura Económica, Mexico). But by far the most complete and interesting interview with Castro, held over several days, is Ignacio Ramonet's *Cien horas con Fidel, biografía a dos voces* (2006), published in two versions in Spanish by Random House Mondadori, Mexico and Barcelona and in a second edition, probably revised by Castro himself, by Oficina de Publicaciones del Consejo de Estado, Havana.

Correspondence between Castro and his friends and collaborators during his imprisonment on the Isle of Pines is published in Luis Conte Agüero, *Cartas del Presidio* (Editorial Lex, Havana, 1959) while documents and details about the Moncada assault can be found in Marta Rojas, *La generación del Centenario en el Moncada* (Ediciones R, Havana, 1964). A more complete collection of documents dealing with the early 1950s is published in Mario Mencía, *El Grito de Moncada* (2 vols, Editora Política, 1986). Mencía has set out to write a lengthy journalistic description of the Cuban Revolution, of which the above two volumes are part, and *Tiempos Precursores* (Editorial de Ciencias Sociales, Havana, 1986) an accompanying volume. Like many semi-official histories of the Revolution, his books tend to be a hagiography of Castro; indeed, judging by some of the textbooks published by the Ministry of Higher Education in Cuba there is a lack of any serious analysis of the Revolution in some official circles, though this is not true, on the other hand, of the research carried out in the universities by academics such as Oscar Pino Santos, Manuel Moreno Fraginals, Jorge Ibarra and Olga Cabrera.

If the Cuban books on Castro tend to be hagiographies, the portraits of him by Cubans in exile are more in the way of demonologies. He is a legendary hero on the one hand and a power-hungry opportunist on the other, and there is little published in Spanish that occupies a middle ground. Several books by exiles can be mentioned as examples. Two of Carlos Franqui's books mentioned above appear in the original Spanish; his *Retrato de familia con Fidel* (Seix Barral, Barcelona, 1981) is a much fuller collection of reminiscences than the English edition. Another long and largely hostile account of Castro's early days, the first part of a longer study, is Norberto Fuentes's *La autobiografía de Fidel Castro* (Ediciones Destino, Barcelona, 2004). Fuentes had been a Cuban supporter of the Revolution until the court case against General Ochoa and others in 1989, which had led to his exile. Two other anti-Castro books are José Pardo Llada, *Fidel y el 'Che'* (Plaza y Janés, Barcelona, 1988) and Carlos Alberto Montaner, *Fidel Castro y la Revolución Cubana* (Plaza y Janés, Barcelona, 1984). The first is the more interesting as it is written by a former friend and collaborator of Castro in the 1940s and 1950s who became an Ortodoxo leader and a well-known radio and TV journalist in Havana before joining Castro in the Sierra in 1958. Though it contains some interesting anecdotes, his portrait of Castro as a wild, obsessively ambitious and ideologically unsound young man reveals more about the author's bitterness at the supposed betrayal of the liberal cause of the revolutionary movement than it does about the ideas and character of the Cuban leader. It suggests once more the powerful hold that Castro continues to exercise on the imagination of Cubans, whether friends or foes.

## Notes

1    C. Franqui, *Cuba, La Revolución: ¿mito o realidad? Memorias de un fantasma socialista* (Península, Barcelona, 2007), p. 417.

2    T. Borge, *Un grano de maíz. Conversación con Fidel Castro* (Fondo de Cultura Económica, Mexico, 1992), p. 112.

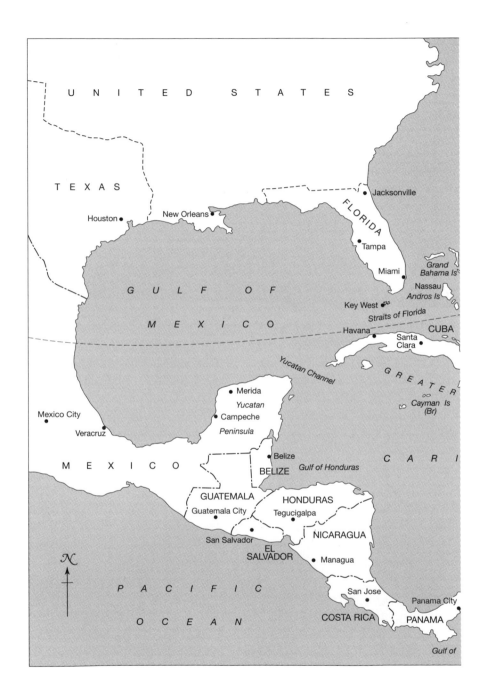

MAP    205

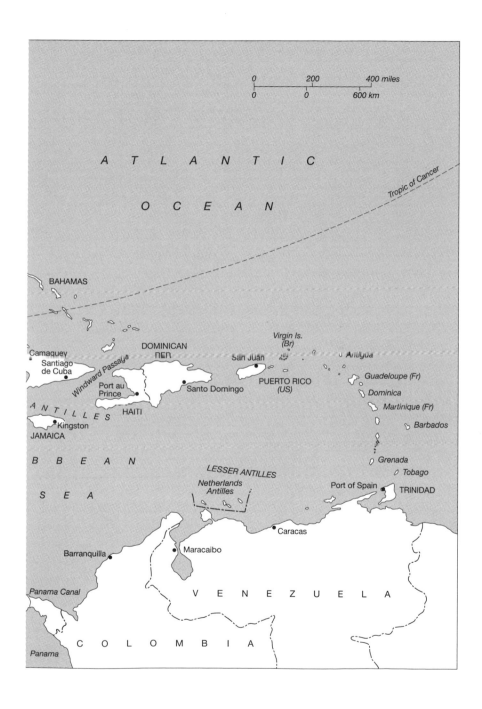

0        200        400 miles

0        0        600 km

*A T L A N T I C*

*O C E A N*

*Tropic of Cancer*

BAHAMAS

Camaguey

Santiago
de Cuba

DOMINICAN
REP.

*Windward Passage*

Port au
Prince

Virgin Is.
*(Br)*

San Juan

Antigua

Guadeloupe (Fr)

Santo Domingo

PUERTO RICO
(US)

Dominica

*A*
*N T I L L E S*

HAITI

Martinique (Fr)

Kingston

Barbados

JAMAICA

B B E A N

*LESSER ANTILLES*

Grenada

Tobago

S E A

*Netherlands*
*Antilles*

Port of Spain

TRINIDAD

Caracas

Barranquilla

Maracaibo

Panama Canal

*V E N E Z U E L A*

*C O L O M B I A*

Panama

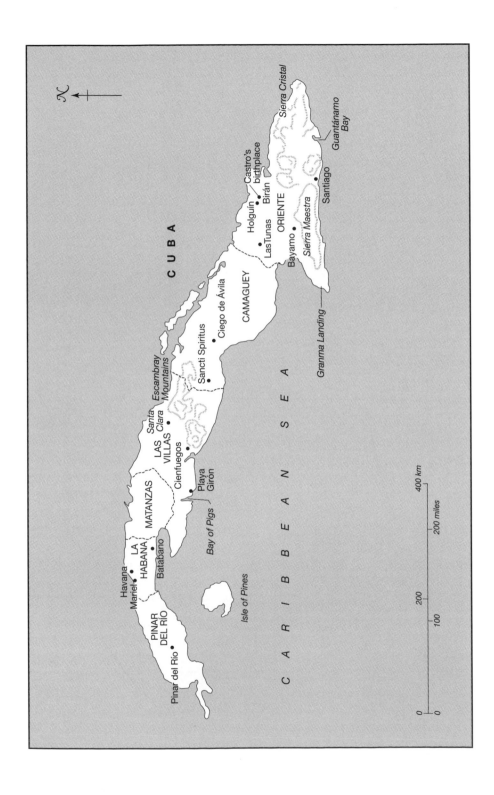

# Index